ALAN RAWSTHORNE

Alan Rawsthorne

Portrait of a Composer

JOHN MCCABE

OXFORD

UNIVERSITY PRESS

OXFORD
UNIVERSITY PRESS

Great Clarendon Street, Oxford OX2 6DP

Oxford University Press is a department of the University of Oxford.
It furthers the University's objective of excellence in research, scholarship,
and education by publishing worldwide in

Oxford New York

Athens Auckland Bangkok Bogotá Buenos Aires Calcutta
Cape Town Chennai Dar es Salaam Delhi Florence Hong Kong Istanbul
Karachi Kuala Lumpur Madrid Melbourne Mexico City Mumbai
Nairobi Paris São Paulo Singapore Taipei Tokyo Toronto Warsaw

with associated companies in Berlin Ibadan

Published in the United States
by Oxford University Press Inc., New York

First published 1999

This publication has been supported by a subvention from The Rawsthorne Trust

British Library Cataloguing in Publication Data

Data available

Library of Congress Cataloging in Publication Data
McCabe, John, 1939–
Alan Rawsthorne: portrait of a composer/John McCabe.
p. cm.
Includes bibliographical references and index.
1. Rawsthorne, Alan, 1905–1971. 2. Composers—England—Biography.
I. Title.
ML410.R233M33 1999 780′.92—dc21 98-24508
ISBN 0–19–816693–1 (hb)

1 3 5 7 9 10 8 6 4 2

Typeset by Best-set Typesetter Ltd., Hong Kong
Printed in Great Britain
on acid-free paper by
Biddles Ltd
Guildford & Kings Lynn

To my wife Monica, with love

PREFACE

IN the book on British composers in the series *Twentieth Century Composers*, Humphrey Searle wrote of Alan Rawsthorne: 'I feel that his contribution to English music is as important as that of any composer working in England today, and that this will be recognized more and more as time goes by.'[1] This generous tribute from one distinguished composer to another indicates the esteem in which Alan Rawsthorne was held by his colleagues during his lifetime; he has, indeed, become regarded as a 'composer's composer', though this summing-up hardly does justice either to the approachable nature of his music or to the remarkable range of technique and expression he explored during his career. There are many received opinions about his music, some of them justified (that he derived his style from a narrow base is undeniable), some of them completely wrong. To pigeon-hole him, as was often done, as primarily of importance in the field of chamber music is seriously to misunderstand the character and importance of his orchestral and vocal works, where (in my view) his most powerful personal statements are to be found.

He achieved enormous success during his lifetime with a few pieces, and a regular flow of performances with many others. He was fortunate, perhaps, to come to prominence at a time when the renaissance of British music was in full flow, yet because of the enormous amount of important music being written in the larger forms by his compatriots, it was easy enough for his more modest demeanour (both as a composer and as a man) to lead to a serious undervaluation of his contribution. This I have always believed, and still believe, to be of lasting significance; it is with a lifetime's love of Rawsthorne's music, and the hope that I can convey something of the richness of his repertoire, that I have embarked on this study.

Though I knew him from 1949, and met and worked with him on many occasions, I cannot claim close friendship; that was the preserve of such people as my piano teacher Gordon Green (through whom I came to meet Alan) and valued colleagues in later years who were closer to him. But listening to his music, and in later years performing it as often as possible, I have found that, far from tiring one of the style, his music deepens on renewed acquaintance.

---

[1] R. Layton and H. Searle (edd.), *Twentieth Century Composers: Britain, Scandinavia and the Netherlands* (London, 1973).

It provides, as fine music always should, an experience which enriches one's own life, entertains, amuses, moves, sometimes even awes the listener.

He wrote many works on a large scale (symphonies, concertos, quartets, and the like), yet always with great economy. Those who complain that he isn't Britten (who wrote operas, massive choral works, a full-length ballet, and so on) rather miss the point—as well to complain that Chopin wrote no symphonies and was therefore not Beethoven. Rawsthorne's contribution was his own, and his integrity is absolute. I hope that by the end of this book the reader will understand some of the continued fascination his music exerts on his admirers, as well as the astonishing range he explored both technically and expressively in a style that developed and changed much more than critics have been willing to admit.

An analytical point should be borne in mind when reading the book. Reference is made, especially in relation to the second half of his career, to Rawsthorne's use of bitonal or polytonal harmonies, and chords are sometimes analysed harmonically (though in a book of this scope the analysis is necessarily fairly basic). One is reminded, however, that André Boucourechliev has written, apropos (among other instances) the famous chord at the beginning of the 'Augures printaniers' in *Le Sacre du printemps*, that though it can be 'explained' harmonically in various ways, it 'must now be considered as an indissoluble unit of sound, and perceived as such for its individual *quality*. In the last resort therefore it is a question of timbre'.[2] One must always remember what analysts sometimes seem to overlook: that the intellectual rationalization of a musical sound does not always precede the invention or use of the sound but follows it. Thus, it may well be that some of Rawsthorne's most striking chord-formations occurred to him primarily as timbre; those who follow him, and are sufficiently interested, can 'explain' the music technically to their heart's content, but the analysis is not necessarily its *raison d'être* but a means of identifying afterwards how the composer instinctively chose sounds which work their magic.

A list of acknowledgements follows this preface, but one source of material should be particularly mentioned at this point, the three-volume survey of Rawsthorne published in 1984 and 1986, compiled and edited by Alan Poulton. In view of the remarkable paucity of major articles about Rawsthorne, with significant exceptions which are quoted elsewhere in this book, Poulton's remains an essential component of any commentator's armoury of sources.

A word should also be said about another invaluable source, the scholarly

---

[2] *Stravinsky*, trans. M. Cooper (London, 1987).

journal produced by the Alan Rawsthorne Society and the Rawsthorne Trust: called *The Creel*, it shares this title with one of Rawsthorne's more familiar works, for piano duet. It should be clear from the context throughout this book which *Creel* is being invoked. The difficulty in writing biographically about Rawsthorne, is that apart from the early materials collected by his sister Barbara and cousin Elizabeth Bridge there is a marked lack of later correspondence (he preferred telephone or telegram as means of communication), which means that the few extant sources are inevitably mined extensively. Finally, I should draw attention to the musical examples themselves. There are a considerable number of them in this book; I felt strongly that this was necessary, in order both to illustrate the analyses and descriptions of the works discussed and to convey, as far as possible, the wide range of Rawsthorne's inspiration, and the variety of his musical character.

J.McC.

ACKNOWLEDGEMENTS

DURING the writing of this book, many people have given most generously of their time and hospitality. Among those to whom particular debts of gratitude should be paid are Mrs Rose Abdalla, John Amis, Mrs Mollie Barger, Sir Richard Rodney Bennett CBE, John Blake, Julian Bream CBE, Elizabeth Bridge, Professor Sebastian Forbes, James Gibb, Sidonie Goossens OBE, Mrs Veronica Leigh Jacobs (who also has generously allowed me to quote from her diaries), Gareth Morris, Brenda Lucas Ogdon, Ronald Smith, Gerard and Carolyn Schurmann, Mrs Topsy Levan, and Edward and Judith Williams. Guy Rickards gave particular help in reading thoroughly and critically, as well as proof-reading.

Gratitude is also due to the Rawsthorne Trust for commissioning the book in the first place, and to the members of the Trust for their reading of the manuscript—in particular, a profound debt is owed to John Belcher, the Chairman of the Trust, and John Turner for the enormous practical help and advice they gave. During my researches, I had good cause to be especially grateful for the kindness shown to me by various organizations whose establishments I frequently cluttered up with my notebooks, papers, and computer, notably the Library of the Royal Northern College of Music (Anthony Hodges and Dr Rosemary Williamson, past and present librarians respectively), the Archive at Oxford University Press in Oxford (Peter Foden, then Archivist, and his staff), and the Music Department of Oxford University Press, both the Printed Music Division (Andrew Potter, Helen Thomas, and Teresa Levonian Cole have been most helpful in providing those scores I did not already possess) and the Hire Library, where Dr Simon Wright was patience itself when confronted with my demands to borrow scores. I am also most grateful to Geoffrey Thomason, of the RNCM Library, for undertaking the index and chronology.

At the Music Books Division of Oxford University Press, Bruce Phillips, Helen Foster, Janet Moth, and Fiona Little have been understanding and calm in guiding through the process of writing the book, and have patiently answered innumerable questions about procedure. I am most grateful for permission to reproduce a good deal of copyright material. Schott & Co. Ltd. (London) kindly gave permission for me to quote Ex. 3.1(a) from Hindemith's *Mathis der Maler*. Ex. 3.6, from *Three French Nursery Songs*, is reproduced by permission of Boosey & Hawkes Music Publishers, London. Ex. 4.4, from the Suite for recorder and piano, is reproduced by kind permission of Forsyth

Brothers Ltd., Manchester. Most of the examples are from works whose copyright is held by Oxford University Press, to whose Music Department I am grateful for permission to reproduce the following examples: P. 1 and 6.7(*a*) (© Oxford University Press 1951); 1.3 (© Oxford University Press 1968); 2.4 (© Oxford University Press 1955); 3.1(*b*) (© Oxford University Press 1949); 3.1(*c*), 7.5 and 6, and 9.7 (© Oxford University Press 1960); 3.2 (© Oxford University Press 1938); 3.4 and 5 (© Oxford University Press 1943); 3.7, 8, and 9 (© Oxford University Press 1946); 4.1 (© Oxford University Press 1943); 4.2 (© Oxford University Press 1941); 4.3 (© Oxford University Press 1973); 4.5 and 6 (© Oxford University Press 1942); 4.7 and 8 (© Oxford University Press 1947); 5.1 (© Oxford University Press 1948); 5.2 (© Oxford University Press 1948); 5.3 (© Oxford University Press 1949); 5.4 (© Oxford University Press 1950); 5.5 (© Oxford University Press 1949); 5.7 (© Oxford University Press 1949); 5.8 and 9 (© Oxford University Press 1952); 6.1(*a*) (*ii*), (*b*) (*ii*), (*c*) (*ii*), 6.2, and 6.3 (© Oxford University Press 1952); 6.4 (© Oxford University Press 1953); 6.5 (© Oxford University Press 1962); 6.6 (© Oxford University Press 1956); 6.7(*b*) (© Oxford University Press 1953); 6.8 and 9 (© Oxford University Press 1954); 6.10 and 11 (© Oxford University Press 1954); 6.12 (© Oxford University Press 1955); 6.13, 14, 15, and 16 (© Oxford University Press 1959); 7.1, 2, 3, and 4 (© Oxford University Press 1959); 7.7 (© Oxford University Press 1963); 7.8 (© Oxford University Press 1962); 7.9 and 10 (© Oxford University Press 1963); 7.11 (© Oxford University Press 1962); 7.12 (© Oxford University Press 1962); 7.13 (© Oxford University Press 1964); 8.1, 2, 3, 4, and 5 (© Oxford University Press 1964); 8.7 (© Oxford University Press 1964); 8.8 and 9 (© Oxford University Press 1966); 8.10, 11, 12 13, and 14 (© Oxford University Press 1965); 8.15 (© Oxford University Press 1970); 9.1 (© Oxford University Press 1970); 9.2 (© Oxford University Press 1967); 9.4 (© Oxford University Press 1969); 9.5 (© Oxford University Press 1972); and 9.6 (© Oxford University Press 1975).

Correspondence, apart from that in the various archives, has been reproduced by permission of the writers; the letter from Elisabeth Lutyens to Isabel Rawsthorne in Chapter 9 is quoted by kind permission of the Trustees of the Estate of Elisabeth Lutyens. I am grateful to the Rawsthorne Trust for permission to quote from unpublished works by Alan Rawsthorne the copyright of which is vested in the Trust, and for free access to documents and other memorabilia in the ownership of the Trust. I am also grateful to Dr Rosemary Williamson for permission to publish short extracts from unpublished Rawsthorne manuscripts, both musical and documentary, belonging to the

Royal Northern College of Music. Material from their own archives is reprinted by permission of the Oxford University Press, to whose Archives Division I am most grateful.

Perhaps most important of all, my deepest gratitude goes to my wife Monica, for her immense patience in reading countless drafts, proof-reading, discussing, advising me, and putting up with large mounds of music and papers littering our house—she knows how much Rawsthorne's music has always meant to me, and to her I dedicate this book, with love.

J.McC.

November 1997

CONTENTS

LIST OF ILLUSTRATIONS

(between pp. 174 and 175)

COMPACT DISC: CONTENTS

THE accompanying Compact Disc contains the following tracks, each of which appears by courtesy of the named copyright owner:

1. *Concertante pastorale*: opening section (2'56")
   Northern Chamber Orchestra / David Lloyd Jones
   Naxos 8.553567 (Music for Chamber Orchestra)
   © 1998 HNH International Ltd.

2. Theme and Variations for two violins: Theme and variations I–III (4'36")
   Nicholas Ward and Pauline Lowbury (violins)
   Redcliffe Recordings RR 006 (British Chamber Music for Oboe and
     Strings)
   © 1991 Redcliffe Recordings

3. Piano Concerto No. 1: second movement, Chaconne (5'40")
   Moura Lympany (piano) / Philharmonia Orchestra / Herbert Menges
   EMI SLS 5080 (3-LP set) (20th Century British Piano Concertos)
   © 1957 EMI Records Ltd.
   Pub. 1962 EMI Records Ltd.

4. Overture *Street Corner* (5'28")
   Pro Arte Orchestra / Alan Rawsthorne
   EMI CDM 7 64718 2 (The Composer Conducts)
   © 1993 EMI Records Ltd.
   Pub. 1958 EMI Records Ltd.

5. Fantasy Overture *Cortèges*: closing section, from letter U (3'36")
   BBC Scottish Symphony Orchestra / Lionel Friend
   Naxos 8.554240 (Violin Concertos)
   © 1998 HNH International Ltd.
   By courtesy of the BBC Scottish Symphony Orchestra

6. Clarinet Quartet: finale Allegro risoluto—Andante teneramente (6'13")
   Nicholas Cox (clarinet) / Redcliffe Ensemble
   Redcliffe Recordings RR 010 (British Chamber Music for Clarinet &
     Strings)
   © 1996 Redcliffe Recordings

7. 'Carol' (3'15")
   Martin Hindmarsh (tenor) / Alan Cuckston (piano)

Swinsty Records FEW 120 (cassette) (Songs and Piano Music by Rawsthorne)
© 1991 Swinsty Recordings Ltd.

8. Symphony No. 1: first movement Allegro tempestuoso (6′49″)
London Philharmonic Orchestra / John Pritchard
Lyrita SRCD 291 (Rawsthorne, Symphonies 1, 2, 3)
© 1977 Lyrita Recorded Edition, England
Pub. 1995 Lyrita Recorded Edition, England

9. String Quartet No. 2: finale Theme, Three Variations and Coda (5′41″)
Flesch Quartet
ASV CD DCA 983 (Rawsthorne String Quartets)
© 1997 ASV Ltd.

10. *The Cruel Sea*: Prelude and Nocturne, arr. Philip Lane (5′34″)
Royal Ballet Sinfonia / Kenneth Alwyn
Silva Screen FILMCD 177 (*The Ladykillers*)
© 1997 Silva Screen Records Ltd.

11. *A Rose for Lidice* (5′04″)
National Youth Chamber Choir / Michael Brewer
Redcliffe Recordings RR 011 (British Choral Music)
© 1996 Redcliffe Recordings

12. Violin Concerto No. 2: first movement Allegretto (8′50″)
Rebecca Hirsch (violin) / BBC Scottish Symphony Orchestra / Lionel Friend
Naxos 8.554240 (Violin Concertos)
© 1998 HNH International Ltd.
By courtesy of the BBC Scottish Symphony Orchestra

13. Violin Sonata (1958): third movement Toccata: Allegro di bravura (3′33″)
Suzanne Stanzeleit (violin) / Julian Jacobson (piano)
Cala United CACD88036 (Fricker, Rawsthorne, Vaughan Williams, Violin Sonatas)
© 1996 Cala Records Ltd.

14. Symphony No. 2 (*Pastoral*): finale Andante (5′13″)
Tracey Chadwell (soprano) / London Philharmonic Orchestra / Nicholas Braithwaite
Lyrita SRCD 291 (Rawsthorne, Symphonies 1, 2, 3)
© 1995 Lyrita Recorded Edition, England

Grateful thanks are due to the companies named above for kind permission to use these extracts from their recordings. Recordings are on compact disc unless otherwise stated.

LIST OF ABBREVIATIONS

Poulton i   *Alan Rawsthorne*, i: *A Catalogue of his Music*, ed. Alan Poulton (Kidderminster: Bravura Press, 1984)

Poulton ii   *Alan Rawsthorne*, ii: *Biographical Essays*, ed. Alan Poulton (Kidderminster: Bravura Press, 1984) (by various writers)

Poulton iii   *Alan Rawsthorne*, iii: *Essays on the Music*, ed. Alan Poulton (Hindhead: Bravura Press, 1986) (preface by Sir William Walton and contributions from several distinguished friends and colleagues of Rawsthorne)

OUP archives   archives at Oxford University Press, Oxford

RNCM archives   archives at the Royal Northern College of Music, Manchester

PROLOGUE

EARLY YEARS (1905–25)

ALAN RAWSTHORNE is usually regarded as the epitome of urbane sophistication, elegant and worldly-wise, very much a man about town, yet in truth he was more of a countryman: he lived in the Essex countryside for the last eighteen years of his life, and spent his first eight years in Lancashire sheep-farming country. He was born on 2 May 1905, at the family home of Deardengate House, Haslingden, in Lancashire (the family moving to Sykeside House on the edge of Haslingden in 1908 on the sale to the Corporation of the previous property). The year 1905 was a significant one for music. It saw the births of the great Bavarian symphonist Karl Amadeus Hartmann and no less than five English composers, William Alwyn, Constant Lambert, Walter Leigh, Michael Tippett, and Rawsthorne. Alan was the second child of Hubert and Janet Rawsthorne (his sister, Barbara, was four years older). They were a comfortably situated and extraordinarily close-knit family. Hubert had qualified as a doctor, though he practised medicine only briefly during the First World War (as a Voluntary Medical Officer). He spent much of his adult life supervising the extensive family land-holdings. Known as the Rawsthornes of Rossendale, they held substantial farms, other properties, and land in an area of rolling countryside in which sheep-farming and the woollen industry were important elements. It was a middle-class background, rural landowners in a hard-working, tough environment, though inevitably as time passed the sale of the properties in order to maintain the family life ate into the collateral they represented, and the income from the estates suffered gradual erosion.

The landscape is one of grey stone mills, churches and housing, moorland hills, and green valleys, with a vast blue sky in summer and a coating of snow in winter; it was said that if it were going to snow anywhere in winter, it would be on Haslingden Parish Church, the highest point of the town. It is always interesting to ponder the extent to which childhood landscape inhabits the subconscious of a creative artist. It is surely far-fetched to find in Rawsthorne's music any real echoes of the moorlands, or the wooded glens which were his childhood environment (it must be remembered that the family moved from there when he was 8 years old), but the melancholy that so often colours his music may well stem partly from the hard winters and the essential toughness of life around him. The economy of his work might equally be traced to the self-enclosed nature of the landscape, with its pockets of habitation, clear moorland outlines, and little wooded copses nestling in the folds of the land below the moors. Even though he lived for so much of his adult life in towns, leading a somewhat nomadic life from one apartment to another, the countryside had made a deep impression in his earliest years. In his *Concertante pastorale* for flute, horn, and strings, written in 1950, one cannot help thinking that the magical beginning, with its autumnal colouring and pastoral melancholy, stems from the early impact of this beautiful, sometimes bleak moorland (Ex. P.1; Compact Disc, track 1); his subsequent removal to the Essex countryside in 1953 was a source of much-needed spiritual refreshment, and had a supremely beneficial influence on his composition.

The family provided a secure background, not only financially but emotionally—there was the deepest mutual affection. Alan's sister Barbara wrote a touching and spirited memoir of her childhood, vividly conveying the delightful childhood she and her brother shared.[1] Their parents took an active part in the local life, Hubert being involved with the Choral and Orchestral Society as well as church, and Council affairs as well as politics. Barbara described their father as

a strange character. He was a Liberal in politics, and a man of great integrity, which I think Alan inherited in a marked degree. He was very reserved and very cautious, and found it difficult to communicate, although he was by no means a recluse or unsociable . . . [he] was meticulous in everything he did . . . He was devoted to his wife, who was 10 years younger than he was, and to his children.[2]

Janet she described as 'pretty, gay, full of a gracious kindliness and compassion, with a great sense of fun. Everybody loved her, particularly young friends of ours.'[3] It must have been, in many ways, an idyllic childhood: Barbara, in her published memoir, refers to memories of the 'whistling wind, and the clack-clack of the cotton workers' clogs as they went to and from work', as well as 'another sound, most nostalgic of all', the 'unmistakable' creaking noise of the 'slipper' brake on the horse-drawn waggons descending the hill, 'loaded with bales of cotton and other goods'. She recalled a local Italian organ-grinder, complete with a monkey 'dressed in a red coat and cap', the local Pace-eggers dancing past the house carrying coloured eggs (on their way to take part in

---

[1] *Diary of an Edwardian Childhood* (Rossendale Borough Council, 1995). This was published after her death in 1991.

[2] 'Alan Rawsthorne. For his Friends—from his Sister Barbara' (undated MS memoir).

[3] Ibid.

Ex. P.1. *Concertante pastorale*, bars 9–18

the Easter 'egg-rolling' in a nearby field), and another group of dancers, the Coconutters (the Coconuts 'fastened onto their elbows, knees and hands', clapping together as they danced). There were dancing lessons in a neighbouring town, whither they went in a horse-drawn cab or on the electric tram, children's parties, an annual seaside holiday, and above all a vigorous life of childhood imagination. They invented characters, including a formidable female named Mrs Mealso, 'who did the most eccentric and outrageous things' and provided a focus for discussion of 'the latest outrage committed by or to her'.[4]

The gregarious nature of the family meant that, in the words of Alan's cousin Elizabeth Bridge,

There was always an atmosphere of modest, unostentatious, gracious living in which everything ran smoothly without a hitch. Our welcome there was never failing and everything seemed to be geared to what would please us. This was largely due to my aunt [Janet] and Barbara . . . This happy state of affairs reached its climax at the celebrations for [Alan's] twenty-first birthday. This event lasted a whole week and was highly organised by Barbara. There was something for everybody—family, friends, students and children . . . so much fun and laughter.[5]

At the same time, Alan was capable of great sensitivity throughout his life: Elizabeth recalled that after the death of her father in 1929 'Alan was particularly kind to my poor mother. He used to play demon patience with her in the evenings and I can almost hear the roars of laughter that surrounded them. He seemed to know intuitively that this hilarity was therapeutic and in some way helped grief.'

A particularly important moment was a family trip to London in 1912, which the children found most enlivening with its motor cars and taxis, the zoo, walks in the parks, and the magic show of Maskelyne and Devant (who sawed a lady in half to piano accompaniment), and in 1913 there was much excitement about the visit to Haslingden of King George V and Queen Mary. Among the home amusements were plays (for example, a charity performance of *Cinderella* in the drawing-room with local children, during which Alan, acting the part of a herald, was able to inform the audience that his trousers had just split, an early indication of his awareness of the ridiculous). Barbara provides a detail of Alan's early years that is interesting especially in view of his later detestation of the military:

My brother had a large collection of toy soldiers, coloured lead figures that stood about 2 inches high—He had every conceivable regiment of the British Army, including Colonial troops, and a field hospital with nurses, orderlies, ambulances etc. He played for hours with these, covering the nursery floor. As he grew older he became interested in strategy, his game took on something of the nature of chess, and I think that his lifelong interest in chess grew directly out of his toy soldiers.[6]

Only ill health cast a shadow over their existence: there was a family history of tuberculosis, from which Hubert's father, aunt, and grandfather had all died.

[4] *Edwardian Childhood.*
[5] 'The Rawsthorne Family', *The Creel*, 1/1 (autumn 1989), 4.
[6] Handwritten biographical note, May 1972.

Janet had had a serious illness in childhood, the effects of which hastened her early death, and Alan suffered considerably from rheumatism as a child (indeed, it prevented his attendance at school during what would have been his earliest school years, though the lack of suitable local schools may also have occasioned the parental lessons in reading and writing and visits from governesses). It is not surprising that Hubert and Janet became very protective of their children. In view of Alan's lifestyle as an adult, when he certainly took little care of himself, it may well be true that his childhood illnesses gave him a certain physical resilience; certainly, Barbara wrote in 1972 that 'he grew out of those complaints he had as a young boy . . . And I think he must have basically been pretty strong to come through, as he did, some of the illnesses he had in later life.'[7]

Both Barbara and Alan took to writing at an early age, with Barbara producing a house magazine called *Nursery Tit-bits* from 1911 to 1914.[8] There were clear rules about the 'Nurseryites Society', of which Barbara made herself President, Alan constituting the rest of the society. This later became a 'Parliement' (*sic*) with equally strict rules. Alan must have been aware of Barbara's fascination with news of the suffragettes' 'Votes for Women' campaign, imitated by Barbara in her newsletter series 'Pockets for Women', complete with letters to Mr Lloyd George and a cod reply from him: 'Dear Madames . . . How dare you tell me to leave the matter to you, and take off the tax on Women's pockets?' Alan later wrote an immense amount of material, and his range of interests was as wide as his imagination. Among the products of his literary career at this stage were a play *King George V* (winter 1916–17), written as a parody of *Henry V*, which he was studying at school. This is an extraordinary work, filled with topical references to the First World War, at its height at this time, and demonstrating an acute awareness of political trends as well as the personalities involved in the war. The characters included David Lord Lloygius, My Lord Balfive, and the Rt. Hon. Mr Quithquas. A motor dispatch-rider, no less, brings a telegram from King George's 'Uncle of Exeter':

> K. GEO. By my faith! Sad news indeed for me!
> Cousin the Count of Hoen hath declared
> A war on France, and that he may invade
> That fair countree he hath marched through the land
> Of Albert, King of Bell. My uncle of Exeter
> Adviseth me in strong, potential language,

---

[7] Ibid.

[8] Extracts from Alan and Barbara's childhood writings are from documents in the RNCM archives.

> For to declare a war on him in turn,
> Nichol, the Grand Duke of Russ doth march
> Against my cous, whom I did think was nice,
> Lords, good is Uncle Exeter's advice. [Exeunt]

Among the large number of writings that survive, it is the range that is astonishing, with a notable leaning both towards introspection (as in a piece about a contemplated suicide) on the one hand and parody on the other. A piratical verse-melodrama *De misero corpore* (1918) is bloodcurdling in the extreme, but replete with the kind of footnotes typical of educational editions of the classics. He also produced a version of the Casket Scene from *The Merchant of Venice* as if it 'had occurred in "Pickwick Papers"', and an extraordinary adventure story *Captain Black* with elements of Bulldog Drummond, piracy, and Rider Haggard, as well as a chilling description of the Witch of Serophis:

A strange incantation rose in a wail as we entered, in weird syllables of a forgotten tongue. A huge temple, crowned with a jet black throne, and scores of wrigling [*sic*] animals greeted our eyes; but what was our horror at seeing that these suppose[d] animals were human beings, but without limbs! A hundred at least were grovelling helpless in this awful state, grovelling and wailing before this throne of terror. And sitting in the throne was a terrible looking old woman, with long black robes, and jet black hair, as straight as strands of wire, hung round her, veiling only sufficient of her awful features as to make them more frightful and terrifying.

There was also a splendid parody of Longfellow's *Hiawatha*:

> Should you ask me, whence these stories?
> Whence these legends and traditions,
> With the odours of the forests,
> With the dew and damp of meadows?
> I should answer, I should tell you,
> 'Longfellow, the poet, wrote them,
> Wrote them down on bits of paper,
> Wrote them so that all might read them:
> Now adapted all, and changéd,
> You may read them in my writings!'
> Should you ask where this Longfellow
> Found these songs, so wild and wayward,
> I should answer, 'There you have me,
> I have not the faintest notion!'

From this time stemmed his love of Dickens and the Sherlock Holmes stories, and he soon began to read Shaw, with profound effect on his later left-wing political views. Even his boyhood poetry, ranging from pastoral sonnets to works of considerable irony, sometimes reflected the growth of mature points of view:

> 'Tis mere thirst for glory
> Gives power of excelling;
> 'Pro patria mori—'
> 'Tis mere thirst for glory,
> It is the same story
> Unchanged in the telling;
> 'Tis mere thirst for glory
> Gives power of excelling.

Though no music has survived from these years, Rawsthorne later recalled that he 'had always been interested in composing since I was a child. I used to compose a good deal. In fact I once started to write an opera when I was about eleven but I didn't get very far. It was on the subject of Siegfried and I suddenly found that Wagner had already written an opera called Siegfried so I abandoned mine and I've never written an opera since.'[9] It is tragic that, right at the end of his life, he had been commissioned, too late, to write what might have been a fascinating opera on John Arden's play *Sergeant Musgrave's Dance*.

Alan's first school was Winterclyne School, Southport, which he attended from 1914, the year after the family moved to Southport. Barbara described the day-schools she and Alan attended as 'small private schools . . . one looks back at them now with affectionate amusement'.[10] Winterclyne was

kept by a large and redoubtable lady. She had very strong religious views and was militant in putting these into practice in her school . . . Serious misdemeanours on the part of her boys meant the slipper administered by her, followed by a prayer for better behaviour . . . she really did know and care about small boys, and would spend whole mornings in her kitchen baking pies and cakes with which to feed them . . . The teaching staff consisted entirely of women, and although the education the boys received would hardly be recognised as such to-day, they did get a good grounding in such things as Latin Grammar and Maths.[11]

Four years later, he was moved to Sandringham School, Southport, about which Barbara was fairly dubious: 'I remember the Headmaster's thinly-veined [veiled?] scorn at the fact that Alan was having piano lessons—these things were for kids and girls.' Alan himself later described the schoolmasters, raw

---

[9] BBC radio interview with Malcolm Rayment for series 'The Composer Speaks', recorded 24 May 1962.
[10] Handwritten biographical note, May 1972.
[11] Barbara Rawsthorne, 'For his Friends'.

amateur recruits to their trade, as 'a mixture of Bill Sykes and Groucho Marx'.[12] Eventually Alan's health once again caused him to leave school, and a private tutor was employed.

Southport was possessed of an amateur orchestral society, and there were occasional visiting recitalists (including Suggia and the young Solomon); in a BBC interview with Malcolm Williamson (1965), Alan referred to his good fortune in learning the cello, suggesting that his profound love of chamber music stemmed from this period. He played the cello in the local orchestra, and wrote to Barbara in January 1918 about going to hear a visit by Clara Butt:

She *did* sing 'Abide with me' . . . sort of swathed in a golden and white bit of stuff, the gold being at about the angle of a Highlander's plaid. Above this was an enormous amount of her manly chest. Below this stretched her beefy arms, and for a skirt she had long strips of yellow over white. The white had extinct flowers on rather larger saucers, and she had a long train. The pianist looked exactly like a small beetle crawling out after her.

An important musical development was a local concert in about 1919, reviewed in a Southport paper. He was described as 'a clever young pianist, whose achievements give promise of a very successful future'. He played the Adagio and Rondo from Beethoven's 'Pathétique' Sonata and followed this with his own Passepied and *Sylvan Sketch* (both of which have disappeared)— 'They were delightful little pieces, and were loudly applauded.' Barbara recalled settings of two poems of de la Mare and one of Blake, in about 1920; the de la Mare settings have recently come to light. The first of these, 'The Sunken Garden', is a remarkably assured, rather statuesque setting in a thoroughly tonal D flat major with the occasional use of F flat to darken the harmonic colouring; there is a Brahmsian rhythmic touch in the middle section. 'They told me' is quicker (Molto moderato), in a conventional E major, though with a sudden C major seventh chord before the final return to E, an effective and (in such a conventional context) dramatic stroke. Both songs are essentially simple, with eminently singable vocal lines.

When it became time to decide on a career, Janet and Hubert were chary of allowing Alan to pursue musical studies. In the post-war period, fixed private incomes were no longer either sufficient or reliable, and Hubert was now too old to begin following his medical profession. In addition, they felt music to be an insecure profession, especially since there was no tradition of musical

---

[12] Rawsthorne, 'Outbreak of War', article (*c*.1946) unpublished in his lifetime, printed in Poulton ii, pp. (viii)–(xi).

talent in the family. Following much family discussion Alan enrolled in 1922 as a student in the Liverpool University School of Dentistry (giving rise to the much-quoted remark that after this abortive effort he never practised dentistry even as a hobby); after a year of considerable unhappiness he switched to the same university's School of Architecture. In a letter to Barbara (5 May 1923) while on holiday in Kettlewell, Yorkshire, he conveyed vividly his general mood:

I have a curious feeling about Kettlewell . . . There is no brilliant haze of sunshine, and though it is quite warm enough for my liking, the air has a sharpness about it that to me is quite ominous.

It isn't jovial wintry snap; it is more like the breath of some demon of the moors who is doomed to hide himself until October. I should like to come here in the late Autumn, when such forces are re-appearing. I am sure they would be cruel, and catch people who strayed on to the hills at night, like the Marsh King in Hans Andersen's story. All this sounds very absurd; but no one can deny that such *influences* exist, any more than they can that human influences exist. And if one finds it difficult to conceive metaphysical force or energy as such, why not imagine it as personified? Indeed, it is not apparent why, if we are permitted to have bodies, such spirits as these (perhaps far more powerful than ours) should not have them too. It's all a question of the trinity of everything.

Though more amenable to him, architecture proved equally unsatisfying as a prospect, and after four terms and further family discussion he was allowed to enter the Royal Manchester College of Music (RMCM) in 1925. It should be stressed that this was not a case of heavy-handed parental opposition: there were no Victorian-style dramatic scenes, but merely sympathetic parental anxiety. What swayed the decision finally was Alan's decisive comment that if he could not study music properly, he would give it up completely, even as a pastime—an indication of the steadfastness of purpose that became apparent as he pursued his own individual path as a composer in later years. In the 1962 interview with Malcolm Rayment he summed it all up with characteristic self-depreciation: 'It was through never passing any examinations that I managed to get my own way in the end. I couldn't really see, as time went on, why the fact that a chap was very interested in music, was any valid reason for his becoming a dentist.'

1

APPRENTICESHIP (1925–35)

WHEN Rawsthorne entered the RMCM (which later became the Royal Northern College of Music), he studied cello with Carl Fuchs, composition with Dr Thomas Keighley (a notoriously ineffective composition teacher to whom Rawsthorne did not in later years refer when discussing his tutors), and piano with Frank Merrick, of whom he said, 'His methods of teaching were really invaluable because one learnt a great deal more about the actual composition of music from him than one would from most piano teachers',[1] and rapidly came to the fore as both pianist and composer. He was good enough to perform one of the Mozart E flat concertos, the Brahms Horn Trio, and, with a fellow student Gordon Green (who became one of Britain's finest piano teachers and one of Rawsthorne's closest friends), the Bach C minor Concerto for Two Pianos. Green recalled him also giving fine performances of Haydn's A flat major Sonata (Hoboken 31) and the Brahms *Handel Variations*, as well as Falla's *Nights in the Gardens of Spain* and Beethoven's C minor Violin Sonata. This repertoire, which also included Purcell (notable not least for Rawsthorne's later disinclination for the school of English musicians most keen to explore our musical past), demonstrates the obvious technical command he must have had. Haydn was to become one of his two favourite composers (the other being Chopin), while his relationship with the music of Brahms became less consistent, changing from deep admiration at this time to a high degree of ambivalence later on. While claiming to dislike Brahms intensely he nevertheless stated that had he taught he would always have encouraged students to go and study Brahms as a model, and his own Second Piano Concerto clearly reveals a debt to Brahms, repaid with obvious affection.

Among influences to which he did admit in later life, one important figure impinges on his family background: Blake. To the casual observer this is a rather surprising influence: Rawsthorne's music seems hardly very Blake-like in its restraint and economy. One assumes it was Blake's literary, rather than visual, work that prompted this admission. In one important respect there is

[1] Radio interview with Malcolm Rayment for series 'The Composer Speaks', recorded 24 May 1962.

a clear family link, since the Rawsthornes were much involved with the Swedenborgian religion, and Blake was himself for a time a Swedenborgian (sharing with the religion's founder frequent experience of visions). This belief was based on the teachings of the scientist, philosopher, and prophet Emanuel Swedenborg (1688–1772), whose missionary work and interpretations of biblical revelation achieved a wide following in Europe and America, outlining a Christianity of liberalism and community fellowship. Hubert's father James had married the daughter of Dr Jonathan Bayley, a leading Swedenborgian minister who came from Salford, and after running a school in Accrington for a number of years, moved to London and built up a substantial reputation through his teachings and books. On the death of James from tuberculosis aged 38, Hubert's mother took him at the age of 2 to live in London with her parents, and later both Hubert and his wife Janet became practising Swedenborgians, though neither Alan nor Barbara followed suit.

Alan's active and promising musical life at the RMCM was seriously disturbed by the death of his beloved mother in 1927 at the age of 49. The whole family was shattered by Janet's death, which cast a shadow that probably never quite left the Rawsthorne children; there exists a charming family portrait photograph of Barbara and Alan with their parents conveying most touchingly the obvious happiness of the family, and in such a close-knit group this event must have been especially tragic. It is interesting to speculate whether the haunted nature of so much of Rawsthorne's music, especially his predilection for the ghostly waltzes that punctuate his career, stems from the resonances in his subconscious from this shock. In 1929 Barbara, Hubert, and Alan moved to Fallowfield, Manchester; three years later, in 1932, Hubert moved to Colwyn Bay, where he remained until his death in 1943. Another important person entered their lives during the RMCM years, the violin student Jessie Hinchliffe, who later became Alan's first wife.

Gordon Green has given a vivid picture of Rawsthorne in their student days:

. . . strikingly handsome; slim, with blonde hair, pale complexion, exceptionally broad forehead and an oval face narrowing steeply towards the chin. Beneath the face the fine bony structure was clearly marked. There was a hint of Modigliani about the head and the face was Chopin-like, but with a mouth even more firmly moulded than Chopin's and without the disfigurement of Chopin's too large aquiline nose . . . [Ours] was a friendship which, I believe, gave Alan much happiness and, for me, was a constant source of stimulation and joy.[2]

---

[2] Quoted in Alan Poulton, 'The Pianist—From Manchester to Poland and Berlin', Poulton ii. 12.

Green described this friendship in some detail:

I found him willing to talk about most subjects; his general reading was wider than mine, and he had thought to greater purpose than I had about those extra-musical matters which so greatly interested me . . . During our student days, and for many following years, we discussed a wide variety of topics—gossip not excluded—usually at a very late hour; in fact, over all the years, one of the characteristics of my friendship with Alan was a reluctance to go to bed and, certainly in the summer months, bed-time was usually indicated only by the singing of birds.

Clearly, a certain bohemian disregard for the niceties of conventional time-keeping was already a strong characteristic.

During this period, Alan was starting to have pieces performed in student concerts. Three Songs to texts of de la Mare, Shakespeare, and Villon (which have disappeared) were performed on 15 March 1927, and in May the same year the first movement of an early (now lost) Violin Sonata, as well as a Chopinesque Valse for piano (a first broadcast for both Alan the composer and Gordon Green the pianist). Two years later saw performances of a Ballade for piano in G sharp minor, dated Christmas 1929, also written for Green (who referred to it as containing 'a recurring thematic reference to *Good King Wenceslas*'[3]), and a group of settings of Chinese texts, the *Tzu-Yeh Songs*. Inevitably there is some inconsistency in the standards of these very early works, which remain unpublished (though the *Tzu-Yeh Songs* deserve to emerge in print). It is interesting to note that, though vocal music appeared intermittently throughout his career, there was much more emphasis on it at the beginning and, to an even greater extent, in the last decade or so. In the summer of 1929 he wrote to Bax, whose music he greatly admired at the time, asking for composition lessons; Bax politely declined but recommended Adam Carse, whose lessons, postponed to 1932, proved to consist solely of contrapuntal exercises.

In 1929 Rawsthorne left the RMCM having taken both the performer's and teacher's diplomas, as well as winning prizes for both composition and piano. Adolph Brodsky, the Principal (who in younger days had given the première of the Tchaikovsky Violin Concerto), wrote in his testimonial (Christmas 1928): 'I think his future lies as much in concerted music as it is in his solo playing. He adapts his tone more than many others to the tone of the string instruments as against the formidable tone of the modern piano. His phrasing is to the point and he grasps the proper style of a given composer.' Anticipating a career as a pianist, Rawsthorne went in 1930 to Zakopane in Poland to

---

[3] Quoted in Alan Poulton, ii. 13.

study with the great pianist and teacher Egon Petri. His experiences there were recorded in letters home and to his fellow RMCM graduate Harry Blech, sometimes most amusingly. Describing his journey in a droshky to the Zakopane *pension* where he was to stay, he wrote to Elizabeth Bridge on 4 July 1930:

As to the number of wheels on a drosky, there should be at least one: indeed it is more comfortable to ride in when there are two. Also these wheels should be circular in shape, and of more or less the same size, but this is not essential—what is essential is that the horse which draws the vehicle should be a savage and self-willed brute and the driver either drunk or a lunatic. I have only driven in one once—in fact, I believe that most people only drive in them once, the survivors being too unnerved for a second attempt. There is a sanatorium in Zakopane with a cemetery attached especially built, I believe, for people who have been for rides in droskys.

He found life in Zakopane more stimulating than expected; writing to Blech on 1 July 1930 he stated that, while he had expected 'music, the mountains, reading and thinking about various things . . . a rather introspective and self-conscious period', he found that 'Zakopane has more resources than I imagined in the way of sophistication' and that 'extremely easy relations' were established among Petri's pupils. 'Twice we have been to a dancing place called "Morskies" and returned in the clear light of day; this is not without its aesthetic value because the dawn here . . . is unforgettable.' He and a German fellow student sometimes went at night 'to the room of Elena Gavrilova, who is the 24 year-old step-daughter of Glazounov and who is well aware that she looks her best in pyjamas.' Despite all this socializing, however, a touch of melancholy crept in:

I suffer most profound fits of depression, thinking I shall never play the piano, nor find any vacant inches [niches?] to fill. Also, that I am all the time seeking some really satisfying modus vivendi and haven't got it really clearly before my eyes . . . It is an extraordinary thing that human beings if they are not actively oppressed by poverty or disease or cruelty of the usual 'slings and arrows of outrageous fortune' must invent nameless phantasies to be miserable about. I suppose it is a matter of temperament rather than circumstances.[4]

Rawsthorne's enthusiasm for Busoni, of whom Petri was a noted interpreter and former pupil, may date from this time (though Merrick's influence must also have played a part). The elusive, sometimes withdrawn nature of Busoni's art, for all its occasional virtuoso display, gives a clue to their musical kinship, and in technical terms, Busoni's liking for augmented harmonies and touches

[4] Ibid. 15.

of bitonality would certainly have struck a response from Rawsthorne. They have other features in common, too (see the opening section of Chapter 3). Szymanowski also lived in Zakopane, but there is no record of Alan ever having met him or being particularly interested in his music.

In September, Alan returned home to Fallowfield. He wrote to Harry Blech (15 September 1930):

I have to come to London next week-end . . . in order to attend an immense family party on Friday afternoon. My dear blissfully innocent creature you have no comprehension of what this means but if you have ever read Galsworthy's 'Forsyte Saga' you may be able to form a guess. Every type therein set forth will be present. My Great-Uncle Edward, the Family Patriarch, a Justice of the Peace and ex-member for Chiswick will champ his toothless gums in reminiscences of the early '40's . . . I can't summon the spirit to contemplate the week-end with equanimity.

In February 1931 he went to Berlin to continue his studies with Petri, going there via Amsterdam. To Elizabeth Bridge he wrote on 24 February 1931:

I had to be taken to the police-station and shown to the police—nothing to do with Beethoven [which he had been practising], but just because it is the custom here. Whenever anyone arrives in Berlin, or removes or does anything of that kind, they always tell the police, and the police take many particulars as to what you are, why you have come to Berlin (which they seem to think a very odd thing to do), whether your father wears artificial teeth and much more.

It is an interesting coincidence that Alan Bush, later to become such a close friend and colleague, gave a concert of his own music in Berlin on 29 January; there is no record of the two Alans having met there, but it seems very likely that they did. Rawsthorne did, however, attend a Schönberg concert, described in a letter to Blech (27 February 1931):

I spent last night in the company of the Berlin Tonkünstler where a German young lady played piano pieces by Arnold Schönberg for an hour and a half [sic], and certain stars shot madly from their spheres and I shot madly into the nearest restaurant and drank a Cherry-brandy. I am still all of a Schönberg—I fear this letter is somewhat confused—but it was a very strange Concert indeed.

Later in life he recalled: 'I remember then wondering whether one should react to these pieces as romantic outpourings, or whether they should be regarded as more intellectual studies. I decided in favour of the first, and I rather think that has continued to be my attitude towards this sort of music, certainly Schönberg'.[5] In his broadcast interview with Malcolm Williamson (1965), he

---

[5] Radio interview with Malcolm Rayment.

maintained that Schönberg had a profound influence on everybody, regardless of whether they followed his methods or not: 'You don't have to be Robespierre to be aware that a French Revolution is taking place, do you?' After his return to England, he shared a flat in London with Harry Blech, being permitted to do so only after Blech had discussed things with the family and convinced them that Alan would be perfectly safe in London ('How lovely that you have had lunch with my father', he wrote to Blech) and searched around for a means of earning a living.

The early 1930s had seen the production of a number of minor works, mostly songs such as 'Le Moulin' (a setting of a French text by the Belgian poet Emile Verhoeren), *Four Poems of Richard Church*, and a more interesting piece, *Esquisses* for voice and chamber orchestra. The range of texts he drew upon is extraordinarily varied; as his own juvenile literary efforts indicate, he was a voracious, wide-ranging reader. Among the works thought to have been written during the period 1930–2, 'Le Moulin' is harmonically unadventurous, with an unrelenting accompanying figure derived pictorially from the mill of the title and a syllabic melodic line that offers little in the way of interest. There is a little more flexibility of vocal technique in a setting of 'Fain would I change that note', which bears the dedication 'For J.', along with subtler shifts of harmony, occasional expressive melismata, and some touches of real individuality, though the 5/8 rhythm forces him into some awkward word-setting. A setting for soprano and smallish orchestra of 'Come unto these yellow sands' is uncharacteristically folk-like. The contrast between the orchestral part, in 6/8, and a more abstract vocal line in 2/4 is imaginative, and he delays the establishment of the E minor tonality, playing tonal games with the listener, even if at a fairly simple level at this stage of his career. The orchestration is straightforward, but with some nice touches—low bassoon fifths after the words 'Hark! the watch-dogs bark bow-wow!', for instance.

Like the Shakespeare setting, *Esquisses* is for high voice and chamber orchestra (flute, piccolo, oboe, clarinet, bassoon, two horns, gong, triangle, celesta, and strings), setting four of Arthur Waley's translations from the Chinese. As Trevor Hold has pointed out, 'the wedding of these First Century B.C. Chinese poems with twentieth-century dance-tunes has a somewhat surreal flavour . . . it is less a song-cycle than a suite of instrumental dances with a vocal part'.[6] The vocal writing remains rather constrained, but there are some imaginative touches in the orchestral part, with an almost soloistic use of the celesta and triangle in the first movement and an air of langorous, somewhat

---

[6] Trevor Hold, 'The Solo Vocal Music', Poulton iii. 68.

luxurious but nostalgic relaxation. It is followed by a Waltz (in 6/8), of decidedly Spanish tinge, a slowish Polka with restrained echoes of Shostakovitch (as in *The Golden Age*), and a final Allegro feroce in B minor in which side-drum and cymbals are added to give extra punch to the orchestral sound. The discretion with which the scoring is accomplished shows clearly his natural understanding of the medium, and the intriguingly *Façade*-like touches scattered through the score add to its charm. There are occasional hints of Rawsthorne's mature style, not least in a very characteristic Polka theme, while the ironic contrast in the Waltz between the singer's last line 'For long years plunged in sordid grief' and the orchestra's final energetic flourish on its Spanish tune indicates his thoughtfulness.

The *Four Poems of Richard Church* (1931), for voice and piano, contain hardly any hints of the composer to come, however. Indeed, so clumsy are some of the harmonic changes, and even the piano writing, that it is difficult to see how they can come from the same period. There are strong hints of the influence of John Ireland, Richard Strauss, and even Reger, somewhat undigested, and the customarily syllabic setting, combined with the overall slowness of tempo and melancholy mood, leads to an impression of monotony. Some unexpectedly pictorial touches colour the piano part, but occasional bursts of more elaborate writing fit uneasily into the overall modesty of the style. Rawsthorne's interest in choosing texts reflecting aspects of nature and their relationship with human emotions is significant throughout all these works, and this is equally true of the little cycle of *Tzu-Yeh Songs* (again from Waley's translations from the Chinese), which though written earlier than the other works (their first performance was in 1929), is much more successful. It is true that there are some transitions needing careful handling by the performers, and there is little real individuality in the music, which falls into the diatonic English song tradition with, once again, hints of John Ireland, but this group of four short settings, performed without a break, has considerable charm. The accompaniment's pattern-making never outstays its welcome, the vocal line is singable and flexible, not just purely syllabic, and there is a true sense of the delicate melancholy underlying the final poem. The ending, inconclusive and questioning, is highly imaginative, and Rawsthorne's use of thematic and accompanimental ideas from the first few bars as material unifying the whole work anticipates the close thematic integrity of his mature music. Coincidentally, Constant Lambert, later to become one of Alan's closest friends, completed his *Eight Poems of Li-Po* in 1929; Lambert's settings are more personal as well as subtler in their approach to touches of chinoiserie, but the Rawsthorne songs achieve successfully what they set out to do.

In 1932 Rawsthorne took up the only full-time job of his life, as pianist and composer at the School of Dance-Mime at Dartington Hall in Devon, the famous liberal arts school founded in the 1920s by Dorothy and Leonard Elmhirst, who wanted to establish a centre for a new classless society based on ideals of community, progressiveness, and radical political and creative thought. Early visitors included W. H. Auden, Benjamin Britten, Walter Gropius, Barbara Hepworth, Aldous Huxley, T. E. Lawrence, Ben Nicholson, and Bertrand Russell. Alan provided occasional compositions, as incidental music for play and dance productions and for individual dance numbers, and gave numerous piano performances at their public shows in places like Teignmouth and Plymouth. His repertoire ranged from Clementi, Haydn, Bach, Purcell and Brahms to Bartók, Casella, Debussy, Szymanowski, and Ibert. Conditions, especially during the winters, were spartan, with all the traditional pitfalls of performing at local theatres, draughty and somewhat insanitary backstage conditions, and the like. There were compensations, in the form of visits to the cinema to see the latest German films, lobster parties, and, not least, the presence of a number of attractive young women among the dancers.

The most significant musical development of the period was the composition of a String Quartet in 1932, performed by the Griller Quartet in June of the following year at Dartington. At the same concert Norman Stone gave the first performance of Six Songs, of which the only extant manuscript is a Herrick setting, 'To Daffodils'; the simple, unaffected piano part shows a new degree of contrapuntal and linear relationship with the flowing, stepwise vocal line. The mood is, typically, melancholy, the harmonies inflected by a new major/ minor ambiguity, which became a fundamental element in Rawsthorne's style. The quartet itself was taken up by Anne Macnaghten's quartet during the 1933–4 season of the Macnaghten–Lemare concerts in London, a prominent series established in 1931 to give young or neglected British composers a public hearing; it also gave women composers a fairer hearing than they later received in the immediate post-war years in London, and the significant works they premièred included Britten's Sinfonietta and *A Boy was Born*. Among other composers represented by works (mostly new) in the 1933–4 season were Helen Perkin, Maconchy (two works), Grace Williams, Britten (two works, including the *Quartetto serioso*), Jacob (two works), Dorothy Gow (two works), Frederick May, and Christian Darnton. The Dartington appointment came to an end when the Kurt Jooss Ballet Company arrived to take up residence, displacing the company already present, Before this, Alan was (as a passenger) involved in a serious car accident, from which it took him some time to recover, and following his resignation from the company in the summer, he returned to London and married Jessie in July 1934; Gordon Green arrived in the morning to find, to his surprise, that he had been 'cast for the role of best man'.[7]

The London performance of the 1932 quartet was well received by the press. *The Times* commented that 'Few "influences" were discernable, and though the form was the most interesting feature of the work, the matter was original enough to fill it without any straining after outlandish modes of expression. It struck an individual note, said what it wanted to say, and promises well for future work.' The *Musical Times* thought it possessed 'genuine string quartet writing . . . at one point near the end, the music took charge of the composer with the strength of an inspiration. It was not the composer making the music, but the music making the composer.'[8] Both the Macnaghtens and the Grillers thought highly enough of it to include it in further concert programmes. The three movements have numerous aspects quite typical of the later Rawsthorne, including an inclination to move from one key to another, and a large number of characteristic rhythmic devices (such as a 5/8 rhythm in the finale that reappears in the Scherzo of the much later First Symphony). There is an interesting tempo progression, gradually increasing the pace from the opening Fugue (Molto Adagio), through the central Andante, to the Molto Allegro quasi Presto of the finale, and the key of the work is B minor, the middle movement ending in G. The Fugue theme itself has a number of Rawsthornian fingerprints, with a trill within the melodic outline, the use of a sharp seventh as the peak of a curling phrase, and the kind of rhythmic instability that he employed in a number of relatively early works, with successive time signatures of 14/8, 5/8, 14/16, and 6/8. In the Andante, the main theme is a simple, childlike melody in G, a type of tune that he hardly ever employed in later works, though the busy, expressive climax and the use of a canon for the final restatement of the main tune are more typical. Following a performance (possibly private) for Eric Blom, Alan wrote to Anne Macnaghten that

I feel there is a connection in style between the first and third movements, but I rather think . . . the middle one is out of the picture. In fact I believe it isn't a stylistic unity in itself; I tinkered at it for a bit, but there comes a time when one says 'Hell!' and the only thing to do is to write another quartet.

Vigour is the hallmark of the finale, with much emphasis on vital rhythmic impulse and a characteristic recalling of earlier material, tranquillo, before a

[7] Poulton, 'Marriage and First Successes in Composition', Poulton ii. 24.
[8] (Mar. 1934).

presto coda, another device used in many later works. Stylistically it is an uneven work, but it has many clear hints of the mature composer and much interesting material. Rawsthorne himself admitted that

it certainly took a long time for me to decide exactly which road I wanted to travel in the way of composing. I tried a great many things—imitations of various composers, out of which I have tried to produce something which is individual. But until I felt at ease in this way I didn't really want to emerge as a composer.[9]

What is remarkable even about the works from the early 1930s is the rapid development of Rawsthorne's personal voice, which comes out intermittently in the 1932 quartet but begins to take command of the overall tone of his next chamber works.

The two unpublished violin sonatas from 1933–4 were written (presumably) for Jessie (the second certainly bears a dedication to her, as well as an inscription, ' "Du hast Diamenten" '). Their importance lies in the sudden emergence of vitally important thematic material from which the mature composer was to draw seemingly limitless inspiration. The first sonata, in A major, has two movements, the incomplete first opening lyrically (Ex. 1.1) with an underlying passion that bursts out later in some massive, almost orchestral passages on the piano. The movement is really too long and inconclusive, with much note-spinning and some unusually muddy textures; rhythmic interest is created at times by changing metres, much as in the 1932 quartet. An interesting feature is the increasing range of intervals in Rawsthorne's melodic repertoire, now incorporating fourths, which dominate the slower second subject group (in E major); equally significant is the recapitulation, where a fortissimo variation of the second theme in the violin is combined with a grandiose piano treatment of the first (a device characteristic both of the mature Rawsthorne, anticipating his dislike of the full, conventional recapitulation, and of Haydn, who liked to dovetail development and recapitulation; Busoni was another who disliked what he felt was unnecessary repetition). The second movement, dominated by a slightly Prokofievian rondo theme complete with tonal side-slips, has similar failings, with some overlong pedal-points holding the music back rather than building tension, but two sections were reused in the Concertante for violin and piano of 1935. There is also the first appearance in his music of what can only be described as 'oom-pah' music, another feature frequently encountered throughout his career. When asked in 1969 (apropos his Concerto for Two Pianos) why he had included a section of this kind in the finale of that work, he replied to the effect that it was a bit

[9] Radio interview with Malcolm Rayment.

Ex. 1.1. Violin Sonata in A major, opening

of 'North Country vulgarity—people expect that sort of thing from me', a typically self-deprecatory remark to be taken with a pinch of salt, but revealing none the less. It is impossible to discover from where he derived this particular kind of inspiration; he does not seem to have been particularly fond of circuses or brass bands, both possible sources of this musical style, though he did enjoy music halls and variety shows. Possibly these gave him this particular stimulus, much as Satie, Poulenc, and others derived inspiration from Parisian music-hall and cabaret.

The A minor Violin Sonata, the second to be written, also contains some clumsy piano writing (surprising in so proficient a performer), with over-use of octaves and bass sonorities. The first movement is really a set of variations on the opening theme (Ex. 1.2), though typically there is a strong developmental tendency as the music proceeds; indeed, there is a somewhat uncomfortable dichotomy between variation technique and elements of sonata form, something Rawsthorne resolved triumphantly in the Symphonic Studies for orchestra (1938). There are an astonishing number of pre-echoes of his later music: the third variation reaches a massive piano climax anticipating moments

Ex. 1.2. Violin Sonata in A minor, opening

in the late chamber music with piano, while the fifth, a light scherzando in 6/8, forms a contrast with the brilliance and virtuosity of the fourth, a contrast employed to entirely personal effect in such later pieces as the concertos for violin and cello. The fourth variation begins with running semiquavers in the piano clearly foreshadowing the Scherzo of the Quintet for piano and wind (1962–3), one of his finest late works; an especially interesting feature is that, while the later Scherzo employs a serial note row, here there is a series of eleven notes at the start, though this implication is not followed through. Perhaps it lay dormant in his creative subconscious for thirty years. The two versions of the second movement are different: what is presumed to be the later copy because of some pencilled performance markings (and the fact that the other copy has a preliminary title 'Theme and Variations', crossed out) starts with an Allegro Appassionato used in the later Concertante No. 2, and both also include other material employed in the Concertante, where it is more focused structurally and the textures have been cleaned up.

Exx. 1.1 and 2 demonstrate how much of the mature Rawsthorne is present in these two sonatas, for all the immaturities they demonstrate as they progress. In the A major Sonata, the lack of motion for most of bars 3–4 is disappointingly weak, but the opening violin tune is strongly characteristic, with its upward leap of a sixth (bar 6), the shift from A minor to G sharp minor at the end of the same bar, the rhythmic shape of the theme at the end of bar 7 and the beginning of bar 9, and (also in bar 9) the lovely harmonic shift to F major, albeit with a sharpened fourth (B♮). There is also the typical false relation (G♯ against G♮) in bar 11; this major/minor ambiguity is already becoming a musical fingerprint. Ex. 1.2, from the A minor Sonata, is even more significant. Admittedly, the cadence back to A minor in bars 10–11 is extraordinarily conventional, though its obvious weakness is emphasized by its placing in a context otherwise so full of personal character.

Professor Sebastian Forbes has pointed out how the first three notes of the piano part are crucial in relating to much of the thematic material throughout the work, sometimes with great subtlety.[10] These notes, indeed, form one of the most important reservoirs of material throughout Rawsthorne's career; it is as if he had already identified his most essential thematic device. The interval of the major seventh (G♯ down to A) is a vital expressive component of his style, and the cell A-G♯-F provides him with innumerable possibilities: it covers a major third (A to F) as well as a minor third (taking G♯ to be equivalent to A♭), giving him the major–minor dichotomy that creates such ambiguity and

---

[10] 'The Chamber Music', Poulton iii. 9.

bitter-sweetness in the sound of his music, while the three notes played as a chord provide the basis for his most characteristic seventh chords (add C or C# to them to create the most essentially Rawsthornian harmonies). Such four-note chords, of course, also include an augmented triad (for example, A–C#–F), the sound of which imbues his music with that elusive, ambiguous atmosphere one might trace back to Busoni and, perhaps through him, to the late works of Liszt. The cadence into B flat minor (bar 9) is, like the move to G sharp in Ex. 1.1, entirely characteristic. These are early illustrations of Rawsthorne's liking for fairly rapid harmonic or tonal movement, which became quicker and even more fleeting once he had worked out his style fully and eradicated disruptive outside influences; it is the speed of his harmonic or tonal thinking that makes his music difficult for some listeners, and requires them to fine-tune their antennae in order to be completely receptive to the progress of the music or to begin to appreciate its subtleties and depths. The extent to which he derived so much inspiration from the interval of a third is remarkable (though one is reminded of Nielsen's remark that it was a gift from God); apart from melodic factors such as alternating major or minor thirds and the use of a sixth (the inverted third) within a curling melodic line (as in bar 6 of Ex. 1.1), there are the harmonic implications (augmented and seventh chords made of superimposed thirds), and the major/minor tonal inflections reflect Rawsthorne's liking for third-related tonal centres, as one must learn to call his keys, reminding one that both Haydn and Beethoven were fond of keys related by a third, and that Sibelius (who was not such a favourite of Alan's) used the third as a vital tonal tool.

Everything comes together splendidly in the Concertante No. 2 for violin and piano (1935), his first publication, taken by a small publishing firm, Cecilian Press, and issued in 1937; it was later (1968) revised slightly and published by Oxford University Press (OUP) under the title 'Concertante'. (There is no indication as to the identity of Concertante No. 1: it has been suggested that it was the A major Violin Sonata, but it could also have been an earlier version of the work known as Sonatina for flute, oboe, and piano, which originally dates from around this period.) The various sections largely derive from the two earlier sonatas, but are given more coherence and force by their juxtaposition and structural tightening in this excellent recital piece, which is (once again) dedicated to Jessie and lasts about eight-and-a-half minutes. The key-scheme is a progression from a D minor-ish opening to a defiant final A minor (almost as if the work were an extended plagal cadence). Rawsthorne is sensitive to the need to relax and increase tension: he does this, after a period of intensely chromatic and tonally shifting music, by arriving at a tonal centre which is maintained for longer or has melodic or harmonic material derived from a repeated note or chord, thus giving the listener the feeling that a more stable position has been reached, however momentarily. Ex. 1.3 gives several extracts to display both the flavour of the music and a sense of its thematic integration.

The opening violin line (Ex. 1.3(*a*)), the first four notes of which became a familiar Rawsthorne 'signature' (his equivalent of Shostakovich's D-S-C-H

Ex. 1.3. Concertante for violin and piano: (*a*) opening; (*b*) from p. 2 line 4; (*c*) from p. 8, 2nd system, bar 1 (piano only)

(*a*)

(*b*)

figure), once again depends on his alternating major and minor thirds, which also provide the piled-up piano harmony underneath, while the second violin phrase again shows his liking for the melodic use of particular intervals (including the sixth in a curling melodic line, and the seventh). The violin line introduces an important new element in Rawsthorne's musical make-up, a recitative-like style (the tempo marking includes the indicative words '*quasi improvvisamente*') that in other works might be marked '*parlando*' or '*libera-mente*', while the piano chords starting in bar 6 are decidedly bitonal in impli-cation, though they can also be analysed simply in terms of augmented chords with false relations. In the succeeding Allegro Appassionato (taken from the A minor Sonata), one notes the individual use of cross-rhythms, indicated by the accents, as well as melodic elements already becoming familiar; Sebastian Forbes has pointed out that the first upward violin phrase clearly fills in the implications of the opening descending phrase of Ex. 1.2, inverting it and filling in the interval of the major seventh with notes from the scale of which it is the skeleton,[11] and the speed with which the harmonic motion now pro-ceeds should be noted (in the first two bars, the bass-line descends from D through D♭ to C and then up to F, outlining incredibly fast tonal shifts). The central Adagio, which first appeared in the A major Sonata and reappeared in its successor, is remarkably near to atonality, though stability is provided by the sustained B♭ in the bass (Ex. 1.3(*c*)) and then by the introduction of a simple upper right-hand theme whose expressive richness is enhanced by the accompanying lines, with melodic and contrapuntal interest of their own. There are also hints of the imaginative use of sequential devices (bars 5 and 6 of Ex. 1.3(*c*), for instance), another important ingredient of Rawsthorne's technical armoury. The final Tempo del Allegro recapitulates, with some vari-ation, the material of the first Allegro, itself clearly related to the Lento intro-duction, and there is a burst of exuberant virtuosity to close the work. The sustained vigour and rhythmic excitement of the final section are most in-vigorating, and the work is a remarkably successful recital piece displaying the virtuosity of both performers as well as the composer's technical ingenuity and expressive mastery. Gordon Green commented of this period that 'Alan was finally realizing where his innate musical sympathies lay (Bax had long since been superseded by Bartók and Stravinsky; Brahms was being displaced by Berlioz and Chopin) and the direction, creatively, he was to take.'[12] The Con-certante is testimony to his remarkable progress in rapidly defining his own musical world.

[11] The Chamber Music, 7.

[12] 'The Pre-War Years', Programme Book for the Alan Rawsthorne Memorial Concert, Wigmore Hall, London, 24 Nov. 1971.

2

MAKING A CAREER (1935–8)

OVER the next few years, Rawsthorne concentrated on composing and trying to make a career for himself (he is reputed to have worked for a short while in a piano showroom, as John Field had done over a century earlier). Gordon Green commented that he 'fulfilled many routine commissions, scoring other people's music for this or that combination and gaining valuable experience thereby. In particular, he made arrangements for the Adolph Hallis Quintet, one of those ensembles favoured by the BBC at the time, playing, excellently, music that was both light and good.'[1] The vast repertoire covered by these arrangements (made under the pseudonym 'A. Jess') ranged from Mozart's 'Turkish' Rondo, a Paganini caprice, and a Chopin mazurka to pieces by Couperin, Smetana, Gung'l, Daquin, Moszkowski, Tchaikovsky, Raff, Clementi, and a host of other names. A list in the OUP archives also catalogues a number of titles under his own name such as 'En bateau', 'Hungarian Sketch', and 'Chinese Dance', hardly any of them known to us (apart from one or two pieces of incidental music and what is presumably a quintet arrangement of the violin and piano piece 'Pierette', so there may somewhere be a store of manuscripts of light music by him. With Jessie a violinist in the BBC Symphony Orchestra, and Alan acting for the BBC as an arranger and copyist, there was plenty of scope for making new friendships and meeting people. Iris Lemare, the conductor, and Anne Macnaghten, the violinist whose string quartet was still an eminent ensemble in the 1960s, were particularly important figures on the musical scene.

Referring to life in the 1930s, Gordon Green wrote that

awareness of unemployment and malnutrition at home and of the ominous rise of fascism in Europe marred our felicity . . . Like many liberal-minded persons of our age and generation, we saw the world as dividing into two camps represented in quintessence by communism and fascism, and we believed that the former was the only power ideologically and materially strong enough to meet the menace of the latter . . . Neither

---

[1] 'The Pre-War Years', Programme Book for the Alan Rawsthorne Memorial Concert, Wigmore Hall, London, 24 Nov. 1971.

Alan nor I could accept the discipline of Communist Party membership. Alan set too much value on individual autonomy.[2]

The artistic and social movements of the 1930s can be seen, with the benefit of hindsight, as a sometimes shattering realignment of society. In Germany, the move to power of Hitler and the National Socialist Party led to the horrors of the Second World War and the Holocaust; in Spain, the Fascists also rose to power (with considerable aid from Nazi Germany among others), following a bloody civil war in which the Republican movement was the focus for support from left-wingers including a substantial number of British artists (composers like Britten and Rawsthorne, poets like Auden, MacNeice, and Spender, and many other writers and painters: Orwell's *Homage to Catalonia* remains one of the most vivid reminders of that time); in Italy, Mussolini's Fascist government reached its apogee. Oswald Mosley's Fascist movement in Britain represented a strong right-wing force. There was, despite the calls of many politicians and others (including, famously, Winston Churchill), a mood of appeasement by the British government towards Hitler.

At the same time, there was a leftward move, or at least a shift in opinion and policy towards more awareness of the community. One of Rawsthorne's closest friendships, from the 1930s on, was with the communist poet Randall Swingler, whose views had great influence on him (they also shared a voluminous knowledge and memory of English poetry). In politics, Britain's Labour Party had achieved government, and the Depression, the Jarrow Hunger Marches, and other symptoms of poverty and deprivation inspired the gradual establishment of policies in health, education, and unemployment benefit that led to the post-war Welfare State. The arts saw the growth of the Modernism of the time; in poetry, Auden, Eliot, and others began to dominate the scene. The arts in general reflected the gradual division of society into left and right. The most spectacular theatrical hit of the era, Noel Coward's *Cavalcade* (1932), was described by Robert Graves and Alan Hodge as 'a variety show which evoked the sentimental charm, the belief in progress, and the patriotism of the Victorian age . . . "Cavalcade" was an immediate success because it appeared just when a stern national effort was being made to overcome the Depression.'[3] It was an era of Victorian revivals as well as avant-garde experiment, the latter partly influenced by the effects of the jazzier 1920s and partly by the political changes taking place.

The previous decade, indeed, had begun to establish some specific artistic

---

[2] Quoted in A. Poulton, 'Biography', Poulton ii. 24–5.
[3] *The Long Weekend*, 2nd edn. (London, 1985), 296–7.

trends. Graves and Hodge summed up one literary area: 'Coward was the dramatist of disillusion, as Eliot was its tragic poet, Aldous Huxley its novel-ist, and James Joyce its prose epic-writer. They all had in common a sense of the unreality of time.'[4] This was the generation of Huxley's *Brave New World*, H. G. Wells's *The Shape of Things to Come*, the rise of pacifism (personified by Sassoon and Huxley) and of communism, the almost religious belief in the power of science to remedy society's ills and at the same time the anxiety (well justified, as things have turned out) that its discoveries might be misapplied and the benefits be forgone. The new technologies expanded, housing devel-opments (Betjeman's beloved suburban areas, for example) spread, and in the cinema the important development of the documentary movement led by John Grierson (who coined the term 'documentary') reflected the growing confidence in the medium in Britain and the concern to reflect ordinary lives. Films like *Drifters* (1929), *Night Mail* (famous also for its Auden text and Britten score), *Coalface*, *Housing Problems*, and many others led to a bur-geoning of documentary-making subsidized by industry (the Post Office, railway companies, tourist associations, and the like) and paved the way for the establishment of the outstanding government service films of wartime and the poetical films of Humphrey Jennings (*Diary for Timothy*, *Listen to Britain*, *Fires were started*).

Anthony Payne summed up the musical world into which Rawsthorne had emerged during the 1930s:

It seemed in the 1930's as if Vaughan Williams had re-created an English tradition by relating himself to our Elizabethan past, but it is becoming increasingly clear that his stylistic discoveries had relevance solely to his own visionary requirements . . . [Rawsthorne's] first public performances in the late thirties displayed a style utterly at variance with the prevailing English fashion. It lacked the religious mysticism, nature poetry, and other programmatic overtone[s] then popular. It was independent of our vocal and choral tradition, and so was not susceptible to literary description, while its concentration on overall expressive structure and pattern-making ran contrary to the picturesque rhapsodising which in many quarters was considered the main hope for a sincere British school of composition. In a word it was considered continental.[5]

In a sense, there is a kind of equivalence between the English pastoral tradition and the new interest in Continental models, and the split between right and left in politics, though Vaughan Williams's socialism straddled the boundaries with immense generosity of spirit.

---

[4] Ibid. 147.
[5] Sleeve-note for the LP recording of Rawsthorne's Clarinet Quartet (Argo ZRG 660, London, 1970).

Rawsthorne produced a number of works during this period, some of whose dates of composition are not precisely known—the song 'Infant Joy' (a Blake setting) and the violin and piano waltz 'Pierette', for instance. The more substantial works are for the most part more easily dated, though at least two are lost: Iris Lemare conducted on Overture for Chamber Orchestra composed in 1935, and a Chamber Cantata for voice, string quartet, and harpsichord on medieval texts was performed at one of the Adolph Hallis Chamber Music concerts, in February 1937 (a series which later saw the première of the original version of the First Piano Concerto). Neither of these was particularly well received by critics. The *Daily Telegraph* reviewer J. A. W. (presumably Westrup) commented on the overture that it 'was a careful and sincere piece of work; but at present the composer is still too much occupied with the technical problems to let his fancy take wing', though other reviewers were more positive about the composer's individuality and imagination. Of the cantata, J. A. W. (clearly not a Rawsthornian) commented in the *Daily Telegraph* (18 February 1937) that it was 'sincere, and even humorous, with not a little technical address; but the obstinate counterpoint and the nervous shrinking from a natural vocal line made an effect of strain and forced expression', while the anonymous reviewer in *The Times* the following day also commented on a voice part 'that seems perversely to avoid any feeling for vocal line'. It is significant that Rawsthorne's difficulty in writing sympathetic vocal music while he was working out his own style was so apparent to the critics, and it is particularly frustrating that these works have disappeared, especially the Cantata, since settings of medieval texts produced two fascinating and important late works, the *Medieval Diptych* and, one of his finest works, the Choral Suite *Carmen vitale*.

Much of Rawsthorne's extant work from this period remains unpublished, but it none the less contains music of high quality. This was revealed by the compact disc recording of his 1935 String Quartet, the non-publication, indeed non-performance, of which, remains a mystery.[6] Certainly he might have wanted to tighten the structure somewhat, especially in the last movement, but there are some remarkable things in the work, and it contains passages unlike anything in his later chamber output, as well as a slow movement of genuine mastery. The opening of the first movement (Ex. 2.1(a)) is immediately gripping, with its quiet throbbing rhythms, potentially rich harmonic and melodic material, and true sense of being a major work about to unfold. It is marked 'Andante con moto', and the rhythms of the first bar and a half

---

[6] The Carl Flesch Quartet, on ASV CD DCA 983 (London, 1997).

Ex. 2.1. String Quartet (1935): (*a*) first movement, bars 1–7; (*b*) third movement, from fig. 5

(*a*)

(*b*)

drive almost all the melodic invention forward. The gradual widening of the music from the narrow span of the opening through to the whole range of the instruments is superbly handled, as is the growth in romantic expressiveness. The climaxes are cleverly graded in intensity, and in every aspect of quartet writing Rawsthorne shows genuine mastery: the variety of texture, from solo with accompaniment to pairs of instruments contrasting and, of course, to block chordal textures, is beautifully handled. So too is the increase and decrease in tension, which is achieved partly by thickening and thinning texture and partly by simplifying the complex, shifting tonality with the occasional arrival at a more sustained tonal centre or a brief but telling pedal note. There are some passionate rhetorical gestures, anticipating moments in later orchestral works, a typically brief recapitulation (though with Rawsthorne it can be dangerously misleading simply to talk in terms of traditional sonata structures even when they seem to apply), and a tiny codetta which is dovetailed with the recapitulation but which also reiterates the idea from the opening to close the movement in a delicate, slightly melancholy E major.

In the succeeding scherzo, Allegro deciso, he inhabits a world familiar from the later Theme and Variations for two violins and the Bagatelles for piano, with vigorous semiquaver groups within basically quaver-driven melodic lines. The quartet writing is again resourceful and varied, with a good deal of perky contrapuntal development of the ideas and a satisfying overall shape. One has the feeling that other similar movements in later works are more memorable, but there is no denying the skill that is being applied. It is in the third movement, Molto adagio, that the heart of the work lies, however. It is unusual for a Rawsthorne slow movement in that, despite some development of material, there is no dramatic climax; instead, the music inhabits a largely spare, bleak world anticipating the later Shostakovich quartets, with an exceptional sense of immense space. In the opening section there is a seamless progression from slow-moving crotchets through quavers to more flowing semiquavers, though without any particular growth in excitement, normally the object of such a device; rather, it is an intensification of the underlying expression. When the opening material recurs towards the end, it is telescoped by the use of canonic devices, a typical way of avoiding the full, lengthy recapitulation of classical procedure.

What gives this movement its particular character is its restraint; the delicate 6/8 Più mosso central section is particularly notable. This kind of siciliano motion was to become a familiar Rawsthorne archetype, but here it is given the character of a ghostly waltz by the use of mutes and the accompanying figure: the atmosphere is uniquely delicate and complex (Ex. 2.1(b)). In the return of the opening material, the order of events is reversed, quavers coming before crotchets. Throughout, there is a tendency to provide more tonal stability than usual by means, for example, of slower harmonic motion from one underlying chord to the next, which is given an added fragility by the frequent sparseness of the instrumentation. The movement is marked by extreme clarity:

the instrumental spacing is superbly calculated to give the music room to breathe and to enable everything, even the slightest hint of contrapuntal working, to be heard clearly. It is one of his finest achievements in chamber music, venturing into territory he never explored so deeply again.

The final Allegro is markedly less successful. The problem is its diffuseness: wisely, the Flesch Quartet, in their recording, make a substantial cut (six pages out of a total of seventeen-and-a-quarter!), but this does not entirely solve it. There is, however, much to admire and enjoy, not least the idiomatic quartet writing. The movement opens with a strong unison E, followed by tiny three-note phrases reminiscent of the 'muss es sein?' phrase from Beethoven's F major Quartet, Op. 135. This forms the reservoir from which Rawsthorne derives most of his material, though there are two other important ideas, a Shostakovichian anapaestic dominant–tonic phrase which enters quite soon and is used as a kind of punctuation mark (most firmly at the conclusion of the work), and a secondary tune which was to reappear in the Fantasy Overture *Cortèges* ten years later (the surrounding textures, with their hints at a march-like feeling, also form a link with the later piece). Canonic workings abound, and Rawsthorne is beginning to incorporate into his vocabulary a liking for sequential treatment reflecting his love of baroque music, though any predictability this might bring is mitigated by cross-rhythms and syncopations. As Sebastian Forbes says apropos this quartet, 'there is always much to be gained by close examination of an example of any composer's early expression of his true voice—immaturity may still be found, but the long term goals are clearly in view, and the qualities of freshness and discovery are wonderfully evident.'[7]

This is equally true of an elegant Oboe Quartet, thought to have been written the same year and first performed on 1 October 1935 at the London Contemporary Music Centre by Helen Gaskell, Jean Pougnet, William Primrose, and Bernard Richards. The review in *The Times* was enthusiastic: it 'finished with a fine fugal movement in which a real musical impulse found full and cogent expression. An interesting technical point was his use of the oboe less as a quasi-solo instrument than as a thicker thread in the texture.' Indeed, this is a more consistently contrapuntal work than the String Quartet: the first movement is predominantly in three parts, enabling Rawsthorne to make the climactic dovetailing of development and recapitulation more telling through its fuller four-part texture. The tonal centre is F, which is affirmed strongly by the opening eight bars, and the opening (Ex. 2.2) reveals how

---

[7] 'The Chamber Music', Poulton iii. 12.

Ex. 2.2. Oboe Quartet (1935), first movement, bars 1–8

many important strands he is able to explore simultaneously: the oboe theme, an important counterpoint on viola (both beginning with a downward fourth, the interval from which the viola countersubject is more extensively derived), and a cello line moving in regular half-bar shifts like a baroque (or jazz) 'walking bass'. The descending chromatic phrase at the end of bar 7 (viola) is used canonically to close the movement, and seems a touch perfunctory, but its weakness has a purpose: the violin irruption at bar 8 is immediately more dramatic by virtue of its contrasting decisiveness, and the use of this contrast between lyrical and more aggressive elements is an important extension of Rawsthorne's resources. So too is the new emphasis on fourths as a thematic resource, and a variation of the first subject just before the close hints at a *rapprochement* with the more diatonic English pastoral school (a false hint, as it happens, though in his last period Rawsthorne frequently employed more open diatonicism). A curious feature is that the highest intensity of the movement occurs about half-way through, with the four-part climax; after this, the music gradually winds down, almost fizzling out into a somewhat casual final cadence.

An interesting feature of the Oboe Quartet is that each movement is longer than the preceding one; this leads, as in the String Quartet, to a certain diffuseness of form in the finale, though the attractiveness of the material goes a long way to making up for this deficiency. The slow movement has other notable features. There is much use of close-knit, slow-moving canonic string writing at the start, and of the oboe's more rhetorical recitative which follows this; the contrast between the two is an important element in the development of the material. There is a più mosso section acting as a kind of second subject group, though the theme is actually a variation of the oboe's main theme, a kind of intense but contained recitative melody over simple minor-key or augmented chords. The ending is equivocal: just a few hints of the main theme above inconclusive low string chords implying, but not affirming, a D minor-ish tonality.

The formal, march-like quality at the start of the finale immediately introduces a strenuously contrapuntal texture, and this is emphasized by the lively fugue which follows the introduction. There are numerous tempo changes during this movement, some changes of metre, and a number of close thematic relationships with other early works: the fugue subject includes rising and falling sixths reminiscent of the Concertante for violin and piano, as well as the rather Haydnesque presence of a semiquaver turn as an integral part of the melodic line, and one string passage recurs almost identically in the Viola Sonata. Not everything about the finale is convincing. The final unison statement of the fugue subject as a kind of brief recapitulation does not seem to arise naturally out of the preceding music, and the repeated Fs at the end of the work are a shade over-emphatic (two fewer, one feels, and it would have been more satisfactory). But there is a strong, determined personality here, and the relative toughness of the finale gives the work a wider range than a traditionally light movement would have done. Furthermore, Rawsthorne makes subtle use of a trochaic rhythm in each movement to enhance the work's overall coherence. Like the 1935 String Quartet, the Oboe Quartet is eminently worthy of proper revival, enhancing what is still a relatively slim repertoire; Rawsthorne's later Oboe Quartet (1970, one of his last works) makes an interesting contrast and equally deserves closer attention than it has had.

Another unpublished, and even less well-known, work from this period needs discussion, the *Studies on a Theme by Bach* for string trio, written in 1936. It gives a clear indication of the extent to which counterpoint had become an important element of Rawsthorne's work. The theme is the first four notes (C♯-B♯-E-D♯) of the fugue subject in C sharp minor from Bach's *Well-Tempered Clavier*, Book I, No. 4, which fits in perfectly with Rawsthorne's characteristic use of thematic cells from which harmony and melody can be derived. It contains within it implications of C minor and major and C sharp minor, and clearly relates to both Shostakovich's D-S-C-H motif and the four-note Rawsthorne tag already becoming familiar as a musical fingerprint. From the outset, Rawsthorne employs this cell developmentally, building typical harmonies and textures from it rather than initially stating it as a straightforward theme (Ex. 2.3). The opening Adagio is largely chordal, with touches of melody (as in bar 3 in the violin), and it gives way to a Fugue (Allegro Moderato) in which the subject, the retrograde of the Bach theme, is combined with a more flowing countersubject right from the start. He contrasts full contrapuntal textures, sometimes increasing in intensity through the diminution of note-values, with much sparser ones, dissolving the thematic material into fragments of just a few notes. Again, he is exploring a technique that he was to incorporate less self-consciously in later music, the gradual dissolution of one subject group to create a vacuum into which another could then step.

The Prestissimo in 6/8 which follows is the first example of a particular kind of scherzando movement that was also to become familiar, with fleeting thirds shifting the tonality at bewildering speed; the third of the piano Bagatelles is a more mature example. Half-way through, a change to 2/4 brings in a Hindemithian ostinato in the cello above which violin and viola indulge in thematic argument, only for the music once again to dissipate into fragments and the returning 6/8 material to burst in fortissimo, a surprising but con-

Ex. 2.3. *Studies on a Theme by Bach* for string trio, bars 1–9

vincing dramatic stroke. In a device common in baroque dance movements, the recapitulation of this scherzo inverts the material, and it is worth commenting that some of the overlapping phrases of the 6/8 strongly anticipate the 'Country Dance' movement of the Second Symphony. There is a brief final Andante, closing the work, after some uncertainty, on gentle unison Cs, pizzicato. The last section is really too short to be a convincing finale, as there is no real climax to the Prestissimo from which it would be logical to lead to an epilogue, and the Fugue itself has some faintly mechanical moments during its contrapuntal peregrinations. But the work, playing without a break, only lasts about ten minutes, and some of the invention is first-rate.

From the same period, there are a number of minor or unpublished works, the dates of some of which can only be estimated. The 'valse-caprice' for violin and piano, 'Pierette', is thought to date from the period 1934–7 and is a delightful piece of light music, a genre in which major British composers of preceding generations excelled. Though untypical in its straightforward diatonic style, 'Pierette' does occasionally present the authentic Rawsthorne voice through a characteristic chord or texture, as well as the Prokofievian tonal side-slips, and it also has a slightly Waltonian bitter-sweetness (the world of *Siesta* or one or two of the more Mediterranean numbers of *Façade* is not too far away). There is, however, nothing original about its basic format, which is for the most part simply a tune with an oom-pah-pah 6/8 accompaniment, and one wonders whether it was written originally for the radio light music broadcasts of the Hallis Quintet and then arranged in this form later. It is delightful in its own way, and just before the end there is a tiny slower section ('poco meno') which may be a delicate, even subconscious remembrance of the Italian organ-grinder who used to entertain the Haslingden populace in the Rawsthornes' childhood. The song 'Infant Joy', to words by Blake, is thought to date from the same period and is a sensitive, melancholy setting of the poem—rather a sophisticated and world-weary sadness than an expression of sympathy and compassion. The vocal line, though as syllabic as in most of the early songs, is more lyrical, with an accompaniment that carries it along with some skill, though the underlying tonal changes seem more haphazard than usual.

The Enemy Speaks, which dates definitely from 1936, is a setting of a text by C. Day Lewis for tenor and orchestra. Rawsthorne handicaps himself by choosing a text 'for its message rather than musical suitability'.[8] The words are imbued with the belief, prevalent in the 1930s, in the scientific future, and, as

---

[8] Trevor Hold, 'The Solo Vocal Music', Poulton iii. 71.

Trevor Hold describes it, the 'hard, polysyllabic "scientific" words, the clin-ical, Audenesque precision of language, the ironical tone and the preaching posture, are all inherently anti-lyrical'. The vocal line itself is declamatory and largely syllabic, as in Rawsthorne's earlier songs, and though the orchestral part has more character, with some delicate chamber-like scoring at times, it seems a curiously unfocused work; the aim is clearly high, with an impressive opening tutti and lofty philosophical expression, but the essential economy of gesture fails to fulfil it. This failure makes the magnificent success of the Symphonic Studies two years later even more impressive by contrast.

The Sonatina for flute, oboe, and piano of 1936 is light in texture, elegant of expression, and charming to listen to. Constant Lambert had some inter-esting things to say: 'Stravinsky juggles with the bar-line only to make us the more conscious of its existence. In Rawsthorne's sonatina the bar-line is only there for practical convenience. It has no more aesthetic reality than in the music of Dowland.'[9] In the first movement, indeed, there is no time signature, so fluid is the rhythmic flow, and while the central developmental sections are contrapuntal and intense (sometimes with a touch of severity), the basic tone is airy and lyrical, epitomized by an open harmonic texture and the impor-tance of fourths in both harmonies and melodic lines. The close is fascinating: above a repeated 5/8 rhythm in the bass clef (both hands) for the piano, unusually marked 'timpani', oboe and flute confirm the basic B tonality with lyrical descending phrases, the oboe finally holding an E♭ which contradicts the minor key of the piano phrases with a distinct hint of B major. The succeed-ing Lento is extremely brief. It is a miniature ternary form in which slowly overlapping counterpoint in the flute and oboe frames a central piano solo, building considerable emotional intensity in a very short time; in this combin-ation of emotional outburst with a tiny structure it looks forward to the com-pression of some of Rawsthorne's last chamber works. The final Presto has a brilliant, virtuosic rondo style, though formally, as one would expect, it is far from conventional: apparently subsidiary motifs reveal themselves as new sub-jects, while the ritornello sections are sometimes so varied from the original as to seem like new material. The counterpoint is scintillating and the rhythmic invention incisive, with much use of syncopations and imitation to maintain captivating forward momentum. At eleven minutes this is hardly a major work, nor, despite its considerable intellectual qualities, is it a particularly significant one, but it reveals, as did the Concertante, just how well Rawsthorne had developed and refined his own personal voice and techniques by this time. The work was only published in 1968. Alan Frank, by then in charge of the Music

---

[9] Article on Rawsthorne in series 'The Younger English Composers', *Monthly Musical Record* (Sept. 1938).

Department at Oxford University Press, wrote to him on 21 September 1965, following a performance, 'we thought it sounded very well . . . I imagine it is not too difficult and since there seem to be such hosts of woodwind players, it ought to find a market.' Frank's view has not led to the work entering the regular wind repertoire, yet as a serious divertissement it deserves to do so.

The Clarinet Concerto of 1936–7 is similarly lightweight. It was written for the great clarinettist Frederick Thurston, a colleague of Jessie's in the BBC Symphony Orchestra, and he gave the first performance with Iris Lemare conducting her orchestra at the Mercury Theatre, London, in 1937. Geoffrey Thomason has pointed out that it is, if we disregard Stanford's Concerto (1904), 'a pioneering work with a claim to be the first significant British clarinet concerto of the present century'.[10] As he was often to, Rawsthorne revised the ending. The shorter, easier one appears in the clarinet and piano score published in 1972, the year after Rawsthorne's death. For her recording (at one time the only compact disc recording available of any Rawsthorne work!), Thurston's widow Thea King, together with the conductor Alun Francis, was able to reconstruct the more virtuosic and exciting version of the finish from a private recording by Frederick Thurston with the composer conducting. It is rather a pity that the decidedly weaker ending was the one to be published, or that performers are not provided with the choice between the two; this must reflect the composer's approval of the simpler one, since he did himself correct the proofs of the printed version.

Alun Hoddinott noted that the customary division of a composer's output into three phases works well in Rawsthorne's case, and that each phase of his work opens with a concerto: 'the concerto that marks the opening of each phase quite clearly initiates new explorations of the composer's musical idiom.'[11] He went on, however, to suggest that though this is less true of the Clarinet Concerto than of the others, it reveals 'the basic patterns of Rawsthorne's creative language'. These include 'an instinctively imaginative conception of textures allied to a sure balancing of solo and tutti'. Rawsthorne's essentially self-effacing personality, and the relative modesty of his musical aims, make it surprising that he should have proved so fine a composer of concertos: as with Haydn, the demands for soloistic virtuosity and to some extent conflict between soloist and orchestra could have seemed inimical to him, yet Rawsthorne was actually very successful in reconciling these conflicting demands. The scoring (for string orchestra) is resourceful, with effective use of solo instruments including some especially eloquent solo cello writing, and he resolved the concerto dilemma by opting for important

---

[10] 'The Clarinet Concerto: An Analysis', *The Creel*, 3/4 (spring 1997), 11.
[11] 'BBC Music Review', *Listener* (31 Mar. 1966).

elements of baroque concerto style, indicated by the titles of the four movements: 'Preludio', 'Capriccio', 'Aria', and 'Invention'. The concentration throughout the work on top and bottom lines, the centre of the texture being simply the harmonic filling, is a further link with baroque procedures, and therefore also with the neo-classicism then fashionable in Continental Europe.

The structures of the movements also avoid traditional concerto forms; indeed, the work could be more aptly called a suite were it not for the numerous interrelationships between the themes, as well as the consistent harmonic language. Geoffrey Thomason states that 'virtually everything of significance in [the 'Preludio'] is generated from semitones juxtaposed either vertically or horizontally', and this emphasis is carried into the remaining movements. Rawsthorne opens with a brief phrase leading to a pause before the first movement starts properly; this use of an opening gesture was to become another characteristic device in many works. Here it is a string phrase pregnant with harmonic and thematic possibilities, answered by a clarinet phrase whose semitonal wavering places the emphasis on the interval rightly commented on by Thomason. The movement proceeds at an ambling, moderate tempo, while the Capriccio (the first use of a favourite Rawsthorne title) is a rarity for him, a fast 3/4 scherzo, descended from the Beethovenian one-in-a-bar style. It is marked by frequent two-bar silences punctuating the music's progress (a decidedly Haydnesque way of keeping the listener in suspense), by the inversion of the main material upon recapitulation, and by the way it changes direction so that what seems a lively and fairly extrovert movement suddenly becomes much more intense and darkly passionate for the main orchestral climax, a shift of mood Rawsthorne also exploits in the Preludio. Rhythmically, too, there are frequent shifts of emphasis created by cross-rhythms or syncopations, helping by repetition and sometimes sequential treatment to develop the intensity. The Aria has a Bachian gravity, featuring slow-moving and gloomy low string parts under a clarinet line which largely exploits the lowest register (there are only two notes above the treble stave, both towards the end and beautifully placed for maximum effect); it is interesting that for substantial parts of this movement the soloist is actually silent, the working-out being done solely by the orchestra. The final Invention, more definitely centred on a key (F) than the preceding three, is lighter in tone, though towards the end Rawsthorne broadens the material into a grander, more sweeping lyrical style which brings the concerto back to the seriousness of purpose with which it began. The final, quicker section follows, with the briefest hint of the main theme rather than a full, rondo-type restatement; Rawsthorne was already establishing his dislike of what he felt was unnecessarily complete repetition.

Having written this work, Rawsthorne was technically in complete command of his resources, with an individual style formed in every detail (occasional influences are to be felt, but only in passing). The work which firmly announced his arrival as a force to be reckoned with was the Viola Sonata. It was completed in October 1937 and revised in January 1954 after the music had been rediscovered in a second-hand bookshop in Hampstead (having disappeared after the première in 1938 at the Wigmore Hall). The printed score states that Rawsthorne 'has taken the opportunity of thoroughly revising the Sonata before publication',[12] but as it happens, the only major revision is a new lead-in to the coda in the finale; others, apart from the addition of metronome marks, are mere details. It is significant that, after the songs of his earlier years, Rawsthorne should have concentrated so much on orchestral and chamber music for strings, for this is a reminder of his early cello-playing days and the involvement with chamber music that this brought. It is also significant that the first major work to present him as a complete composer, technically and imaginatively assured, was for a stringed instrument. Lambert described it as 'his most important work so far. The introduction has a fine rhapsodical sweep, the succeeding Allegro and Scherzo have a thoroughly convincing intellectual energy . . . , which is well contrasted with the sombre imagination of the slow movement.'[13]

Ex. 2.4 presents the opening paragraph, which is exceptionally grand in tone in a sonata for such an intimate instrument as the viola and full of interesting detail. The Maestoso introduction is very Hindemithian in its chromaticism, as well as in its combination of interdependence and independence of the two instruments; the unison G#, unadorned by other notes, at the beginning of bar 8, is the first unison to be encountered, and it momentarily gives this note (which, after all, is the dominant of C#) the status of a new tonal centre. There is a toughness of fibre about the sound, and a majesty, which marks the emergence of Rawsthorne as a strong personality: even though the sound has Hindemithian elements, it is essentially quite different and utterly personal.

The rising fourth in the left hand (bar 1) immediately gives the impetus to the impressive piano line either side of the first barline: this majestic theme contains the typical Rawsthorne four-note 'fingerprint' (A-G#-F#-F♮), and in the viola part thirds and their inversions, sixths, form an essential part of the melodic vocabulary (the falling thirds are especially significant, since so much of his harmonic and melodic vocabulary derives from this interval). They are also present in the piano writing from the very first chord, and in the keyboard

---

[12] Published by OUP (London, 1955).
[13] Article on Rawsthorne in 'The Younger English Composers'.

Ex. 2.4. Viola Sonata, first movement, bars 1–8

writing one notes especially bars 5–7, where the two parts (both doubled in octaves) constantly force each other to move by becoming suspensions. To take one example only, from the end of bar 5 the upper part moves from A♭ through G to C, while the bass E goes to E♭; the tonalities that are thus invoked shift from E major through E minor to C minor. This kind of very fast harmonic thinking even in music of slow tempo makes the unison G♯ at bar 8 so vital in providing a moment of arrival. The rising fourths are important not only as a melodic and tonal device but also in the way they act at times almost as a classical dominant–tonic cadence. This traditional procedure forms part both of Rawsthorne's handling of tonality, to help him state new tonalities more decisively, and of his melodic material, tying in these two elements together so that they are virtually indivisible. The last one-and-a-half beats of bar 1 in the piano, for instance, use the fourth both as the starting-point for the melody and as the important affirmation of what turns out to be only a passing tonality, and the same is true of the rising fourths in bars 6–7.

This degree of close thematic working, so inextricably bound up with harmonic and tonal processes, makes the introduction extraordinarily impressive, but the C sharp tonality only achieves its pre-eminent position in the Molto Allegro main body of the movement: seventeen out of the sixty-nine bars of this vitally rhythmic toccata are entirely or partly based on C sharp, and after a lyrical Andante interlude moving to a return of the opening gesture of bar 1, a Molto Allegro closing section (acting as a brief recapitulation of the toccata main theme) is entirely based on C sharp. The link to this Andante interlude is unique in Rawsthorne's output in using piano harmonics, chords of C major (root position) and A flat major (first inversion) at the extremes of the piano played fortissimo and then sustained as harmonics in the middle of the keyboard, an extraordinarily dramatic stroke. The choice of C major dramatically to break the tension is cunning, since as an immediate neighbour of C sharp it occupies an important place throughout the work.

The driving momentum of the Allegro is paralleled by the extraordinary ferocity of the next movement, a scherzo marked 'Presto non assai' in which 100 out of the 190 bars are again centred on C sharp; strong hints at a modal C♯–E–G emphasis remind one of the importance of the intervals of a third and a tritone to the composer. It starts pianissimo (Ex. 2.5(*a*)) with a dance-like

Ex. 2.5. Viola Sonata: (*a*) second movement, bars 1–12; (*b*) third movement, bars 25–9

(*a*)

(b)

6/8 theme in viola triplets taking its cue from the four-note Rawsthorne tag once again, enabled by an upward fourth to expand (middle of bar 3) and given a dark edge by the low C♯ on every beat; the obsessive nature of the movement comes to the fore in the last fifty-three bars, with a massive crescendo and diminuendo over a C♯ pedal turning a somewhat uneasy jig into a veritable dance of death. It is an astonishing *tour de force* of dramatic power. Formally, the scherzo is of great interest: the first episode is a variation of the opening 6/8 triplets transformed into a waltz theme on the piano in 3/4 time but still shadowed by the viola's persistent triplets, following which the first section returns, reversed (thus bars 1–28 and 78–105 together form a single palindrome, interrupted half-way through by the interlude). Once the shattering climactic fortissimo has been reached and passed, the music ends with an elusive chord built up on the piano, over (what else?) a low C♯ sustained by the pedal. It is a remarkably inventive movement in both its strong emotional grip and its formal subtlety.

In the Adagio third movement, the opening chord of C–E implies C major, but that is immediately cancelled by a low octave C♯ in the piano, and the movement (only thirty-three bars long) returns no less than seven times to this bass note. Its character is extremely dark and lugubrious, maintaining the extraordinarily intense character of the work as a whole up to this point: a lamenting secondary subject is based on repeated notes constantly circling back to their initial starting-point, and when the sombre opening theme returns on viola it is surrounded not by dark chords and octaves underneath but this time by low pedal-points plus, in an inspired piece of 'orchestration' for piano, winding phrases at the top of the keyboard (Ex. 2.5(*b*)). It is worth noting that the outer notes of the upper-register music in bar 25, for instance, alternate ninths and sevenths, the parts moving in contrary motion (E–D♯ to D♯–E and so on). This is another Rawsthorne fingerprint, as ubiquitous in later years as the four-note tag or the shifting tonality, and very useful for moving within chords without changing them too much. The use of the high piano register, pianissimo and *lontano*, prepares the way via a tonally indeterminate cadence and a lightening of texture for the extreme change in the finale, which follows without a break (Rawsthorne was already fond of linking movements). This Rondo, marked 'Allegro commodo', is in F major, a key hitherto of relative unimportance in the sonata, and opens with a bland, Hindemithian, and rather amiable main theme. The contrast with the rest of the work has led a number of commentators to regard it as a let-down. Lambert wrote: 'Where the work disappoints, to my mind, is in the final Rondo, which is pleasing and well-made but lacking in the intellectual fire of the rest of the work. It seems rather too easy a get-away from the problems posed earlier on.'[14] Other commentators early in Rawsthorne's career noted a difficulty he seemed to encounter with last movements. Ralph Hill remarked that his first movements are often 'bold, vigorous, and full of fine craftsmanship—the result of truly musical ideas worked out with individuality and imagination; but his finales are often curiously inconsequential.'[15] This one is, however, very charming. The tune itself and its developments and contrasting material are memorable and effective, while there is a return to the sonata's earlier intensity through some strong and determined contrapuntal working. Shostakovich's influence crops up in the first episode, when a perky tune against staccato repeated crotchet thirds reminds one of the Russian's First Piano Concerto and other works from that period, though Rawsthorne's invention remains distinctly his own. This cheer-

---

[14] Article on Rawsthorne in 'The Younger English Composers'.
[15] 'Radio Music', *Listener* (7 June 1940).

ily nonchalant lyrical tune develops toccata figuration, bringing it into line with the first movement's Molto Allegro to some extent, though it is lighter and less persistent. Before the splendidly vigorous, even triumphant conclusion, in a resounding F major, there is a curious little incident in the piano's upper register when the main theme, normally innocent and simple, is transformed by a few chromatic changes into something more sinuous and less straight-forward, a momentary shadow banished by the closing section.

The sonata is formidably difficult for both players: intonation is difficult for the violist (the part explores the whole range of the instrument with great thor-oughness), ensemble needs to be very precise so that the often subtle cross-rhythms and changing metres come across clearly, and the pianist must be good enough to play at least Rawsthorne's solo piano music, if not the First Con-certo. But it is surely one of the most important viola sonatas, along with those by Brahms, Hindemith, and Shostakovich, and its neglect by violists and concert promoters is inexplicable.

3

INTERNATIONAL RECOGNITION
(1937–9)

THERE are several clear influences, or at least kinships, to be detected in Rawsthorne's music, and a number are cited with fair regularity; some (the Baroque in general, and Handel in particular, as well as Haydn) are discussed elsewhere in this volume. His music certainly shows a high regard for Prokofiev and Roussel, though this emerges only subtly and very occasionally. Among the few overt references are the opening of the Second Violin Concerto, whose solo violin theme has a clear relationship with that of Prokofiev's Second Violin Concerto (a favourite of Rawsthorne's) extending to register, style (single, uniformly spaced notes), and the outline of common chords as part of the melodic shape. The side-slipping tonality pervading his music, though accomplished in his own individual manner, also has a Prokofievian flavour. Roussel is a more distant influence: it is more a matter of their common liking for augmented harmonies and a certain steely refusal to give way to sentimentality (sentiment is a different, nobler matter). There is little in common between the two composers in terms of emotional world, or the actual sound of the music. Similarly, Frank Martin, to whom Rawsthorne is often likened, is linked merely through his shifting tonality: again, neither the sound nor the world of the two composers is especially similar, and it could be argued that of the two, it is Rawsthorne who has the greater emotional range and stylistic development. On his own admission, Bartók was a strong influence, something noted by many commentators, but it is easy to overstate the case: there are some technical points in common, notably the use of small thematic cells, but Rawsthorne seems much more concerned with the flow of the music and the dovetailing or overlapping of events. His work, in short, seems less sectional than Bartók's, perhaps partly because it is largely not folk-derived.

There is, however, one composer whose influence is invariably cited: Hindemith. In one respect this is almost inevitable, since in the 1930s, if a British composer wished to escape from current British thinking and adopt a Continental influence, Hindemith, Bartók, and Stravinsky were the models to explore; the dictatorship of the post-Schönberg school was a post-war phenomenon. It is a curious fact, however, that very little of his mature music actually *sounds* like Hindemith—the opening of the Oboe Quartet of 1935, perhaps (Ex. 2.2), a few bars in the finale of the Viola Sonata, a generic orchestral sound here and there (perhaps in the first movement of the First Symphony, for instance), and one or two other fleeting moments. But even these few seconds of music could not have been written by anyone other than Rawsthorne, and there is no direct Hindemithian quality elsewhere.

The strongest debt, and the main reason for the attribution of this influence, is something that, so far as I know, is unique in music. It is simply that Rawsthorne derived a very large amount of material, throughout his career, from a theme appearing in its purest form in Hindemith's *Mathis der Maler* (and beautifully quoted in Walton's great *Variations on a Theme of Hindemith*). Ex. 3.1(*a*) gives the Hindemith in its original form, and the illustrations of the way it pervades Rawsthorne's thinking are: (*b*) the familiar main theme of the *Street Corner* Overture (1944), where the relationship is clear though the rhythmic style, orchestration, and harmonies differ considerably from anything Hindemith might have written, and (*c*) the 'Country Dance' Scherzo in the Second Symphony (*Pastoral*) (1959). However, Ex. 3.1(*d*) presents the bassline from the Sarabande from the *Two Studies for 'Doktor Faust'* by Busoni; clearly, this work (first performed in 1919) outlines a very similar theme, and it should be recalled that Hindemith, who must have heard it during the 1920s, was a regular visitor to the Donaueschingen Festival established in 1922, becoming one of its musical directors two years later. Significantly, Busoni was on the board of directors from the start. Perhaps, after all, the origin of this motif lies in the music of Busoni, perhaps through the prism of Hindemith's influence. Busoni himself has already been cited as a possible influence, and two comments of Anthony Beaumont are particularly relevant. Discussing Busoni's Violin Concerto and the virtual absence of literal recapitulation in it, he says that themes 'are transformed from movement to movement in ingeniously secretive ways', a remark that could easily apply to one of the essential factors in Rawsthorne's handling of his material.[1] Beaumont's summing-up of Busoni's cosmopolitanism includes reference to 'a certain fleetingness, an elegiac, melancholy tone alternating with positively plebeian humour', and apart from the earlier composer's constantly fluctuating tonality and instinctively narrative style there are other features common to both, such as a love of augmented chords and even, from Busoni's works around the

---

[1] *Busoni the Composer* (London, 1985), 49.

Ex. 3.1. (*a*) Hindemith, *Mathis der Maler* Symphony, third movement, 6th bar of fig. 15; (*b*) Rawsthorne, *Street Corner* Overture, from 4th bar of letter A; (*c*) Rawsthorne, *Pastoral Symphony*, third movement (Scherzo), from letter C; (*d*) Busoni, *Doktor Faust*: Sarabande, ground-bass theme

(*a*)

(*b*)

(*c*)

(*d*)

Molto sostenuto e gravemente

turn of the century, the melodic interlocking fourths that became such a feature of Rawsthorne's music. For them to have so much in common does suggest that Busoni at least made a striking impact on the younger man at an early stage of his career.

But it is Hindemith who is normally regarded as the major figure in the background, with the theme from *Mathis der Maler* thought of as the well-spring of much of Rawsthorne's thematic material throughout his career. Indeed, Rawsthorne is sometimes, and quite unfairly, regarded as a one-tune composer simply because of the pervasive nature of this influence: after all, Hindemith was only one of a number of sources for Rawsthorne's style. There are other ideas which run at least as consistently through his career, too, notably the four-note 'fingerprint' B-C-D-E♭, which occurs as obssessively in his output as the *Dies irae* in Rachmaninov's. The crucial question to be asked is whether, therefore, Rawsthorne's dependency on the *Mathis der Maler* tune robs him of his individuality, and the obvious answer is that it does not, for the simple reason that there is hardly a bar in his music that could have been written by anybody other than Rawsthorne. He merely took a musical element that was around at the time and, because it fitted absolutely his way of thinking about music, made it a pivotal part of his music just as, for instance, Britten used the augmented fourth melodically, harmonically, and tonally.

Rawsthorne was not given to public utterances of a social or political nature, except on rare occasions: he was too private a person and artist for that. But even in such an early work as the Concertante for violin and piano of 1935, one can sense the expression of a growing social anger in the violent cross-rhythms and aggressive dissonances of the quicker movements, as well as the influence of jazz in the bluesy harmonies of the central Adagio—though he was influenced by jazz only remotely, far less than Walton or Lambert for instance, and then perhaps it is a question of coincidence rather than direct influence, since the false relations which pervade so much of his music inevitably lead to this kind of harmonic colouring anyway. Indeed, in some ways Rawsthorne was remarkably untouched by the influence of jazz. What is more significant is that, by the time he had completed his Viola Sonata, he was beginning to define his particular formal methods.

That work showed that he was working within apparently traditional formal parameters (sonata form, ternary form, rondo) but so imbued with variation technique and the consequent close relationships of one theme to another, and of thematic material to harmonic and even tonal, that traditional terminology is hardly adequate any more. To talk, in the Scherzo of the Viola Sonata, of ritornello and episodes, or of ternary form, is useful but inadequate; the cross-relationships of various aspects of the material are so detailed and ubiquitous that such a clear separation of themes or harmonies is not strictly relevant. The three works which brought him to international attention were all essentially variation works, in two cases integrating this with other forms. The first of them has the title that summarizes this most important fundamental aspect of his technique: the Theme and Variations for two violins, written in 1937 (Compact Disc, track 2). Even here, Rawsthorne's approach is not entirely conventional. The work consists of eight individual pieces, ending with an additional Fantasia (variation IX) which alternates reminiscences of earlier movements with a new contrapuntal variation, the whole being initiated by a movement which, though simply called 'Theme', is in effect an alert, sprightly two-part invention. The salient points of the material, the first three bars of which are quoted in Ex. 3.2(*a*), include once again rising fourths (notes 1–2, 3–4, and 9–10), the Rawsthorne four-note tag (notes 5–8), and of course an immediate tonal shift (from B minor to B flat). One can also note how he instantly starts developing material and exchanging ideas between the two instruments: the second violin anticipates notes 4–8 of the first so that this part of the theme is in reality an imitation of the countersubject lying beneath it.

Ex. 3.2. Theme and Variations for two violins: (*a*) Theme; (*b*) variation 2: Siciliano, bars 1–6

(*a*)

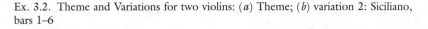

(*b*)

This ingenious part-writing, allied to development of material, enables Rawsthorne to give the two instruments absolute equality throughout the work, which is an astonishing display of compositional virtuosity. It is achieved without recourse to special effects: the scintillating little Scherzetto (variation VI) is muted throughout, but this is the only example, and the double-stopping consists almost exclusively of sixths and, occasionally, thirds. There are only two three-note chords and one four-note chord in the entire piece, and with one exception relatively few octaves: the exception is the Ostinato (variation VII), in which violin 1 plays vigorous D octaves and open strings virtually throughout, a device repeated at the end of the Fantasia when both instruments drive forward to their final unison Ds. The two-part writing is sometimes, as in the Theme, the Cancrizzante (variation III), and the Canone (variation VIII), rigorously contrapuntal. At other times, as in the Siciliano (variation II), it enables Rawsthorne to convey the harmonic implications of the music (Ex. 3.2(b)), the bitter-sweet nature of which clearly derives from the clashes between major and minor implications.

In his own programme note, the composer said that he was 'convinced that the theme appears in each variation', implying a certain casualness of approach belied by the detail that analysis reveals. However, the theme is not always used complete: the Scherzetto is based largely on notes 5–8, handled at terrific speed but very quietly, with much imitative working, and the overlapping thirds of the Rhapsodia (variation IV) reduce the opening intervals from fourths to thirds, C-E–E♭-G and so on (thus creating tonal centres a minor third apart). These are, as it happens, the opening notes of the theme on which his next work, the Bagatelles for piano, were to be based, and they recur in a different transposition for the crucial fugal section in the Symphonic Studies. It is perfectly reasonable, and quite common, for a composer to derive much inspiration from one cell in several works from the same period: in the two-violin Rhapsodia, the overlapping of these notes enables Rawsthorne to create atmospheric and mysterious three- and four-note chords which enlarge the textural range of the work.

The emotional scope of the Theme and Variations is enormous. The Fantasia's cumulative power produces genuine grandeur, achieved partly by its own decisive identity and partly by the remembrances of earlier variations (chosen to relax and then increase the tension), and the Rhapsodia is freely expressive. The Scherzetto has great wit, with exquisite placing of a single portamento and just a few pizzicato duplets against the general 6/8 rhythm. There is a playful dryness, a kind of straight-faced good humour, about some of the more contrapuntal music, whether sprightly or more stately. Yet there is

Ex. 3.3. Theme and Variations for two violins: variation V: Notturno, bars 1–5

romantic warmth, too: David Cox referred to an important aspect of 'Raws-thorne's whole attitude to his art: the avoidance of obvious romantic expression . . . rarely is it associated with external ideas',[2] views which quickly became received opinion about his music. Surely the titles of the movements in the Theme and Variations for two violins give a clear indication that at least some of them are character pieces—not programmatic, perhaps, but nevertheless distinct and generically personalized. And what could be more romantic, or more beautiful, than the opening of variation V, the Notturno (Ex. 3.3), with its evocative harmonies and free-flowing lyrical line, so redolent of a Chopin cantilena?

One important aspect of Rawsthorne's skill is the way he cleverly controls the work's overall shape. Two-part invention texture recurs almost as a ritornello does in a thematic context, and the Rhapsodia and Notturno together form the emotional centre. The Scherzetto's lightness and airiness provide just the right contrast before the Ostinato sets up the momentum to be carried right through to the conclusion. The work thus becomes an organic whole despite the great variety within it. It is still recognized as a chamber-music classic, though it is regrettable that most international top-flight virtuosi are

---

[2] 'Style and Idea', *Listener* (28 Mar. 1963).

notable for their neglect of what is possibly the finest achievement in writing for violin duo alone. The first performance was given by Jessie with her duo partner Kathleen Washbourne at the Wigmore Hall in 1938. The performance at the London Festival of the International Society for Contemporary Music in the same year created even more interest, and it became Rawsthorne's first important work to be recorded for the gramophone, by Decca. The record release was greeted by the columnist 'Terpander', in the *Gramophone* (April 1939) in a review which, though highly favourable to Rawsthorne's compositional mastery and technical assurance, contained the startling assertion that his musical structures were 'remarkable for their rather grim, humourless logic'.

The Four Bagatelles for piano were written in July 1938 while Alan and Jessie were on holiday at the Norfolk home of their composer friend Patrick Hadley, and were given their first performance by Gordon Green (to whom they are dedicated) in a broadcast in Oslo; Green received the completed manuscript shortly before embarking on the boat to Norway. They have since established themselves in the repertoire, one of his few works to do so consistently, and in later years a number of virtuoso pianists enjoyed playing them, including Andor Foldes, who became a great supporter of Rawsthorne's music. The Viennese première of the First Piano Concerto (1950) was due to the enthusiasm of its soloist, Paul Badura-Skoda, for the Bagatelles, and they have received several gramophone recordings, the first by Denis Matthews in 1943. (Matthews liked to hold the low E♭ pedal note at the end of third bagatelle by using the middle pedal; when he recorded it, the studio piano had only two pedals rather than three, so he had to ask someone else to hold down the low E♭ for him.) The first bagatelle is marked 'attacca' to the second. It seems, however, more satisfactory to regard the whole work as essentially one entity and play it through without any disruptive pauses. The powerfully dramatic opening Allegro leads effortlessly, through the lilting Allegretto (which has been likened to a more reticent Anglicized equivalent of the 'Forlane' from Ravel's *Le Tombeau de Couperin*)[3] and the ghostly scampering Presto non assai, into the beautiful final Lento. There is one interpretative problem, however: the power of the Allegro creates a strong impression, but there is no comparable emotional pillar later in the work to which the epilogue can provide a satisfactory conclusion. James Gibb, one of Alan's closest friends and leading interpreters, refers to a conversation with Gordon Green, who 'formed the opinion that the *Bagatelles* would be improved as a set by the addition of

---

[3] 'The Piano Music', Poulton iii. 59.

Ex. 3.4. Four Bagatelles for piano, No. 1: (*a*) bars 1–15; (*b*) bars 44–51

(*a*)

another one in robust vein, similar, perhaps, to the first and to be inserted between the third and the last. Alan had agreed to this and promised to write one.'[4] However, the work was published (an event delayed until 1943 by the wartime shortage of paper) without an extra movement, which never materialized. The interpreter, therefore, must bear this in mind; one solution seems to be to give the climax of the Presto (when the opening Allegro theme returns in the form nearest its original shape) as much power as possible, both by emphasizing the dynamics and possibly even by a touch of allargando leading up to the climactic, fortissimo C minor chord.

The opening of the first bagatelle (Ex. 3.4(*a*)) shows the authority both of Rawsthorne's idiomatic keyboard writing and of his invention. The main theme of the work, thirds zigzagging upwards to create both forward momentum

⁴ 'The Piano Music', Poulton iii. 59.

(*b*)

and a typical major/minor ambiguity (in the first few bars, the theme strongly implies C major, C minor, B major, G major, G minor, A major, F minor, G major, and so on), is a virile statement. The bass-line, equally forceful in providing momentary tonal centres, also includes much use of his favourite four-note tag (initially G to B, bars 1–2). This cell is marked *q* in Ex. 3.4(*a*), and is much used during the Bagatelles, sometimes as part of the melodic invention but always in a subsidiary capacity to the right-hand theme, which is marked *p*. His liking for sequential writing is shown by the phrases marked *x* and *y*. The vital cross-rhythms in bars 11–14 are very characteristic of his music at this time, and form an important rhythmical element in the developmental sections of the Symphonic Studies. The brilliance of Rawsthorne's keyboard writing is clearly shown in Ex. 3.4(*b*), the eminently practical crossed-hands layout enabling him to state the theme in the top line (right and left hands alternating) and concurrently in the bass, in augmentation. It is also notable how superbly his four-note signature fits the keyboard and enables him to create virtuosic textures that are thoroughly idiomatic and very playable (see the first two bars of Ex. 3.4(*b*)).

Rees Stephen Allison remarks that the 'precedent for the Bagatelles both in title and formal design are the sets by Beethoven—particularly those of Opus 119 which generally are comparable three part structures, with curtailment or variation of the final recapitulated section. The prevalent structure . . . shows

Ex. 3.5. Four Bagatelles: (*a*) No. 2, bars 1–4; (*b*) No. 4, bars 1–4 and ending

(*a*)

the same two contrasting sections followed by a transformed recapitulation of the first.'[5] Though this is not a straightforward set of variations, the thematic transformations to which the main tunes are subjected are derived from variation technique. The Allegretto, a gently nostalgic siciliano, shows this clearly. Its ternary overall shape is dominated by the opening variation of motif *p* (Ex. 3.5(*a*)), motif *q* producing a 'new' secondary subject before the return of the first theme, initially in the left hand inner part (what pianists call the 'tenor thumb' register, a favourite of Rawsthorne's for varying recapitulatory textures). The overall tonal scheme of the Bagatelles derives substantially from the opening unison C. This key centre (one of Rawsthorne's favourites throughout his career) is the music's constant, returning at many important junctures, and though there are inevitably excursions to other keys, often fleeting and full of typically rapid harmonic and tonal movement, it is either to C or to keys very near to it physically (especially C sharp) that the music returns. The sense of a strong home key is maintained throughout, even when, exceptionally, there is a lengthy pedal on E♭ (the last fifteen bars of the Presto), or, as in the final Lento, a movement begins on another note (D in this case). The beautiful closing cadence (Ex. 3.5(*b*)) in a peaceful C major is made to seem inevitable through the emphasis on the note C throughout the work. The inevitability of the ending is also partly due to the presence, either implicitly or explicitly, of the notes of the common chord in the thematic material of the music.

As can be seen from Ex. 3.5(*b*), the opening of the Lento inverts motif *p*, in a two-part texture that gradually fills out through occasional octaves for harmonic emphasis, to full chords, though the music never becomes so emphatic as to destroy its equilibrium ('poco più forte' is the loudest dynamic marking here). The flickering Presto is essentially a 6/8 scherzando, whose main theme

[5] 'The Piano Works of Alan Rawsthorne', Ph.D. thesis (Washington, DC, 1970), introduction.

(*b*)

leading to:

simply combines the thirds of motif *p* in a familiar style of piano writing; motif *q* is less in evidence here than elsewhere, being relegated to inflections of the decorative passage-work. The importance established gradually during the Presto of the note E♭ is cancelled immediately by the first note of the Lento, and the route taken to the final C major is a subtle one, touching it significantly only once before the final cadence. This cadence contains a further Rawsthorne characteristic, his love of Neapolitan harmonies or notes (the flattened second, D♭, in this instance).

Referring to Rawsthorne's piano writing in connection with the Bagatelles, but with more general application to his other keyboard music, Gibb wrote: 'He especially enjoyed exploiting the blurring of outlines afforded by use of the sustaining pedal, disguising the seams between one phrase and another and leaving the listener in doubt as to when one phrase ends and the next begins.'[6] Among Rawsthorne's favourites were Chopin and Debussy, in both of whose music subtle pedalling and half-pedalling are most important interpretative

---

[6] 'The Piano Music', 59.

aspects, as is precise articulation of rhythm. He was gently helpful to performers when advising them on points of performance; in the Allegretto bagatelle, for instance, he was at great pains to help the performer convey the dotted rhythms clearly and with just enough lilt (the short notes, he said, should not be skimped, but neither should they be overemphasized in order to avoid such skimping). Can one also sense, especially in the final Lento, the influence of Busoni, in his more elegiac mood?

During 1938–9, Rawsthorne produced a number of shorter works, including one or two choral arrangements and some songs. The *Three French Nursery Songs*, dedicated to Gemma Blech and recorded in 1942 by Sophie Wyss for Decca, were first performed in February 1938, and exist in alternative versions with piano or chamber orchestral accompaniment. They are charming miniatures, new settings of French children's rhymes. Utterly Rawsthornian touches of rhythm or harmony, along with some characteristic side-slips into remote keys, coexist with an acute appreciation of the authentic French folksong style: it is strange that he should so easily draw upon a Continental European folk style while still resisting the blandishments of English folk-music. Ex. 3.6 gives a taste of the delicacy and slightly melancholy wit of the settings. One should note the artistry with which he uses a fairly corny traditional cadence (bars 6–7) to give it a special, expressive quality by using it as part of a typical key change from B minor back to the C minor with which he started. The shift to G sharp minor (bar 12) is also characteristically affecting. The element of pastiche, and the decision to write a work of such essential simplicity, enabled Rawsthorne to write more convincingly for the voice than in most of his earlier solo songs. The restriction he seemed to feel in writing melismata is not relevant here, where they would be out of proportion to the music's innate modesty of aim.

Though they remain unpublished, the two songs Rawsthorne contributed to the *Prison Cycle*, which he wrote in 1939 conjointly with Alan Bush, are a distinct advance in vocal writing. These settings of poems by the German-Jewish poet Ernst Toller, who had committed suicide in 1939 at the age of 46, were brought to Bush's attention by a refugee German group, the Free German League of Culture, established to present artistic works of various kinds by German progressive artists, and it was Bush who suggested sharing the task with Rawsthorne; the latter contributed the third and fourth of the five numbers. Toller's poems reflected his experiences as a prisoner following the Munich revolution (known as the Bavarian Workers' Republic) of 1919. The songs were performed towards the end of 1939 by Anne Wood, with Bush at the piano, but the manuscript was mislaid for thirty-five years. Though there

Ex. 3.6. *Three French Nursery Songs*, No. 1, bars 1–13

are five songs, there are only three texts: one poem, 'Sechs Schritte her' ('Six Paces Here'), was set as an introduction and epilogue (Bush), and as an interlude (Rawsthorne) at the centre of the work. It deals with the frustration and claustrophobia of pacing to and fro in the prison cell. Rawsthorne's ability to convey a complex, troubled mood with a few notes is perfectly in tune with the brevity and economy of the expression, and the words are set as simple, grave phrases between discreetly contrapuntal piano motifs. The fourth song, 'Über mir', depicts the swallows nesting outside the prisoner's window; again, the vocal line is simple but poignant, the setting being a melancholy siciliano akin to the second of the Bagatelles. Few co-operative works of this kind really come off, but this is something of an exception. The authorship of Rawsthorne's brief contributions is immediately recognizable, and Bush's more florid writing stems more obviously from the English lyric tradition (coloured by his habitual toughness of thought), but the totality is eminently convincing. Though performed initially by a mezzo-soprano, the cycle has most recently been sung by a baritone voice, the darkness of which suits it admirably.

This was not Rawsthorne's only collaboration with Alan Bush. In January 1939, Bush's London String Orchestra made its début with a programme including an item entitled '100 Years of the Viennese Waltz', for which Bush had arranged waltzes by Haydn, Beethoven, Hummel, Ries, and Lanner, and Rawsthorne had arranged pieces by Schubert and the Strausses (the score of this has disappeared). The concert included Bush's string orchestra version of his earlier masterpiece for string quartet *Dialectic*. Bush also organized and conducted a 'Pageant for the People', first performed on 1 April 1939. Other participating composers included Arnold Cooke, Erik Chisholm, Christian Darnton, Norman Demuth, Elizabeth Maconchy, and Bush himself. Rawsthorne's contribution was an arrangement for mixed voices of the Czech partsong 'Homeland Mine' (published by the Workers' Music Association in 1940) and the finale, a setting of words by Randall Swingler (later to become almost Rawsthorne's resident provider of texts) entitled 'For Peace and Liberty.' The orchestration was for wind band and percussion. Here too, the material seems to have disappeared: Rawsthorne's bad luck with mislaid manuscripts seems to run like a leitmotif throughout his career.

In view of Rawsthorne's post-war eminence in film music, one must note that his career in this genre began in 1939 with two documentaries, *The City* (directed by Ralph Elton and produced for the GPO Film Unit by Alberto Cavalcanti) and *Cargo for Ardrossan*, directed for Realist Films by Ruby Grierson. One curiosity stems from this period, the Light Music for String Orchestra. Originally called *Three Catalan Tunes*, it was published under that title by the Workers' Music Association (for whom it was written) in 1938. Eleven years later, Alan Frank wrote to Rawsthorne suggesting that the title be changed, perhaps to 'Divertissement' or 'Light Music', and in 1957, returning the score to OUP, Rawsthorne wrote to Frank on 24 June:

You will be astonished, now we are very old, to receive the enclosed papyrus. I have even found the original manuscript, like a Dead Sea Scroll, in a cave near Saffron Walden. When subjected to fluorine tests it has been found to resemble the proofs in many respects. I am worried as to the title. Who is going to believe that I wrote these tunes myself, as Habakkuk must be saying to himself at the moment? Gen. Franco might not recognize them but others would.

OUP finally republished the work in 1958. Its chief interest lies in the evidence of Rawsthorne's sympathy with the Republican side in the Spanish Civil War, shown in his use of Catalan folk-tunes (once again, a Continental rather than an English folk source). Musically, the interest is negligible: the three linked pieces, lasting less than four minutes in all, are entirely conventional in harmonic and rhythmic setting. The orchestration, clearly aimed for amateur players, is very straightforward. One senses that Rawsthorne, writing for performers of less than professional standard, found his imagination somewhat restricted, as he did later in his *Overture for Farnham* for school orchestra (1967).

In these immediately pre-war years, Rawsthorne's most significant major works were emphatically for professionals: the Symphonic Studies, the First String Quartet,[7] and the original version of the First Piano Concerto, with orchestra of strings and percussion. The concerto will be discussed in the next chapter; however enjoyable this original version may be, there is no doubt that its true qualities emerge only in the full orchestral dress which was provided in 1942. The mixed reception accorded its first performance in 1939 (by Adolph Hallis with the London Symphony Orchestra conducted by Iris Lemare) might well have stemmed from an awareness that the work was somehow unfinished in its small orchestra setting. The First String Quartet is also problematical, not least because the Rawsthorne manuscript jinx struck once again. It was originally the second movement of a two-movement string quartet, commissioned for the Venice Festival and due to be premièred there by the Sibelius Quartet of Helsinki. Because of the outbreak of war the festival was cancelled, but Rawsthorne was able to reconstruct the finale from his rough sketches. It was performed in 1940 by the Blech Quartet and published in 1946 by OUP with the subtitle 'Theme and Variations'.

Like the Theme and Variations for two violins, this single piece makes individual movements of the theme and each of the six variations, though in this case it is played without any break, and it makes a satisfactory concert item. That so many quartets have played it over the years both in Britain and abroad

---

[7] i.e. the first of the 'official', published quartets; reference will continue to be made to these by their official numberings, and to the earlier examples by their years of composition, 1932 and 1935.

testifies to its effectiveness. It has, however, little that is new in extending Rawsthorne's expressive or technical equipment. Indeed, some of the most striking invention is an extension of aspects of the two-violin work. The two-part counterpoint, lyrical but rigorous at the same time, which opens variation 5 (Allegro preciso) derives from similar writing in the earlier piece, and the rhapsodic solo violin lines of variation 2 (Andante appassionato) similarly echo the earlier Rhapsodia. The most interesting is perhaps variation 4 (Adagio, poco misterioso), in which the violins and viola pile up and superimpose sixths to create a quiet web of ambiguous tonality while the cello restates the theme, its phrases separated by pauses as if hesitating to disturb the mysterious atmosphere above it. The tonal centre of gravity of the piece is A, but some variations start in a different key or progress to one (the third, Allegro, starts in A but finishes in G sharp). The harmonic language, while entirely characteristic, shows signs of enlargement, with the more frequent use of straightforward minor or major chords over more extended periods than hitherto, as in the second variation. There are two variations in 6/8, sufficiently different in mood to avoid any danger of repetition but sufficiently close to provide a fleeting sense of recapitulation, the first a sprightly tarantella and the second a more aggressive one reminiscent of the brilliant finale of the First Piano Concerto. It is, perhaps, not such an insistently memorable movement, but it is effective none the less, and after some dissolution of the material and further hesitant pauses, it brings the piece to a lively conclusion. The clarity and delicacy of the highly idiomatic quartet writing is further evidence of Rawsthorne's increasingly subtle mastery, but it is a very good example of his craft rather than an inspired addition to his repertoire; perhaps in this instance it is the composer making the music rather than the music making the composer.

Bearing in mind that the First Piano Concerto was not really fully realized until its full orchestral version a few years later, the crowning achievement of this immediately pre-war period is undoubtedly the orchestral Symphonic Studies, still generally regarded as one of Rawsthorne's finest achievements. Suddenly, as if at one bound, the composer of intimate, precisely judged chamber and small orchestra music became the master of large-scale symphonic thought—for, though in some ways 'Concerto for Orchestra' might have been a good title, its essence lies in his remarkable synthesis of variation technique with the demands of a genuinely symphonic argument.

The work is dedicated to John Ireland and was completed in 1938, being first performed the following year at the Warsaw Festival of the International Society for the Promotion of New Music, the performers being the Polish Radio Symphony Orchestra conducted by Stanley Chapple (Roberto Gerhard,

Ex. 3.7. Symphonic Studies for orchestra, bars 1-4

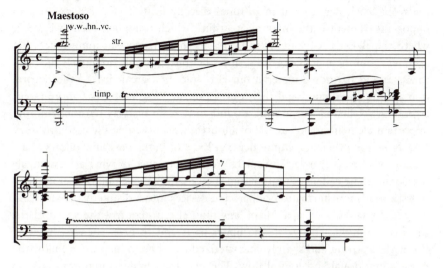

later a stablemate of Alan's at OUP, was a member of the jury which selected the work). The British première came in 1940, with the BBC Symphony Orchestra conducted by Sir Adrian Boult (Rawsthorne's efforts to get Iris Lemare a BBC engagement to conduct the work fell foul of the BBC bureaucracy of the time). The work was recorded in 1946 under the auspices of the British Council, by the Philharmonia Orchestra under Constant Lambert. Rawsthorne told Malcolm Rayment that it

arose in a rather curious way. I had decided on a little piece of self discipline at this time and wrote an exercise every day for a certain period of my life . . . The two prerequisites of these exercises were that they should first be complete, however short, and secondly that they should be as far as one could make them, able to sound well—that is to say, not exercises purely concerned with putting down notes as many exercises are. So I tried one little exercise in the particular way of constructing melody, by taking a short phrase of three notes and then making a short addition, then starting again and adding yet more . . . I became fascinated with one or two of these little exercises and it was out of them that I constructed the Symphonic Studies.[8]

This rather academic-sounding inspiration belies the dramatic power of the work and its majestic opening (Ex. 3.7). The almost Beethovenian Maestoso introduction presents the main theme, which in true Rawsthornian fashion provides a reservoir for virtually all the material of the work, and the five move-

---

[8] BBC radio interview for series 'The Composer Speaks', recorded 24 May 1962.

ments (this term is preferable to 'sections' despite the continuous nature of the work) each derive their main tunes directly from it (Ex. 3.8(*a*)–(*e*)). An important element is the interval of a third, which is implicit even in Ex. 3.7, where the B-E-C♯-A-F outline indicates its importance—an importance that assumes monumental proportions, since the third not only dominates the main thematic and harmonic material but also colours a great deal of the decoration around the themes and their development. Descending (or, more rarely, ascending) chains of thirds swirl around and create or relax tension. Another important element is the interval of a fourth, which is especially used as a tonal base as well as a thematic component; in Ex. 3.8(*e*), the bass-line follows a succession of fifths (i.e. inverted fourths) with a sequence of what are essentially dominant–tonic cadences to underpin the variation above, another example of Rawsthorne's transformation of baroque devices into a distinctly personal language. It enables him, apart from anything else, to control the speed of the tonal or harmonic change in the upper parts and to give listeners, however fleetingly, a strong and sharply characterized bass-line to help them follow the music's emotional and logical flow. The opening phrase is important also in presenting, in its first five notes, the possibility of no less than three triads: E (without the G and therefore neither major nor minor), A major, and (changing F♮ to F♯, as in the main theme of the first Allegro) F sharp minor. When the first movement proper commences with its own principal subject derived from and extending this motto theme (Ex. 3.8(*a*)), this element of bitonality (or even tritonality) is therefore implicit from the start, and it is worth noting that this new principal tune includes, in its first two bars and one beat, all twelve notes of the chromatic scale. Rawsthorne's later excursions into his own version of serial technique (as in the Third Symphony and the Quintet for

Ex. 3.8. Symphonic Studies: (*a*) first Allegro di bravura, bars 1–4; (*b*) Allegretto, bars 1–10; (*c*) second Allegro di bravura, bars 1–4; (*d*) Lento, from fig. 35; (*e*) Allegro piacevole, bars 1–7

(*a*)

(*b*)

(*c*)

(*d*)

(*e*)

Ex. 3.9. Symphonic Studies, Allegro piacevole, fugue subject from fig. 48

piano and wind instruments) can thus be seen to be a logical consequence of the chromatic nature of his invention even at this early stage.

Other close thematic relationships can be traced, too. Francis Routh has devoted considerable attention to detailed examination of the way in which even themes that appear to be completely new can be traced back to the *Urmotif*.[9] For example, the cor anglais theme in Ex. 3.8(*b*) and the cello and bass line in the two preceding bars both derive from transformations of the work's opening four notes, either by altering the note order (and filling in the missing notes either chromatically or diatonically) or by adding a chromatic shift of one of the notes. The thirds of the main theme give rise to much other material: the ostinato figures in the slow movements (Exx. 3.8(*b*) and (*d*) clearly come from this source, and of course the ostinato provides pairs of thirds which, played together, produce the customary major/minor conflicts so integral to Rawsthorne's thinking. The examples give an idea of the character of each movement: the first Allegro di bravura is contrapuntal and dynamic, the second (Allegretto) lighter and more hesitant thematically, and the final Allegro piacevole a touch more openly diatonic, giving a sunnier aspect to the theme than it has hitherto had. The slower movements (the first Allegretto, the second Lento) are different in that the Lento begins more freely, with recitative-like phrases on woodwind solos (some quite cadenza-like in their freedom) before Ex. 3.8(*d*) starts the movement's lyrical flow. In the finale, the sunny, relaxed mood of the opening imperceptibly leads to a darker mood and a ferocious brass fugue on a theme (Ex. 3.9) clearly based on the

---

[9] 'Alan Rawsthorne', *Contemporary British Music* (London, 1972), 43–54.

thirds. The degree to which so much apparently diverse material stems from the bare opening phrase is astonishing.

Recapitulation in the conventional sense is absent; instead there is repetition (either exact or merely referential) of phrases or even substantial sections of music from one movement in the context of another. The opening phrase recurs powerfully at the end of the first movement, in a magically quiet and simplified outline at the close of the second, and (more substantially again) in its original form before the final Allegro molto flourish that finishes the work in a vigorous and triumphant B major—the most convincingly uninhibited such conclusion in Rawsthorne's repertoire. (The end of *Carmen vitale* is equally decisive, but there the triumph is tinged with the medieval sense of inevitable doom). The tonality of B is predominant throughout, constantly recurring either in passing or as an important focus for the music; the recapitulatory moments through the work often use the same tonality for each appearance of a particular idea to reinforce its place in the tonal scheme. There is, however, an important relationship with the key of F, a tritone away (bar 3 of the opening), which gives the choice of F as the tonal centre for the finale's fugue particular importance, making the return to B for the close equally striking. Rawsthorne employs a typical formal device, that of a movement which starts relatively unconcernedly and gradually builds tension towards a shattering climax, often with the use of an accelerando. Here, the most striking examples are the two slower movements, where the climaxes are of highly charged intensity, and of course the finale, where the fugue bursts out of a storm far removed from the mood at the start of the Allegro piacevole. The fugue itself reminds one of the finale of Vaughan Williams's Fourth Symphony (though it should be added that Rawsthorne, always courteous and reluctant to criticize others, admitted that Vaughan Williams's music was not to his taste), but the way in which a fairly innocent, lyrical mood turns into something much darker reminds one irresistibly of the way Nielsen and, later, Shostakovich used this process. One should also draw attention to the enormous variety of texture, from massive power to the frequent moments of delicacy and great sensitivity, to be encountered during the course of the music.

The Symphonic Studies remains, in sum, a majestic work, emotionally gripping and often very moving. For a composer whose music had hitherto exploited to a great extent his love and knowledge of stringed instruments, the degree to which the other instruments form the driving force of the sound in this work is remarkable. A. E. F. Dickinson noticed this, though he interpreted it rather oddly:

The treatment of the orchestral *ensemble* is decidedly in favour of the wind and brass and percussion groups (including plucked, but not bowed strings). The old gibe that Wagner's orchestration sounds like an elaborate swell-organ cannot be levelled at Rawsthorne's instrumental polyphony; but in so far as it implies a lack of sympathy for string-tone, the criticism is truer of Rawsthorne than of Wagner.[10]

('Lack of sympathy for string-tone', indeed! The Symphonic Studies contain some moments of extremely beautiful and very expressive string writing.) There are many felicitous touches of orchestral colour, from the flecks of celesta tone (only for a few bars in the Third Symphony does he use it again in an orchestral work) to some carefully balanced textures, with dynamics individually considered for each instrument. The music is completely imagined in terms of the relevant instrumental sound, and Rawsthorne is always aware of the need to be practical in the layout so that, for instance, the horns can between them play quite elaborate and wide-ranging lines by dovetailing the parts and sharing the music. Full orchestral tuttis are surprisingly rare, in view of the impact of the music, but they are placed to achieve the maximum effect; thus the climaxes are carefully graded, as part of his overall formal control.

Robert Simpson has stated that the main elements of a true symphony are: 'the fusion of diverse elements into an organic whole . . . The continuous control of pace . . . The reserves of strength necessary to achieve [the first two]', and he later sums this argument up by saying that a symphony must 'travel'.[11] In every way, including the ebb and flow of intensity and the need to use the rate of harmonic motion as part of the structure, the Symphonic Studies admirably fulfils these needs. The work is, in its way, a one-movement symphony, whose five sections add up to a satisfying whole. It is also, however, a kind of extended free passacaglia, since the opening four notes in particular have such a pervasive part to play in the creation and development of all the material in every way; this is far more than simply a set of variations on a theme. Wilfrid Mellers stated that in this work 'Rawsthorne exploited an expanded version of the seventeenth- and eighteenth-century technique of division on a ground',[12] while elsewhere, he described this type of variation form thus: 'the principle of development is cumulative over an harmonic skeleton that is hardly more than latent; and . . . it is this skeleton which gives such tautness to the often very passionate melodic and figurative elements.'[13] Contrasting the

[10] 'The Progress of Alan Rawsthorne', *Music Review*, 12 (1951), 87–104.
[11] 'Introduction', R. Simpson (ed.), *The Symphony*, i (Harmondsworth, 1966), 13.
[12] 'Rawsthorne's Recent Developments', *Listener* (Nov. 1950).
[13] 'Alan Rawsthorne and the Baroque', *Tempo* (Mar. 1946).

earlier pieces with this major orchestral work, Peter Evans says that 'the Symphonic Studies demonstrate impressive powers of organization across and within five linked movements; this is a remarkable first orchestral score by any standards'.[14] By so successfully integrating so many aspects of form with his own individual style, Rawsthorne achieved music of immense power and authority, and stamped himself firmly on the international music scene as a composer of major promise.

[14] 'Alan Rawsthorne', in *The New Grove Dictionary of Music and Musicians*, ed. S. Sadie (London, 1980).

4

THE WAR YEARS (1939–45)

SIX months after the first performance of the Symphonic Studies in Warsaw, Hitler invaded Poland and the consequence was the outbreak of the Second World War. For a composer who had just achieved his first international successes and was recognized as a major talent, it was as disruptive a blow to Rawsthorne's career as the First World War had been to Elgar's. Elgar had been particularly successful in Germany (not surprisingly, in view of the technical basis of his style), and the onset of the First World War suddenly deprived his career of its international context and pushed him back into the more insular world of English musical life. Something similar happened to Rawsthorne. For any composer reaching maturity, such an event must inevitably be a serious dislocation of the natural development of his work.

Wartime is, of course, a tragic disruption of ordinary life for everyone, but in Rawsthorne's case a number of other factors affected him as well. He had already settled into a somewhat bohemian existence, in which drink played a major part; he was seldom seen actually drunk, but his steady drinking undoubtedly contributed to the illnesses from which he suffered during the second half of his life. His marriage, too, was unsettled. Though Jessie and he loved each other deeply, and continued to do so for the rest of their lives, they were ultimately incompatible; referring to the break-up of the marriage after the war, the distinguished harpist of the BBC Symphony Orchestra Sidonie Goossens wrote that 'he obviously wanted a different environment and a different type of woman'.[1] Jessie was, perhaps, more conventional by nature, though she tried hard to match his bohemianism. He had a magnetic attraction for many women: it is significant that in many cases, he (and indeed Jessie) remained on good terms with them to the end of their lives, an indication of the liking so many people felt for him. He was generally regarded as a gentle and lovable man, whose weaknesses were accepted and were, indeed, a cause for anxiety on the part of his friends.

Rawsthorne's political philosophy was basically anarchistic, but not in the

---

[1] Letter to the author, 22 Feb. 1997.

sense of violent overthrow of authority. Conradian spies and bombs would have seemed ludicrous to him. Though politically he was a left-winger, his real belief was in a society based on voluntary co-operation, allied to the association of individuals and groups. An important aspect of anarchism was a mistrust of all forms of government, something to which Rawsthorne held fast throughout his life. Late in life, he expressed this feeling in an article on his journey to Russia in 1963: 'For myself, I have a rooted mistrust of all Governments, and a dislike of orthodoxies.'[2] He was, in short, a follower more of Kropotkin's tenets than of the revolutionary tendencies of Bakunin. Though anarchism has some superficial resemblances to communism, it is in essence antipathetic to it: anarchists believe that mankind would be better, not worse, without governments or state control, save for the righting of injustices. (It was the split between the anarchist and communist sympathizers that contributed substantially to the failure of the Republican cause in the Spanish Civil War.) Rawsthorne's innate pacifism was put to the test when he was called up. Unlike some of his friends, whose beliefs led them to a position from which they could only become conscientious objectors, Rawsthorne felt sufficiently strongly that despite his abhorrence of war, he had no option but to take part. A vital element in this decision was the belief that if ever a war was just, this one was; his large number of Jewish friends, the news emerging gradually about the concentration camps, and his deep human sensibilities could lead him to no other decision. For a committed pacifist, however, the emotional strain must have been enormous.

With the outbreak of war, Alan and Jessie moved to Bristol, whither the BBC had transferred their music department, including the Symphony Orchestra, and he continued composing. He also did some volunteer wartime work and lectured at Bristol University, teaching English to foreign students and giving lectures on music appreciation. However, in the following year, 1940, a bombing raid in November destroyed the flat shared by the Rawsthornes and Sidonie Goossens and her husband Hyam Greenbaum (affectionately known as 'Sid and Bumps', to whom the two John Fletcher songs are dedicated), and there is no doubt that this event, coming on top of the dislocation of Rawsthorne's life in several aspects, was traumatic. The air raid occurred as the Rawsthornes were having a celebratory drink with friends, possibly to mark either the première of the choral work *Kubla Khan*, which had taken place earlier that day, or the completion of the First Violin Concerto sketch. Both manuscripts were lost in the bombing. Constant Lambert, on tour with

---

[2] 'The Composer in the USSR', *Sunday Times* (13 Oct. 1963); see Ch. 8 below.

Sadler's Wells Ballet, was staying with them, and went upstairs to rescue his own scores, coming down to report that the roof was on fire. The Rawsthornes' dog, Jill, was rescued, and the group reconvened in a local pub; when the neighbouring building caught fire, Lambert hosed the pub wall with water, famously quoting Gorky the while. They apparently thought that the local fire brigade would put out the blaze in their apartment building, a hopelessly impractical view that is somehow characteristic of Rawsthorne's unworldliness. His own version of the story was that he had sketched half of the concerto when the raid occurred, and that, having recommenced it, he had again only half completed the sketches when he was called up to join the army. Sidonie Goossens comments that 'mercifully the three consecutive bombs that we heard whistling down [while sheltering in the pub] were all duds—otherwise that would have been the end of us all'.[3]

The Rawsthornes' letters home from Chew Magna, where they found refuge in the cottage of the BBC producer Julian Herbage, are revealing, in both what they say and what they omit. Rawsthorne wrote to his father and sister:

We have been, alas, bombed out of house and home during the Bristol 'blitz' on Sunday night. The city was a complete inferno and some of it is still smouldering. I expect (and hope) that you won't have realised this from the accounts that are allowed to appear in the press. Not even the walls of our house remained; I think it must have had high explosives as well as incendiaries. But we were lucky to get out before the fire got too fierce. Jessie, thank heaven, got her fiddle. Otherwise we have nothing. It is a pity— books, scores, manuscripts—some of them are irreplaceable.

Well, well. This is really to tell you that we are safe and sound and that friends . . . have taken us into the haven of their country cottage. How long we shall be there I don't know, but messages will reach us. Julian Herbage is on the B.B.C. Music Staff and of course we shall keep in touch. Everyone has been so kind, though many are in the same boat.

Excuse more now. I am in Bristol doing a host of things and buying a few necessaries. I've borrowed an overcoat! and am going back in a few minutes into the country.

They keep dynamiting unsafe bits of ruins and the time-bombs are still popping off— sorry to write a rather gloomy letter—we are reasonably cheerful!

Jessie's letter to Barbara Rawsthorne (1 December) has a touch more desperation than Alan's determinedly stoic effort: 'I've got my fiddle—that's all. Everything has gone—the place is burned to a cinder. I don't care a bit, about my few possessions—but—Alan . . . all his manuscripts—his new fiddle concerto—music—books——even his new overcoat.' Her hesitant style hints

---

[3] Letter to the author, 3 Oct. 1997.

at the trauma they had suffered, not only being bombed out of their home but losing in the process what was her husband's longest work to date, and one of his most important. He did reconstruct it, the première being at the Cheltenham Festival in 1948, but the setting for soloists, chorus, and small orchestra of Coleridge's *Kubla Khan* was never reconstructed, despite the survival of the vocal score in the BBC's library. The loss in particular of the concerto must have been a further devastating blow to an already unsettled man.

Rawsthorne joined the army in 1941. In his programme note for the concerto's first performance, he laconically stated that the interruptions 'thus occasioned by being successively blown up and called up [have] caused a considerable period of time to elapse between the initial stages of the work and its completion in 1947'. Barbara Rawsthorne, in her manuscript memoir 'For his Friends—from his Sister Barbara', commented:

As may well be imagined, Alan was supremely unhappy in the Army. The frustrations of trying to fit a musical job into the red tape and general inefficiency of Army methods, combined with the outrage that war did to his moral sense, would have broken him completely if he hadn't had a basic 'something' which enabled him to survive this horror—as it enabled him to survive other crises in his life.

He entered the Royal Artillery as Gunner Rawsthorne, a somewhat unlikely concept, and was at one stage responsible for the Quartermaster's stores; he was famously delighted on one occasion when, confronted with a new recruit named Hastings, he searched around and found for him a rifle numbered 1066. The army, in its wisdom but ignorant of what a 'composer' actually did, put him down as a 'compositor', so for a while he was given a mechanical job, repairing tanks, among other tasks; fortunately for all concerned, his basic mechanical ineptitude was eventually discovered (even boiling an egg was a technological challenge for him) and he was moved to the Education Corps. He wrote to Barbara in August 1941 about 'trying to form a Military Band and Symphony Orchestra here, by transferring musicians from other units to this one. But you have no conception of the red tape, frustration and general inefficiency of Army methods. The Headquarters we tried to visit yesterday, for instance, had been moved elsewhere five weeks ago, and we chased it all morning without result.' (He used to dismiss his war service, in later years, with a phrase about sitting in a hut in Wales, peeling potatoes.) The RNCM archives contain some notes outlining a series of lectures ('Notes for Gramophone Talks on Music'), with headings and some revealing comments:

Tudor times—a spirit of adventure and robustness; an interest in foreign music and in keeping abreast of the times.

Jazz bands. This type of sound becomes very monotonous if we really listen to it.

Music must stand on its own legs as well as on the support of a programme.

Music should only be connected with extraneous ideas when the composer has so directed, & not always then. E.G. titles of pieces by Schumann etc.

There is a list of records (the sources of which are also listed, including HQ, Eastern Command) covering the range of music from medieval organum and Morley through to Vaughan Williams, Warlock, and Walton, and more detailed notes on some pieces or genres. On Tchaikovsky's Fifth Symphony, he wrote: 'The symphony to a certain extent a dramatic form. Material must be allowed to develop according to what is inherent in it. Tunes etc. must be true to themselves like characters in a play.' He comments that one must think 'of the material of chamber-music as of remarks made to a few friends', and that the art of musical form 'may be said to consist in presenting material in its right perspective; in making important things sound important in relation to the rest.' Referring to the overture to *The Marriage of Figaro*, he suggested that it was not 'the sentimental comedy of the English, but the intellectual comedy of the Latins, where feelings are not so much invoked as intelligence, and where no moral sense is allowed to dull a sense of the amusing'. Charlie Chaplin he invoked 'as example of the sentimentally-comic figure' (anticipating the critical stance of several decades later).

There were some brighter moments during this period, however. Rawsthorne was beginning to be much in demand as a composer, and inevitably, along with many others, found himself asked to write 'useful' music for special occasions. The BBC (who in 1942 transferred the Symphony Orchestra to Bedford) asked him to write some music for their programme *Radio Newsreel*, which was received with much enthusiasm by the authorities, though in the event an internal BBC memo from Kenneth A. Wright reveals that 'the Overseas news reel people . . . have in fact never been able to use it, though I am not clear why'. Alan had to obtain six weeks' leave from the military authorities to fulfil this commission. The BBC also started to commission him to write incidental music to radio plays, part of the enlightened policy of radio producers in those days to commission new music of quality. Plays such as *The Happy Hypocrite* and *The Golden Cockerel* (based on the tale by Pushkin) gave him valuable experience and enabled him to explore textures or techniques that he did not employ elsewhere. He was also able to rise resourcefully to the challenge of writing vocal lines to be sung by actors, whose voices are more akin to those of ballad-singers than trained classical artists. His experience of conducting orchestras in recording incidental music of this kind enabled him confidently to accept concert engagements, such as the invitation to conduct the BBC Symphony Orchestra in his Symphonic Studies: like many composers, Rawsthorne enjoyed conducting his own music and was reasonably adept at it. When the fully scored version of the First Piano Concerto was premièred at the Proms, also in 1942, he declared that 'The main difficulty in conducting at concerts, I have found, is in getting yourself on to the platform in the first place, and it has been authoritatively observed that the longest distance on the surface of the earth is from the artists' room to the rostrum.'[4]

Further encouragement came in the form of a definite agreement with OUP as his exclusive publishers; they had already taken some of the earlier music such as the Symphonic Studies, Bagatelles for piano, Theme and Variations for two violins, and First String Quartet, following Walton's recommendation that they take an interest in Rawsthorne's work. The hesitancy with which OUP approached the idea of paying a retaining fee is indicative of the practice of the time. An internal memo of 26 May 1942 reveals that 'Walton is the only composer who gets retaining fee. Neither V-W nor Lambert do—it might get about'. The following day it was reported that 'Sir Humphrey [Milford, the long-time head of the company] feels it is an exceptional case & we might . . . make a gesture especially as Rawsthorne turned down the Boosey [and] Hawkes offer of a cash retaining fee per year in order to get options on all his works.' The first regular contract was dated 17 June 1942. OUP were sensitive to the difficulties the Rawsthornes were under. The internal memo of 26 May refers to Jessie: she 'finds difficulty in keeping up with commitments & financing him now he is in [the] army. They lost all their possessions in [the] blitz & needed ready money.' On the copy of a note to her a week later is pencilled a list of manuscripts destroyed in the bombing, including the Clarinet Concerto, *Kubla Khan*, *The Enemy Speaks*, a Trio for piano, flute, and oboe, folksong arrangements, and a Chamber Overture, presumably the one performed by Iris Lemare in 1937. OUP renewed their agreement each time from then on until Rawsthorne's death. On 12 January 1945, a memo from Norman Peterkin, of OUP's Music Department, to Sir Humphrey Milford said, 'it is important to keep Rawsthorne as a purely Oxford composer during the next few years . . . & keep him out of the clutches of Boosey & Hawkes . . . get Rawsthorne to extend the agreement either for another 3 or 5 years'.

---

[4] 'The Longest Walk on Earth', article for Programme Book of the 1949 Henry Wood Promenade Concerts.

The music of the early war years was mostly, and in the circumstances under-standably, small in scale, with the exception of the sketched violin concerto and the composition of *Kubla Khan*. In 1943 there was *Salute to the Red Army*, a pageant written by Louis MacNeice and produced by Basil Dean to a commission from the Ministry of Information. It was in honour of the celebrations for the twenty-fifth anniversary of the establishment of the Red Army. According to William Glock, Rawsthorne's contribution, an *Ode* for soloists, chorus and orchestra, 'had brilliance and dignity and a great variety of impact'.[5] The score of this work has disappeared, but fortunately the vocal score of *Kubla Khan* does survive. To his sister, Rawsthorne wrote in December 1939:

I am setting 'Kubla Khan' to music—a foolhardy occupation. It is a sort of commis-sion from the BBC which both I and they thought had been entirely scotched by the outbreak of war. But it was in connection with some exchange broadcasts with Basle, and the Swiss apparently don't share the BBC's view that whatever you're doing you must stop it. So I have to start work on the thing. Not a very good time for writing music, the present. Well, well. I have been saying loudly and rudely for some time, that if our Government didn't behave differently we should become involved in a war, and here we are. But that is very cold comfort, and the pleasure one can take in being right is small. Perhaps there is consolation in the thought that bad as our Government is, the French seem to have a worse one.

(The exchange commission was Honegger's *La Danse des morts*.) In this wartime atmosphere, Coleridge's exotic text, an unexpected choice for this composer in any case, must have given Rawsthorne a particularly difficult task. There must be some reason why he never reconstructed the work, despite the later efforts of Leslie Woodgate, chorus master of the BBC Chorus, and Humphrey Searle to persuade him to do so. The task would not have been time-consuming, for the orchestration was simply strings and percussion (like the original version of the First Piano Concerto)—though it should be added that investigation of the vocal score suggests that a full orchestral version would be more satisfactory, since some of the textures cry out for the variety of colours that wind instruments would have added.

The first performance was in a studio broadcast in June 1940 conducted by Reginald Redman (a performance which Rawsthorne thought excellent). Those who heard it were deeply impressed. Humphrey Searle wrote that he 'always hoped he would write the work again, but he never did—perhaps he

---

[5] *Observer* (28 Feb. 1943).

wasn't happy with it', adding that he himself refrained from setting the same text until after Rawsthorne's death.[6] Ralph Hill's review in the *Listener* (7 June 1940) was highly favourable: 'a sensitive and subtle interpretation of the poem . . . the music is picturesque and evocative of the varying moods of the poem. The score is rich in melody and rhythm, and the writing throughout is strikingly characteristic of the composer's masterly style.' Bernard Stevens is even more forthcoming: 'All who heard it [at the first broadcast performance], including the present writer, are of the opinion that it remains one of his finest works', and he describes the final main section leading to a minatory choral 'Beware!' as 'not only one of the most moving passages in all Rawsthorne's music but in all Twentieth Century choral music'.[7]

What is most striking about the work is the resourcefulness of the choral writing, from simple stepwise movement and fairly conventional, imitative overlapping entries to more complex textures created by the use of a wordless chorus as accompaniment to a solo, unusually elaborate melismata on a single syllable (his freedom in writing for the voice is markedly developed from earlier days), incantatory repetition of key words, or even the simultaneous setting of different parts of the text (something almost entirely absent from his later choral works, but very effective here). Rawsthorne's liking for augmented harmonies, and for shifting minor tonalities moving down by a semitone, is eminently suited to this strange and mysterious poem, and the final section, an extended tenor solo setting the passage 'A damsel with a dulcimer, In a vision once I saw', is particularly atmospheric. The richness of the climactic build-up, with much contrapuntal working in chorus as well as orchestra, leads to the great choral shout of 'Beware!', followed by a coda ending in a mood of desolation. The occasional fast sections possess great vigour, without too obviously drawing on the example of *Belshazzar's Feast* to do so (a failing of some British choral works of the late 1930s and 1940s), and the final cadence is a simple drop from D♭ to F, the Neapolitan sixth (D♭) being an increasingly important element in Rawsthorne's style (another link with Haydn—and, indeed, Schubert).

The two settings of poems by John Fletcher, 'Away, Delights' and 'God Lyaeus', are reputed to be the source of the Red Army *Ode*, for which they were given a choral and orchestral setting; however, they fit their original voice-and-piano format perfectly, the instrumental writing being particularly effective. These are perhaps the best-known of all Rawsthorne's songs, and

---

[6] 'Biographical Essays', Poulton ii. 47.
[7] 'The Choral Music', Poulton iii. 42.

Ex. 4.1. 'Away, Delights': (*a*) piano introduction, bars 1–5; (*b*) p. 4, bars 8–13

thoroughly deserve a regular place in the repertoire. In the first, as Trevor Hold has pointed out, the extent to which the opening piano phrase (Ex. 4.1(*a*)) permeates the whole song, appearing in every part including both the bass and the vocal line at different times, links the piece with the seventeenth-century English fantasia: 'The voice, though *prima inter pares*, is one strand in a polyphonic texture.'[8] The poem is particularly suited to a composer who liked to set words with sensitivity to their natural rhythmic flow, as well as a preference for responding to the underlying feeling of the text rather than mere

---

[8] 'The Solo Vocal Music', Poulton iii. 75.

straightforward pictorialism. There is, too, a hint of drama in the carefully judged approach to the refrain 'Alas, for pity go' ('stay' in the second verse) (Ex. 4.1(*b*)). Perhaps by a subconscious remembrance of the older composer's interest in earlier English music, there is a distinctly Warlockian exuberance about 'God Lyaeus', the toccata-like keyboard figuration in a thumping 4/4 metre accompanying a fluid vocal line, with sequences and frequent cross-metres adding to the rumbustiousness of 'God of youth, let this day here | Enter neither care nor fear'. It is perhaps rather short for easy recital programming (a mere twenty-two bars). 'We Three Merry Maidens' ('Nous étions trois filles'), also written in 1940, is more substantial. Written for Sophie Wyss, it harks back to a slightly more complex version of the style of the *Three French Nursery Songs* in setting a traditional French text. The double metrical technique, its simple duple-time vocal part contradicting the triple-time piano part, adds to the charm of another delightful piece, whose combination of innocent vocal freshness with technical sophistication gives it an extra dimension in addition to its surface charm: the three young maidens tease their simple country bumpkin with infinite grace.

Equally delightful is another piece from 1940, the piano duet suite *The Creel* (after which the Rawsthorne Society's journal is named), still one of his most popular pieces, and deservedly so. Rawsthorne was fond, rather oddly, of both cats and fish (Lambert's affectionate name for him was Old Fish-Face, or The Fish with an Ear for Music), and in these four pieces inspired by Izaak Walton's *The Compleat Angler* he essayed in miniature a surprisingly comprehensive survey of the components of his own style and techniques. 'I have always felt that fishes have been somewhat shamefully neglected in music, whereas many less worthy creatures are copiously represented', he wrote to Hubert Foss, then OUP's Head of Music, on 7 June 1940, and the vivid characterization of the Pike, Sprat, Carp, and Salmon, complete with Izaak Walton's description of them, is an appropriate tribute. The intention was originally to write the suite for children, but according to Rawsthorne's own programme note 'it proved to be rather too ambitious for this purpose'. The characteristic phrases are all here, including the four-note 'fingerprint', the tune beginning with an upward fourth setting up a dominant–tonic relationship, the major/minor ambiguity and the augmented chords, the trills forming a natural part of the thematic outlines, and so on, but the invention is fresh and memorable.

The first movement, 'The Mighty Pike is the Tyrant of the Fresh Water', is suitably majestic, with a Handelian grandeur emphasized by a gravely ceremonial character, complete with what sound like timpani flourishes. 'The Sprat; a Fish that is ever in Motion' is a perpetual canon (Ex. 4.2(*a*)), 'in which the

Ex. 4.2. *The Creel*: (*a*) 'The Sprat', bars 1–3; (*b*) 'The Salmon', last 7 bars

(*a*)

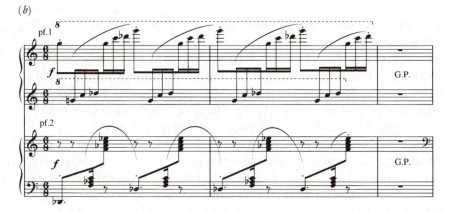

(*b*)

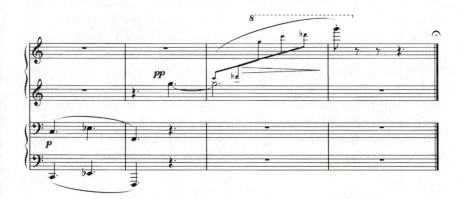

two players chase one another up and down the keyboard, and then go back to the beginning'[9]; it is marked to be repeated *ad libitum*, and since it is Vivace, it is easy for the players to come to grief and end up playing at the same time instead of a beat apart. Like the first movement, it is centred on B minor. 'The Carp is the Queen of Rivers; a Stately, a Good, and a Very Subtil Fish' is based in B flat major, with a melancholy tinge even from the start. It has a touch of the slow waltz, a dance form which impinges on Rawsthorne's music throughout his career, though often implicitly rather than explicitly. 'The Leap or Summersault of the Salmon' brings the suite to a witty, lilting conclusion with a 6/8 piece, Allegro non troppo, rather like a sprightly siciliano, with wider leaps in the melodic line and a delicious final upward flick of the tail (Ex. 4.2(*b*)). It is no surprise that the work has retained its popularity; perhaps the most intriguing performance is that reputed to have been given in Paris by Yvonne Lefébure and Benjamin Britten, though on what occasion is not known.

Three other short works are thought to derive from the early 1940s. The Theme and Four Studies for piano, which were discovered among Rawsthorne's papers after his death and first performed by John Ogdon at his Memorial Concert at the Wigmore Hall in 1971, have something in common with the Four Romantic Pieces from 1954: the theme itself relates closely to the finale of the Concerto for String Orchestra (1949) and the score for the film *Lease of Life* (1954). It is typical of Rawsthorne that, within the works composed during any period of a few years (say, two or three), there is a commonality of material, with the same phrases, textures, or rhythmic devices occurring in perhaps three or four pieces and hardly ever appearing in precisely the same form thereafter. There are, naturally, exceptions to this, but it is relatively easy to date most of his works fairly precisely by finding these bits of common material and working out which other pieces contain them. There are numerous devices, for instance, that he uses only in the works of the mid-1930s like the Concertante, Viola Sonata, and Theme and Variations for two violins and which do not recur in exactly the same way elsewhere; if there are similar phrases later, the emphasis on certain intervals or rhythms is changed and they have new implications for tonal and thematic development. For this reason, one might place this work in the middle or late 1940s. However, the composer Gerard Schurmann, who became a close friend and colleague of Rawsthorne's, stated of the Theme and Four Studies that 'I can say with absolute certainty that it was composed before 1944, probably a few years

---

[9] Composer's programme note.

Ex. 4.3. Theme and Four Studies for piano: (*a*) Theme, bars 1–6; (*b*) Study No. 3, bars 19–20

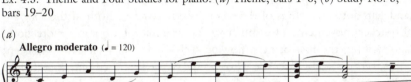

earlier',[10] and Jessie herself put the date as possibly 1940; Rawsthorne had the habit of setting himself to compose something every day, as a task, and she pointed out that after being called up, he would not have had time to do this.

Whenever it was written, the work forms a relaxed and warmly lyrical contribution to the piano repertoire. The fourth study was originally designated as the first of Two Improvisations, and there is an air of spontaneity about the whole work, though it is never in any way careless. The Theme itself (Ex. 4.3(*a*)) is diatonic, with fewer accidentals than customary, and pursues a clear path from a traditional tonic, C, to a traditional dominant, G (bar 6). The four studies are, essentially, variations on the Theme, but less complex or sophisticated than those in earlier variation-derived works such as the Bagatelles. Each

[10] Note in the programme for the Memorial Concert, 24 Nov. 1971.

one pursues a single pianistic style or texture, such as the stately, even sombre Handelian dotted rhythms of the second study (Grave). Both of the substantial quicker movements owe much to the example of Chopin's more florid piano writing, the first being a flowing 6/8 Allegro in which the persistent semiquavers cascading over the whole range of the keyboard only solidify into slower motion for the climactic closing section with Lisztian double octaves, while in the third (which clearly anticipates the third of the Four Romantic Pieces in its perky rhythmic style at the start) a substantial virtuoso movement is developed, looking ahead to Rawsthorne's late Ballade and backward to Chopin's ballade style (Ex. 4.3(b)) as well as developing the Lisztian bravura from No. 1. For all that it is a minor work, less intensely worked out than usual and more relaxed in tone, it makes a welcome, lyrical addition to the piano repertoire, and the final study is a beautiful resolution, clearly modelled on the last of the Bagatelles but without its tonal complexity or contrapuntal working.

Another keyboard work, 'Left, Left' for two pianos, is one of Rawsthorne's curiosities. A further example of the unfortunate propensity of his manuscripts to disappear, this is a short (just over three minutes), brilliant little pot-pourri of tunes associated with the Republican struggle in the Spanish Civil War. The 'Bandiera rossa' and many other tunes make fleeting appearances; Rawsthorne's technical skill at laying out the music for the two pianos and leading naturally from one tune to the next is considerable, and though there is hardly a trace of his own individual style in it, it is in its own, rather curious way an amusing divertissement. The appearance at the end of 'John Brown's Body', arranged with some hilarity, gives the whole enterprise a somewhat surrealist air. The piece was written for the Peppin sisters Mary and Geraldine, a celebrated two-piano duo of the time, and fortunately a recording by them has survived.

The mystery concerning the Suite for recorder (or viola d'amore) and piano has been cleared up in recent years, though since the original manuscript is still missing at the time of writing not all the questions have been definitively answered. In September 1940, the music publishers Schott & Co. announced 'a series of contemporary works for recorder (or flute) and piano'. They were 'reluctantly obliged to delay publication of the complete series owing to the present emergency' (the wartime paper shortage).[11] Rawsthorne was announced as a participant in the series, but his work never materialized and,

---

[11] 'Publisher's Note' in Lennox Berkeley, Sonatina for recorder and piano (Schott & Co., London, Sept. 1940).

though known to have been written, disappeared. Meanwhile, in the early 1940s the viola d'amore specialist Harry van der Lyn commissioned him to write a work for viola d'amore and piano, the score of which, once more, vanished. In 1992 the Rawsthorne Society received a photocopy of the viola work, and the recorder player John B. Turner deduced from seeing it not only that it would fit the recorder perfectly well, with just a few relatively minor changes, but also that the solo part had been altered by someone other than Rawsthorne in order to suit the viola, double-stoppings and other violistic devices being added in another hand.[12] Confirmation of Turner's thesis came with the discovery of what appeared to be a Performing Right Society listing of works, presumably produced towards the end of the 1940s, in which it is listed as 'Suite for recorder (or viola) and piano', and of later correspondence dating from 1948 in the OUP archives relating to possible use of the work as the basis of a suite for oboe and piano (which never appeared).

Performance of the recorder version has thoroughly vindicated Turner's deductions and brought the piece successfully before the public. Like the Theme and Four Studies for piano, it is more relaxed and diatonic than usual for Rawsthorne, and is accessible and lyrical in tone. The opening Sarabande (Ex. 4.4) is based on a tune related to the early dance tune *La folia*, used by Corelli and many others and, in the later 1940s, by Rawsthorne in his score for the film *Saraband for Dead Lovers* and (more distantly) the slow movement of his Concerto for String Orchestra. There are hints of a newly expanded lyrical manner in the falling seventh and rising sixth of bar 6. The Sarabande's Handelian grandeur gives way to a Fantasia based, uniquely in Rawsthorne's output, on an English folksong, 'Wooddy-Cock'. Perhaps this was a tribute to Arnold Dolmetsch, whose repertoire included Farnaby's piece of that title from the Fitzwilliam Virginal Book, and Rawsthorne's treatment, possibly in homage to the thematic integration typical of Elizabethan instrumental music, is effectively a set of divisions on a ground. A lyrical Air, with some charming tonal side-slips, is followed by a closing Jig, brief and delightful, vividly recalling the leaping salmon from *The Creel*. The tonal scheme of the work is unusually loose (F, D minor, A minor, G minor), and the tone of the whole thing gentle and rather delicate. It makes a slender and graceful contribution to the recorder repertoire.

The variety of 'useful' music produced during the war years was considerable. Rawsthorne continued writing music for documentary films, including *Street Fighting* and *Tank Tactics*, produced by the Army Film Unit for the

---

[12] 'Rawsthorne's Recorder Suite', *The Creel*, 2/3 (spring 1993), 121–3.

Ex. 4.4. Suite for recorder and piano, first movement, bars 1–7

Ministry of Information as training films. In a radio interview later, he indicated his philosophy of writing film music: 'the music might have been fulfilling its purpose better unobserved than if it had called attention to itself.' In the case of the latter film, the music 'was directly suggested by tanks—the sort of noise they make and the way they move about'. The most important of his wartime documentary film work was *Burma Victory* (1945). Roger Manvell wrote:

the music by Alan Rawsthorne is combined with sound effects in a fine atmospheric sequence early on in the film, when General Wingate's Chindits were landed by air in Central Burma hundreds of miles behind the Japanese lines. In the dawn the gliders, which have successfully survived the fearful, hazardous flight over mountains eight thousand feet high, land in the clearing, their only audience birds of prey waiting for the fruits of disaster. Here Rawsthorne's music combines with the animal cries from the jungle to help spread an atmosphere of tension over the pictures on the screen.[13]

Rawsthorne described it in a letter to his sister Barbara, writing from the London flat he and Jessie had acquired:

I feel that writing film-music is less exhausting, at my time of life, than picking one's way over the ruins of the Kurfürstendamm, and this film, plus a large chunk of leave

---

[13] *The Film and the Public* (Harmondsworth, 1955), 66.

(long overdue) plus a short time of doing nothing whatever, (Army fashion), should see me through what now remains of my military career. I am due to burst forth upon the astonished civilian world no later than the end of next November—a worse, I fear, rather than a better man, as a result of the last five years.

Rawsthorne's ill luck persisted, however, for towards the end of the war the flat in Ormonde Terrace was hit by a German doodle-bug (how many composers, one wonders, have been bombed in two separate cities?). Jessie was alone in the flat at the time, but escaped uninjured, and there is no record of manuscripts going missing on this occasion.

The most important concert works of the war years were orchestral: two overtures and the fully scored version of the First Piano Concerto. The original version of the concerto, scored for an orchestra of strings and percussion, had been appreciated for its clarity, wit, and effectiveness. A few critics struck a sour note; the reporter for the *Star* commented (15 March 1939) that it 'lacks originality and warmth, and means but little when all is said and done', though being fair-minded went on to report that it 'was heartily applauded' (one wonders why, if it was so unattractive). The *Daily Mail* commented that 'Had the slow movement been slightly profounder, the concerto might have proved something more than mere entertainment' (causing one to ponder the implications behind the assessment of entertainment as 'mere'). In later years Rawsthorne felt that the fuller scoring was infinitely preferable to the original, and there is no doubt that the depth of expression in the slow movement is revealed satisfactorily only in the orchestral version, to say nothing of the added brilliance that his inventive scoring for winds and percussion gives to the quicker movements. From an entertaining work in which the string orchestra's capabilities are perhaps over-stretched (especially at the finale's climax, where one desperately needs the trombones to thunder out the 'Bandiera rossa'), it becomes a scintillating, immensely characterful, 'full' concerto, whose place in the repertoire, seems assured, not least because pianists and audiences alike respond to its subtle vivacity. It clearly relates to the neo-classical concerto style which, partly as a reaction against what was perceived as the sometimes overblown rhetoric of the grand romantic manner, was an important part of musical aesthetics in the 1920s and 1930s, though in Rawsthorne's case it is perhaps nearer to Busoni's 'Young Classicality', an attempt to recapture classical ideals, than a self-conscious revival of the classical manner. More than any other British concerto, it seems like a parallel to the Ravel G major, than which it is not a whit less assured or personal.

The first performance was given at the 1942 Proms, with the London Philharmonic Orchestra conducted by the composer (who had, of course, to obtain leave from the military authorities to do so) and Louis Kentner as the soloist. The hallmark of both first and last movements is the rhythmic verve with which the music drives forward, especially in the opening Capriccio, where Rawsthorne's debt to the Baroque is at its clearest. The toccata-like figuration of the opening (Ex. 4.5(*a*)), with piano semiquavers outlining the underlying harmony and the orchestra interjecting rhythmically, gets the music going with an irresistibly dashing air, and the vigour hardly lets up; even the second subject (a close relative of the tunes listed in Ex. 3.1) has strong forward momentum. Considerable power is built up by canonic treatment of the

Ex. 4.5. First Piano Concerto: (*a*) first movement, bars 1–6; (*b*) first movement, bars 4–5 after fig. 1; (*c*) first movement, Presto coda, bars 3–8; (*d*) third movement, after fig. 59, bars 5–13

(*a*)

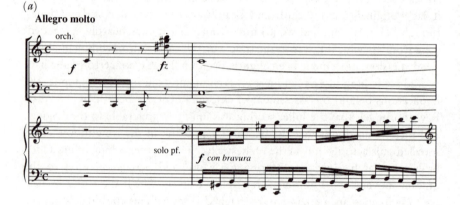

(b)

(c)

Ex. 4.5. *Continued*

(*d*)

second theme, allowing the piano to burst through and take command, a dramatic stroke of concerto theatre. The orchestration is delightful, with admirable use of the percussion (the frequent little touches of xylophone chattering are particularly imaginative). Characteristically, though the movement looks at first sight like a sonata-form structure, it does not behave like one: the recapitulation is greatly abbreviated, omitting the second subject group altogether, and the final quicker section (Presto), which looks like a coda, is actually longer than the recapitulation, developing some of the material still further. It might be better to describe it as ternary-sonata form, with its first subject group being stated, then subjected to development, and a similar process taking place with the second subject and the bipartite third section (recapitulation-coda). Though neo-classical clarity and vigour is all, a full-blooded cello variation, decorated by piano arpeggios derived from the harmonic content of the very opening, has a thoroughly romantic sweep. The underlying tonal centre is C, with the most significant secondary centre being E (for the start of the second theme); this is hinted at in the very first bar of the piano part, where the ascending arpeggiato figuration has an E major chord over a pedal on C. There is a move to G for the start of a more relaxed subsidiary theme, though the xylophone in particular persistently reminds one of the essential toccata character of the movement. The Presto changes from the basic 4/4 metre to a quicksilver 6/8, and builds up a final crescendo over a C pedal; the triple metre links it to the Tarantella rhythm of the finale.

There is a new emphasis on using fourths to unify the thematic material: Ex. 4.5(*b*), (*c*), and (*d*) come from the opening section and coda of the first movement and one of the virtuosic episodes in the finale, where the octave statement of the episode theme in the bass is decorated by brilliant descending fourths in the right hand. In all these examples, it will be seen that Rawsthorne is also using the fourths to shift the tonal implications of the material, and in Ex. 4.5(*d*) he superimposes a duple metre (in the bass) on a triple metre (the right hand), a similar device to that with which he builds up the tension towards the end of the Capriccio. Though the thematic integration of the score is less thoroughgoing than that in, say, the Symphonic Studies (where it is truly extraordinary), there are all sorts of almost subconscious links of this kind helping to bind the work together. The finale's Tarantella is a rondo, bubbling over with lively invention (the themes being, of course, closely related but nevertheless distinct) as well as the deftest orchestration. Rawsthorne was, as the Symphonic Studies had demonstrated, a natural master of orchestration, and knew precisely how to gauge the weight of the sound to enhance the impact of the structure, as well as possessing an instinctive ear for instrumental colouring. The reappearances of the ritornello tune are mostly curtailed, and its final appearance is utterly unique, so far as one is aware: after a sensitive, brief, and very touching piano solo, the orchestra builds up to its big climax and the resounding brass statement of the Spanish Republican song 'Bandiera rossa'. The music quietens down to some simple, utterly Rawsthornian chords, a few flicks of rhythm on the tambourine, and just a couple of tiny fragments of the main theme, pianissimo, on the solo instrument. Then a few bars of very quiet accelerando, with G♯–C♯ dominant–tonic relationships skeletally outlined, and it is all over, with a rather 'Salmon'-like flick of the tail. This nonchalant conclusion has an insouciance both charming and Haydnesque; one is also reminded that Busoni's *Rondò arlecchinesco* finishes with a quiet tap of a tambourine.

The tonal scheme of the work as a whole explores, if reduced to its basics, a close intervallic relationship: the Capriccio's C is replaced by the fascinating scheme of the Chaconne (starting in F minor and closing in D minor), while the Tarantella starts in D flat, corrected immediately to its enharmonic C sharp, on the tonic note of which it finishes. The slow movement we now have was actually the second to have been composed (Compact Disc, track 3). While composing the original version of the concerto, Rawsthorne received one of his first film commissions. He commented: 'When I had finished the film I came back to the concerto, tore up the slow movement, and wrote what I think was a much better one. Why a film about a new traffic plan for the City of London enabled me to do this, I can't imagine; perhaps "slow movement" had something to do with it!'[14] If so, it is unusual for anything to do with traffic to be a cause for gratitude, for the result remains one of the most haunt-ingly beautiful of all his slower pieces. The basis of this Chaconne is decep-tively simple, a sequence of eight chords which, for each variation, is repeated a semitone higher (Ex. 4.6(a)). This plan is followed rigorously for seven sec-tions, taking us up from the opening F minor to B minor; the eighth section, however, moves up a tone to C sharp minor, and only then does it drop the semitone to the C minor thus unexpectedly delayed. After this, Rawsthorne refuses to follow the scheme slavishly: having now altered it slightly, he further disrupts the regularity of the eight-bar length of the sections and makes the tonality more elusive, so that the tenth and eleventh variations form a single unit which gradually vanishes through fragmentation and a momentary sense of having lost the way (see Ex. 4.6(b)). An emphatic, sudden tutti, marked 'forte', brings us back to a more clearly defined A minor, and from then on the cycle of stepwise upward modulations is resumed, going up to C sharp minor (as the music once again fragments itself) and a final, despairing cadence on a D minor chord with a chromatic descending horn phrase (derived from the top trumpet line in the theme, and played by the pianist in the original string orchestra version).

However, a further aspect of the Chaconne theme should be noted. Although the theme itself, thanks to a harmonic twist in the tail in bar 8 (which becomes a dominant cadence to the new tonic of the next bar), constantly modulates up a semitone, it contains within it an equally constant downward pull, like a force of gravity fighting the attempt of a flyer to become airborne. Bar 1 is in F minor, but bar 3 is in E minor, bar 5 E flat minor, and bar 7 a sort of D (major). When the tonality starts to dissipate and the music to lose its sense of direction, it is the piano's aria-like cantilena that becomes the only purposeful element, and even this eventually fades into indeterminacy, partly through its use of duplet rhythmic phrasing in the right hand over the fragile waltz-like accompaniment (Ex. 4.6(b)). The harmonic or tonal implications of the theme and its development through the Chaconne variations are more complex than they sound. Nevertheless, this easily assimilated format, with fairly regular repetition of the ground bass, enables the listener more easily to follow Rawsthorne's still rapid harmonic movement. It is, so to speak, given a handle that it is easy to grasp, a structure that is easy to follow. Herbert Howells eloquently wrote that 'by some hint from slow-shifting common-

[14] Quoted in *Oxford Music Bulletin* (OUP, London, 1 Jan.–1 Apr. 1950).

Ex. 4.6. First Piano Concerto, Chaconne: (*a*) bars 1–16; (*b*) 10 bars before fig. 44

chords that are themselves involved in subtle false-relation, the man of Lancashire (superficially consigned by careless criticism to a spiritual home somewhere in mid-Europe), seems suddenly to stand in direct contact with the
gravity of Tallis and the later Tudors'.[15] Wilfrid Mellers found there to be a
similar relationship with the past in this movement:

[15] 'A Note on Alan Rawsthorne', *Music and Letters*, 32 (Jan. 1951), 24.

The ground-bass technique was one of the first . . . means whereby early baroque composers endeavoured to compose works built on a dance foundation which could none the less attain to considerable dimensions, and its apparently stringent limitations seem to have inspired Purcell, Couperin and Bach to some of their most intensely passionate, because *intensely* disciplined, music. [This] chaconne . . . likewise achieves a peculiar emotional power from a latent tension between the passionate contour of the melodic line . . . and the relentless pulse of the ground-bass . . . The disturbing effect of the music comes from the combination simultaneously of eloquence and tension in the line and harmony with regularity and objectivity in the rhythm and structure.[16]

Illuminatingly, he compares this characteristic with that of Couperin's more tragic B minor *Passacaille* (whose ground-bass also modulates upwards, though concluding with a tonic cadence; the Couperin piece also contains a startlingly Rawsthornian harmony towards its climax!).

Interpretatively the concerto is relatively straightforward. Like the Ravel G major it requires the utmost sensitivity in the slow movement and brilliant clarity in the outer ones, with as much technical precision as possible. In that respect, it has a Mozartian transparency. The one real problem concerns the metronome marks, which are different in the various editions. The first study score is a facsimile of the manuscript, as is the full score of the string orchestra version, but the two-piano score is engraved, and thus presumably postdates the first performance (though one would imagine Rawsthorne to have revised the full score before publication). The differences are shown in Table 1. To add confusion, another printed study score was issued in the 1970s with a mixture of these metronome markings. Rawsthorne very often changed metronome markings after a first performance, or even before it, and a realistic view of this complex situation would simply be that it is all a matter of personal taste—metronome marks, as he himself felt, are simply a guide. The Chaconne is, as it happens, not only much more expressive at a slower tempo,

TABLE 1. Metronome Marks in the First Piano Concerto

Movement	Facsimile study score	String orchestra score	Two-piano score
1	♩ = 152	♩ = 152	♩ = 144
	Coda: ♩. = 192	Coda: ♩. = 144	Coda: ♩. = 184
2	♪ = 76	♪ = 96 (pencil, by another hand)	♪ = 92
3	♩. = 144	♩. = 144	♩. = 158

[16] 'Alan Rawsthorne and the Baroque', *Tempo* (Mar. 1946).

making a better contrast and more adequately fulfilling its place as the emotional heart of the work, but it is also given more than a touch of the Sarabande, a style of which Rawsthorne was particularly fond. Of the several recordings issued to date, Moura Lympany's, which is in any case an outstandingly sympathetic performance, seems to strike the best balance between tempos, and interestingly enough there are in the Capriccio numerous subtle changes of tempo which equate to a kind of tempo rubato; the lilting passages of variable metre, with little hints of a waltz rhythm invading the predominantly 4/4 toccata, need a tiny bit of extra space to convey the expressive ebb and flow so apt for Schumann or Chopin. This kind of sympathetic response to the music's inner rhythm is something Rawsthorne anticipated from his interpreters, and it helps to convey the expressive subtleties which pervade the music.

In its full orchestration, the concerto became one of Rawsthorne's most frequently performed orchestral works, though its popularity was overtaken by the immense success of the Second Concerto after its première in 1951. Equally popular, and still retaining its hold at least on the fringes of the repertoire as the concertos have done, is the Overture *Street Corner* (Compact Disc, track 4). Oddly enough, its successor, the Fantasy Overture *Cortèges*, has not established itself to anything like the same extent, though it is if anything even finer. *Street Corner* was commissioned by the armed forces' Entertainments National Service Association (ENSA—affectionately dubbed 'Every Night Something Awful' by the forces) and written in 1944. The first performance was given the following year in Leamington Spa by the New London Orchestra conducted by Constant Lambert. After a brisk introductory call to attention surprisingly reminiscent of the overture to *The Bartered Bride*, the music proceeds to evoke 'a Saturday night at the cross-roads of a busy industrial town'.[17] It is cheerful and optimistic, music to chase away the gloom and despair of wartime (or any other cause for depression), and it lifts the spirits brilliantly. It was, in a sense, part of Rawsthorne's war effort—music 'specially composed and used by a nation at war as a means . . . of helping to defeat the enemy', he wrote in a manuscript held in the RNCM archives. 'I do not mean that the overture itself is particularly lethal, nor that it was used as Joshua used his trumpets in his assault on Jericho.'

Far from being aggressive, the overture is consistently jolly, but with an unforced merriment that owes much to the subtlety with which Rawsthorne characteristically employs contrapuntal techniques. The main theme (see Ex.

---

[17] Composer's programme note.

3.1(b)) is full of typical side-slips, sequences, and little rhythmic kinks to give it consistent interest: Rawsthorne creates a new theme half-way through the overture by taking the fifth and sixth bars of the tune, playing them more smoothly at half-speed, and then expanding from this to create the new melody (which is, therefore, not really new at all). This is then subjected to canonic treatment, first in two parts and then in three, an apparently academic device which sounds anything but stuffy because the tunes are so attractive and the orchestration so apposite. A habanera rhythm adds an extra touch of colour to the proceedings. Though the piece *sounds* like a fairly conventional sonata-form allegro, as so often with Rawsthorne it does not behave like one. The canonic tune acts more as a kind of trio section, with developmental passages either side of it, and when the main theme returns it is given only the briefest of references by full orchestra, hardly a full-scale recapitulation (though there is a delightful interlude in which a solo violin explores a phrase from it rather pathetically, as if left standing in a corner of the market while its parents have gone off to do some shopping). The biggest statements of the main tune have a rollicking quality provided by an oom-pah accompaniment, a touch of the cheerful vulgarity of which, at his best, Rawsthorne was a master. Quite why this should be a source of embarassment to some over-fastidious listeners it is difficult to see, especially when similar moments in Poulenc or Shostakovich are warmly welcomed as evidence of their common touch.

Cortèges, a much larger-scale overture (fourteen minutes compared with five), achieves a rare balance between polyphony and intellect on the one hand and sheer delightful entertainment on the other, though it essays (and achieves) greater depths of expression. There seems to be no record of the reason for the work's existence. Gerard Schurmann has written: 'I do remember Constant [Lambert] discussing the idea with Alan that he should write a kind of processional piece with balletic overtones, and it wouldn't surprise me if he had also suggested the French title.'[18] (Schurmann also referred aptly to the 'almost Mendelssohnian Allegro in the middle'.) It is dedicated to Lambert, though it was actually Basil Cameron who conducted the London Symphony Orchestra in the first performance, at the Proms in July 1945. For the première, Rawsthorne wrote a programme note saying that the work 'is constructed out of musical elements of a processional character, varying from a funeral-march to a lively tune in light-infantry *tempo*'. Commenting on the developmental section late in the piece, before the build-up to the final climax, he referred to the new subject that is introduced as 'hardly a military march,

---

[18] Fax to the author, 18 Apr. 1997.

but [it] might be said to exhibit, like its author, certain temporary and ephemeral military characteristics', though in fact it was first used in the 1935 String Quartet. It finds a more fitting home in this splendid overture. There is, once again, a striking call to attention, a unison statement of the notes D-E♭-G-F♯ marked 'Allegro Molto Vivace'. After six bars, and a pause, the timpani enunciate a funereal rhythm at quarter-speed (Adagio), and the two alternate, already developing some of the motifs, until the Adagio predominates in a section marked by the funereal rhythm and a sweetly lyrical theme on flutes and viola (Ex. 4.7(*a*)). The emotional feeling is restrained, but there is no doubting the underlying passion, expressed through the beautiful cantilena of the tune, the typically ambiguous major/minor tonality, and the precision with which Rawsthorne places his widening of the harmonic horizons is exquisite.

The Adagio is fully developed, accumulating considerable emotional force, and after reaching its climax winds down to hold the music momentarily in suspense. Then comes the main Allegro section, a fugue in 6/8 time whose theme (Ex. 4.7(*b*)) is marked by the repeated rising fifth motif and the phrase *x* which, in augmentation, later forms a smoother 'new' theme in the manner already familiar from *Street Corner*. The seamless flow of invention, with several themes closely related to the fugue subject, is interrupted by the briefest reference to the Adagio, and the fugue resumes, varied and developed. A change

Ex. 4.7. *Cortèges*: (*a*) from 2nd bar of letter B; (*b*) from 2nd bar of letter D

Ex. 4.7. *Continued*

(*b*)

to 2/4 brings the 'ephemeral military' tune, and it takes its place in the various inventions being whirled around in an invigorating contrapuntal display. A return to 6/8 brings back the fugue, inverted this time, culminating in a wonderful passage which ties together the various strands of the work, combining the two main themes in a dazzling (and superbly orchestrated) display of contrapuntal wizardry (Ex. 4.8). (A reduction of this kind cannot adequately convey the exhilaration of the crackling high spirits, or the complex but airy texture inflected by gurgles or discreet whoops of delight.) (The final section, from letter U, can be heard on the Compact Disc, track 5.) After the powerful climax, there is, as the composer's note says, 'a wisp of the more lively strain for a brief moment and with this, one might say, the composition disappears round the corner'. Lambert, introducing a broadcast performance, commented that a clue to the elusive nature of the ending might be found in the quotation from A. E. Housman affixed to the score (a quotation mysteriously absent from the printed edition):

> Tomorrow, more's the pity,
> Away we both must hie
> To air the ditty
> And to earth I

Whatever the impulse behind it, this is an extraordinarily touching, as well as witty, conclusion (with even an echo of *Till Eulenspiegel* about it). Where *Street Corner*'s final C is positive and affirmative, the D major chord at the end of *Cortèges* is whimsical, a final glimpse of the passing parade. It is a piece whose neglect is more than usually inexplicable.

Ex. 4.8. *Cortèges*, from 6 bars before letter X

Ex. 4.8. *Continued*

5

BROADENING THE CANVAS
(1945–50)

ROBIN HULL's comment that the First Piano Concerto 'brings out . . . the justice of suggesting that this composer, though less spectacularly gifted than Britten, may yet stand in evident range of equality with him' indicates just how high expectations were at the end of the war.[1] Rawsthorne's works began to receive wider international performance once again. *Cortèges* was played at the ISCM Festival in London in 1946 and received its American première in 1948 at Carnegie Hall, with the National Orchestral Association conducted by Leon Barzin. *Street Corner* rapidly became a firm favourite, and Sir John Barbirolli made it part of his regular repertoire: as late as 1968 it appeared in his programmes with the New York Philharmonic. Other works received regular international performance, including the Bagatelles, the two-violin Theme and Variations (the recordings of which helped to spread Rawsthorne's name), and in particular the First Piano Concerto, which acquired a number of distinguished champions, including the Hungarian virtuoso Andor Foldes, who remained a loyal and enthusiastic interpreter. Over the years, apart from many British performances and several recordings, the concerto was played in, among other places, Venice, Gelsenkirchen, Lausanne, Canada, Israel, Malta, and Naples; Moura Lympany gave the New York première in 1952. After playing it in the USA in 1967 Foldes wrote to Alan Frank (7 February): 'after a time-lag of eight years—i.e. since my playing this concerto in Australia at the Concerto Festival in Sydney—I find my re-encounter with this work refreshing, challenging and thoroughly enjoyable.' Perhaps its greatest success was the Viennese première in 1950, with Paul Badura-Skoda as soloist and the Vienna Chamber Orchestra under Franz Litschauer: Denis Brass, of the British Council in Vienna, wrote to Frank on 4 November 1950:

Ever since I introduced him to the Bagatelles a year ago . . . Badura-Skoda has been anxious to give the first performance of the concerto in Vienna . . . I always expected this work to appeal even in this conservative town—but I never expected the wild

---

[1] 'What's New?', in A. L. Bacharach (ed.), *British Music of our Time* (Harmondsworth, 1946), 228.

ovation that it brought. The packed audience in the Mozartsaal clapped and stamped like a lot of students and the soloist was recalled eight times. The last movement had to be repeated as an encore.

On his return to civilian life in 1945, Rawsthorne resumed his bohemian exist-ence. One focal point of it was the pub used by many of the BBC people, the George, known affectionately as the 'Gluepot' on the basis that once there, you were likely to stay till closing time. Elisabeth Lutyens mentions 'someone remarking that if a bomb dropped on the George a large proportion of the musical and literary world would be destroyed. Looking around one could see John Ireland, Alan Rawsthorne, William Walton, Constant Lambert, Humphrey Searle, Lawrence Leonard, Louis MacNeice, Bertie (W. R.) Rodgers, Dylan Thomas, Roy Campbell, Uncle Tom Cobleigh and all!'[2] Rawsthorne's normally amiable temper was seldom seriously ruffled, though he could, when deeply offended, fly into a spectacular rage. On one occasion, in a pub with his cousin Elizabeth and a group of friends, he became enraged when a drunk insulted a Jewish man. Fortunately the publican intervened and evicted the drunk; Rawsthorne had suffered the Army only in order to fight Fascism, and he hated to see such racist attitudes in post-war Britain.

It was not a happy period for his marriage. He sometimes stayed away for several days, and there seems little doubt that in reality he needed female com-panionship of a different kind; his large number of women friends, however, did not lessen the affection that he and Jessie felt for each other. It seems simply to have been that, however devoted they were to each other as friends, he could not live with her. Yet, even after they eventually separated in 1947, Jessie would look after him in their original flat when he was ill, and to the end of her life she remained loyal to him and his memory. Not until his mar-riage to Isabel Lambert, Constant's widow, did he find a thoroughly compat-ible companion.

Among the closest friends of Alan and Jessie were Marion Leigh, the widow of the composer Walter Leigh (who had been killed in action near Tobruk in 1942), and her children. Their daughter, now Veronica Leigh Jacobs, kept a diary from 1950 giving a vivid picture of their social life at the time. It por-trays a wide range of visits to restaurants, shows, and concerts, with Alan becoming almost a surrogate father to Veronica, who often stayed with Jessie. It must have been an unusual (and exciting) life for a young schoolgirl at home during the holidays: 'After breakfast Jessie & I went shopping. We had lunch at Rosie's (roast duck & champagne!) and we had a quiet afternoon reading.

---

[2] *A Goldfish Bowl* (London, 1972), 140.

Alan, Mum and the boys came & we had tea and went to "Aladdin".' Alan's legendary generosity is much in evidence: when Veronica had acute appendicitis, he 'sent a Fortnum & Mason basket of Treats to hospital'.[3] The diary also offers occasional insight into Alan's peregrinations from one lodging to another, as in April 1950: 'He is going to move to Baker St. from St. James's Place.' She was able to meet what must have been a dazzling array of people, including various composer friends of Alan's such as Gerard Schurmann, Edward Williams, and Elisabeth Lutyens (Alan lived for a time with her and her husband, the conductor Edward Clark), relatives and friends, and numerous distinguished musicians, including, of course, Harry Blech, as well as younger composers such as her brother Julian and, later on, the young Richard Rodney Bennett. Alan's presents were a remarkable, and very thoughtful, collection, including a music stand (to be useful to Veronica when attending her first National Youth Orchestra course, in 1951), gramophone records (including Tchaikovsky's *Nutcracker*), birthday gifts of the complete Thackeray one year and a bracelet band for an antique watch another, and a calf leather jewel-case.

Rawsthorne inevitably became involved in committee work. With Walton, Denis Matthews, and Harry Blech he was one of the founders of the Haydn/Mozart Society, and he served on other committees such as the Composers' Guild. Topsy Levan, the secretary of the guild, wrote to Isabel Rawsthorne after Alan's death: 'I had quite a bit to do with him, and came to realise what a very nice person (not all distinguished composers *are* very nice) he was.'[4] The composer Thomas Pitfield (who also studied at the RMCM in the 1920s) recalled one Composers' Guild meeting

during the anti-Communist period in Britain and the U.S.A. . . . there were some very unpleasant exchanges concerning the BBC, an 'Establishment' conductor and the composer Benjamin Frankel, over a work of the latter, turned down because of his political allegiance. William Alwyn was the chairman and was on the verge of tears as the atmosphere became more clamorous. At the point of near-ignition Alan spoke up, making an oblique aside at the intolerance by saying he had no objection if the Conservative Party were to perform . . . (short pause for thought) Stainer's *Crucifixion*— which immediately released tension and provoked a gust of laughter.[5]

In all this, one is reminded of Sir Thomas Beecham's remark, in his biography of Delius, that in England,

---

[3] Mrs Veronica Leigh Jacobs has kindly allowed me to quote extensively from her diary of these years.
[4] Letter of 26 July 1971.
[5] 'Some Recollections of Alan Rawsthorne', *The Creel*, 1/4 (spring 1991), 127–8.

when a creative artist achieves celebrity, there is immediately set on foot a species of conspiracy to divert him from the work in which he is engaged, and to propel him into some utilitarian duties or function which could be performed with greater efficiency by a thousand other persons of average executive capacity . . . he suffers the infliction of a vast correspondence, the bulk of it utterly inconsequent, and all of it clamouring for instant acknowledgement.[6]

(In fairness, one should add that it might be equally disturbing to receive no correspondence at all.)

Among the tasks which help composers to earn a living are writing essays and giving lectures, and Rawsthorne gave a good many of the latter, including broadcast talks. In a broadcast on the subject 'The Composer' he said:

There seems to be a vague idea that composers are people who sit twiddling their thumbs in some world of their own until they are seized by something called 'inspiration', and that they then scribble something down in a moment of hysterical abandon and resume the thumb-twiddling until it all happens again. It is also considered that the composer ought to live in a draughty attic with no money—this view, by the way, is rarely held by composers themselves.[7]

Plus ça change. He returned to this theme in his interview with Malcolm Rayment:

This country, unfortunately, has very little interest, from an official point of view, in cultural matters altogether. In fact it seems to me a pretty barbarous situation which I don't think would be thinkable in France or Germany or other countries as regards public support and recognition, not only of the art itself but also of artists. Here it seemed to be considered still rather indecorous for the composer to want to eat, let alone drink.[8]

He did little teaching, though a few composers had some lessons from him (Gerard Schurmann became more of a friend and protégé than a pupil). Though he never took up a regular academic appointment, he was an occasional visitor to the summer schools at Bryanston and Dartington, usually discussing the music of Haydn and Chopin as well as giving composition lessons.

Rawsthorne's creative work during the war years had inevitably been limited, but on being demobbed he returned to full-time composition. The most immediate products of this period marked his 'graduation' from documentaries to feature films, including a fictional treatment of the discovery of radar, *School*

---

[6] *Frederick Delius* (London, 1959), 159.
[7] BBC radio talk, 4 March 1949.
[8] BBC radio interview for the series 'The Composer Speaks', recorded 24 May 1962.

for Secrets (1946, originally entitled *Top Secret*), written and directed by Peter Ustinov, whom he had met in the Army Education Corps. Though not entirely successful, the film had a brilliant score, with a particularly effective, very fast overture for the credit titles (not unlike the later Overture to *Practical Cats*). More significant work was done for *The Captive Heart* (1946), directed by Basil Dearden, and *Uncle Silas* (1947), directed by Charles Frank. The former is an articulate, moving story of prisoners of war, relating their lives in a prison camp to those of their loved ones back home. (Rawsthorne also based on the score a concert piece entitled 'Prisoners' March', which was published and recorded.) Though the main theme occurs several times in the course of the film, it is reserved for especially significant usage (in contrast with the tendency in recent years to make an entire score out of a single fragment, a technique which saves the composer from having to invent more than one tune). It is also significant that, although there is quite a lot of music in the film, Rawsthorne is careful (it was presumably his decision) to leave some scenes of great dramatic intensity without the distraction of music. The film is strong enough not to need reinforcement of this kind, and as a result the tension is increased. There is also a remarkable scene in which the assembled company of prisoners sing 'Roll out the Barrel' to drown out the German military music being relayed to them, a powerful moment anticipating similar moments in later films and positively Ivesian in impact. Ernest Irving, Music Director for Ealing Studios, wrote of *The Captive Heart* that Rawsthorne

possesses a keen eye for the dramatic points in a film, and has shown that music which can follow the outlines dictated by the 'visuals' of a film need not be without form or void of content . . . his 'effects' are all simple and direct, relying upon the structure of the music for its appeal both to the intelligence and the sub-consciousness. He has an easy technique in symphonic development with all kinds of contrapuntal devices well under control, used in sympathy with the action and never running away from the job in hand; the weary march of the Dunkirk prisoners is a two-part canon, which matches the dragging broken rhythm of the tired and dispirited prisoners to a nicety.[9]

Even more successful is the score for *Uncle Silas*, a splendidly effective barn-storming melodrama about heiresses and inherited fortunes, with Jean Simmons very much put upon by her wicked uncle Derrick de Marney. The great American film composer Bernard Herrmann used to say that this was one of the finest film scores ever written. From a powerful overture, it proceeds through a wide variety of types of music, some pastiche, some highly dramatic, some (for the young heroine) vivacious and delightful. In the

[9] 'Music for the Films', *Tempo* (June 1946).

ballroom scene, Rawsthorne produces genre music of the highest class, including an orchestral recomposition of part of his earlier violin and piano piece 'Pierette' and dances of different kinds, well worth extracting for concert performance if the opportunity should arise (as with most of his films, the original manuscripts have disappeared); the music for the Christmas mummers is especially impressive. There is in particular a remarkably powerful nightmarish train journey (brilliantly conceived by composer, director, and editor), and vividly baleful music for other scenes of Gothic drama. Significantly, at perhaps the film's most dramatic moment, the opening of a secret entrance into the room where the heroine is held captive, there is no music at all, however; once again, acute sensitivity to the needs of the film (and the audience's intelligence) led Rawsthorne to let the scene speak for itself.

The following year, 1948, Rawsthorne produced the score for Basil Dearden's *Saraband for Dead Lovers*, Ealing Studios' first colour film, a lavish and intelligent period tragedy concerning Sophie Dorothea, the spurned wife of George I. The old dance tune *La folia*, familiar from variation sets from Corelli and Vivaldi to Rachmaninov, forms the main motif of the score, appearing in a grand, full-orchestral dress with a vigorous violin countermelody for the credit titles and in other arrangements aptly conceived for the demands of the drama. In one scene it is sung, and a published version with piano accompaniment from the same year (by Rawsthorne and Ernest Irving) extends and elaborates the arrangement, making it an effective, rather romanticized version of the tune. The most full-blooded music is reserved for the most important romantic moment, and there is once again a powerful, tense scene (a sword fight in a darkened hallway) when Rawsthorne refrains from disrupting the intensity, relying solely on the intermittent natural sounds until the fatal climax of the scene is reached. There is also a brilliantly filmed and edited carnival sequence in which he deploys a wide range of extrovert orchestral virtuosity, bringing out the cruelty and raucousness of the boisterous merrymakers. Above all, he is supremely adept at conveying an atmosphere of doom-laden mystery, as at the beginning (where a mournful birdcall matches the music), and expressing profound compassion for characters whose personal lives are inextricably and tragically bound up with political considerations.

The Dancing Fleece and the Anglo-American production *Pandora and the Flying Dutchman* are also important. The former (1950) was made by the Crown Film Unit and is a twenty-minute ballet film, with a continuous score for small orchestra. The film promoted the British wool industry, and though the manuscript disappeared, a piano short score, entitled *Wool Ballet*, has survived. Rawsthorne's experience in working with dance at Dartington in the

1930s gave him a good background for this first professional ballet score. It is all recognizably Rawsthorne, with numerous characteristics in evidence. The use of nursery song inflections in the melodic line (there is more than a hint of 'Oranges and Lemons', for instance, though it is fair to add that this is potentially quite a Rawsthornian tune anyway) and an occasional polka accompaniment make it a lighter piece than he was usually able to write in films, with a number of phrases that have a clear basis in traditional ballet style. It is a charming score, with much use of piano and celesta, and hardly any note-spinning.

Pandora's music was written in 1950 during the composition of the First Symphony, though it was not shown until the following year. The *Time Out Film Guide* describes the film (a reworking of the Flying Dutchman legend, directed by Albert Lewin) as 'a lushly romantic story [told] so skilfully that it possesses the inevitability of myth . . . Lewin combines a script of exuberant literacy with a visual splendour often bordering on the surreal'.[10] On the face of it, Rawsthorne might seem an odd choice of composer for such a film, but his proven ability to convey an atmosphere of mystery and doom-laden romance was most appropriate. One of his tasks during the composition of the music was, according to Gerard Schurmann (who assisted him on this and a number of other films), 'to teach Ava Gardner, one of the stars, to sing a night-club song, which he accomplished, much to her delight, in the course of several intrepid evenings'.[11] The music matches in the subtlety of its colouring the dark pastels and grey-blue tones of the film, shot through with occasional but significant flashes of red or yellow. Schurmann himself researched a fourteenth century Dutch tune, which formed an important part of the film. There are also strong links with Rawsthorne's First Symphony, notably in the horn chords from the second movement's introduction (see Ex. 5.9(*a*)), which are an integral part of the film score, especially in the sarabande-like music underscoring an inner flashback to the seventeenth century. A particularly subtle cue is for Pandora's swim out to the Dutchman's apparently deserted ship, leading to her first meeting with him: here, an open, diatonic style, scored very simply, is tinged with a delicate sense of foreboding that exactly conveys the ambiguous feeling of the scene.

It was perhaps inevitable that, given the pressures of producing a number of important film scores and incidental music for radio plays, Rawsthorne should in the immediate post-war years have produced relatively little in the way of concert music. There are one or two songs. 'Precursors', for high voice

---

[10] 2nd edn. (London, 1991).
[11] 'Recollections of a Long Friendship', Poulton i, 5.

and piano, is thought to date from the period 1945–7 (Louis MacNeice's poem appeared in 1944). The text praises optimism in the face of hardship, and Rawsthorne echoes the powerful nature imagery of the first verse with vigorous, driving semiquavers in the piano, and the grey flatness of the second with a cool two-part counterpoint. The final verse, with the light 'shining through', reverts to the opening vigour, though not entirely convincingly; there is some impressively powerful writing in the song, but also a degree of uncharacteristically poor balance between voice and piano, the low vocal tessitura being masked by a strong, complex piano part in the same register, and the melodic material is not really memorable enough to carry the listener forward.

Far more successful is the beautiful 'Carol' (1947), a setting of W. R. Rodgers written originally for voice and small orchestra of fifteen players for a radio play, *Circle on Circle*, and arranged, with piano accompaniment, the following year (Compact Disc, track 7). This mood of intimate melancholy was more natural to Rawsthorne (at times it came too easily), but the detail of this apparently simple song is fascinating. The vocal melody of the first of the four verses provides the material for the second and fourth (slightly varied each time), with a looser relationship to the third. The atmosphere of dark winter, the 'flashing mirrors' of the snow, the 'lovely child' in the cradle, the doves forgetting to grieve and 'gravely to his greeting fly'—all these are beautifully etched with little touches of pianistic texture (including hints of chiming bells in the right hand) (Ex. 5.1(*a*)). It is worth looking at the bass line, which has an almost baroque linear importance of its own as well as providing the essential tonal underpinning. The combination of bleakness and warmth is perfectly balanced, coming to rest in a final few bars of consummate subtlety and beauty (Ex. 5.1(*b*)).

Ex. 5.1. 'Carol': (*a*) bars 1–3; (*b*) last two lines

(*a*)

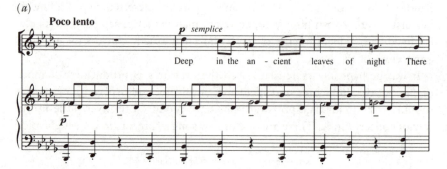

(b)

Rawsthorne's productive relationship with the Cheltenham Festival began in its second year, 1946, when the First String Quartet was performed there. The following year saw the first of his numerous Cheltenham premières, a performance of the Oboe Concerto by Evelyn Rothwell with the composer conducting the Hallé Orchestra. It was repeated at the Proms in the same month, July, this time with the BBC Symphony Orchestra. Rather than being simply a light divertissement, the concerto has its darker side. This might possibly reflect the difficult state of Rawsthorne's life at the time, with a failing marriage, a drink problem, and, to make matters worse, frequent changes of residence (at one time he lived at 106 Baker Street, not far from the home of his beloved Sherlock Holmes). Whatever the reasons, there are some signs of haste: the jig-like finale, though enjoyable and with some intriguing shadows colouring its apparent insouciance, is stretched a little thin, with a not entirely convincing affirmation of a unison C at the close. It also draws a little too closely on the experience of the First Piano Concerto's final Tarantella and the skittering triplets from the First String Quartet and *Cortèges*, in all of which the invention is fresher. The middle movement, marked 'Allegretto con morbidezza', is also somewhat attenuated, but provided it is played at a properly flowing tempo (he unhelpfully did not provide a metronome mark, but 'Allegretto' rather than 'morbidezza' should be the clue), it emerges as a nostalgic waltz, entirely distinctive in character and very touching.

The substantial first movement approximates to a baroque French overture, with a quicker central section flanked by a slower one, though the opening section is quieter and more withdrawn when it reappears at the close. The passionate theme on the strings at the start proves to have considerable importance, for it plays an important linking and unifying part in the main Allegro section. There is no grand build-up to a principal climax; instead, the music thins out to make way for the more reflective return of the introduction. There is a complex interplay of feelings in this beautifully wrought movement, and it is worth noting that the occasional nerviness of the main Allegro theme is echoed in the 'Allegretto con morbidezza' in a most delicate episode of hesitant but affecting music containing almost more rests than notes in the string part. While the work as a whole does not offer a truly virtuosic challenge to the soloist, it provides nevertheless the opportunity for displaying a variety of tonal colourings, as well as command of different types of articulation, and if relatively lightweight it is certainly not as empty-headed or vacuous as some of its successors among oboe concertos.

The year after the Oboe Concerto, Cheltenham had another Rawsthorne première, this time the First Violin Concerto, which had finally reached fruition after so many frustrating years and abortive attempts to complete the sketches. The first performers were the Hallé Orchestra and Sir John Barbirolli, with the fine Dutch violinist Theo Olof, who remained loyal to the work and deeply loved it; he played it in Amsterdam with Eduard van Beinum and the Concertgebouw Orchestra, and in 1972, during the memorial Rawsthorne performances, returned to Cheltenham to play it again, this time with Sir Adrian Boult. This performance, for all its occasional orchestral shortcomings (due, no doubt, to shortage of rehearsal time), has been released on compact disc, and shows Olof (as in his recording of the Britten Violin Concerto) to have been a marvellously full-blooded lyrical player, with a real virtuoso technique when required.[12] He was also deeply committed to the Theme and Variations for two violins, of which he gave numerous performances with Herman Krebbers. Olof's warmth was particularly suited to this concerto, for its most essential quality, especially in the first movement, is passionate lyrical intensity.

---

[12] Theo Olof's recording of Rawsthorne's First Violin Concerto, with Sir Adrian Boult, has been issued on BBC Radio Classics CD 15656 91952, and his recording of the Britten Violin Concerto, with Sir John Barbirolli and the Hallé Orchestra, on an EMI CD, CDM 5 66053 2.

It has such a natural melodic flow that one might be misled into fancying the structure relaxed or even casual; Colin Mason, writing about Rawsthorne in the 1954 edition of *Grove's Dictionary* (edited by Eric Blom), referred to his successes in variation forms 'to which [his] idiom is perhaps more suited than to big symphonic structures . . . there is only one symphony compared with four concertos for soloist and orchestra in which structural demands are always less severe than in a symphony.' Apart from begging several questions, this remark completely misses the point of the concerto's extraordinarily bold and challenging formal approach.

There are two movements, played without a break (making the longest continuous span in Rawsthorne's output until *Madame Chrysanthème* in the mid-1950s), and both of them are built up of contrasting sections. In the first, thematic integrity, with the subjects closely related, and tonal subtlety maintain an effortless flow of music despite the natural ebb and flow of intensity. In the second, the sections are more clearly differentiated by contrasts of texture, tempo, dynamics, and material, though the invention is integrated with that of the first movement. In adopting this sectional approach, Rawsthorne is relying on two things: his ability to unify the material so closely that there are no abrupt jolts other than those with expressive or dramatic effect, and the consequent ability of this formal thinking to replace the traditional symphonic- or sonata-form procedures with a process that acquires equal authority by different means. It brings him close to Chopin's processes, especially those of the ballades and the F minor Fantaisie, on which Rawsthorne wrote a famous article, particularly revealing not only for its intrinsic value as a classic piece of Chopin commentary but also for what it reveals about Alan's own thought processes (far more than he ever revealed in interview). There is something essentially ballade- or narrative-like in much of Rawsthorne's music, and in the article he observes that it

is of the highest importance when writing movements of any degree of organization to compose the form at the same time as the music, and this is what Chopin is doing in these pieces. This creative conception of form is one of the (admittedly many) things which make Haydn, for instance, so great a master. Forms in music differ from those supplied by H.M. Inspector of Taxes; they are not there to be filled in.[13]

Referring specifically to Chopin's ballades, he comments that we 'find in [them] not the invention of a new "form", but patterns of behaviour which are viable for these pieces alone, and where the emergence of "form" is as creative an act as the texture of the music itself. The logic is the same logic as

---

[13] 'Ballades, Fantasy and Scherzos', in A. Walker (ed.), *Frédéric Chopin* (London, 1965), 43–4.

drives forward a sonata movement, though the resultant shape may be different.' Later, he says that Chopin 'recognizes form as sensation, not to be calculated in numbers of bars'. These remarks could be applied to a great many movements by Rawsthorne.

The concerto's first movement in particular is a magnificent achievement. Sebastian Forbes has written a detailed examination of the tonal and thematic schemes underlying the concerto to which I am greatly indebted for an understanding of the complexities hidden beneath the seemingly spontaneous flow of the music, and it is essential reading for anyone who wishes to achieve a thorough technical knowledge.[14] Earlier versions of the first movement exist in manuscript, but these differ considerably from the final version performed in 1948 and subsequently published. It is not surprising that this should be so, since reconstructing a major work must be difficult (doubly so when the effort is also interrupted). It opens with a recitative-like (ballade-like!) passage unfolding on the solo violin, above a held G, the notes G-G♯-B-B♭, which gives us a typical collection of tonal possibilities: G major, G minor, and G sharp minor. The second phrase immediately expands outwards, the bass moving down to F♯ and the violin up to C♯ to give us a momentary F sharp tonality. Already, Rawsthorne is moving harmonically very quickly, with an underpinning of sustained bass notes that enable the listener to follow what is happening; despite the slow tempo (Adagio Espressivo e Rubato), and the feeling that this is merely exploratory groping for some more definite melodic shape, there is also characteristically swift harmonic motion. The first main section is a lilting 9/8 in which the main theme is audibly derived from the opening cell, a cantilena rising and falling in turn; Rawsthorne himself described the process in his programme note thus: 'an introduction . . . consisting of amorphous fragments of the general material out of which the principal melody is eventually constructed. The melody itself is of a gently flowing narrative character.' After an increase in speed and tension, the second main section breaks in with a passionate 3/4 theme starting with the four notes of his musical fingerprint, this time descending (C-B-A-G♯) and then rising (reversing the process of the first theme), and there is a substantial section in which the intensity, maintained for a remarkable length of time, is gradually unwound.

The solo cadenza is placed at almost exactly the half-way point, earlier than in traditional concerto forms—an inspired stroke which fulfils several formal purposes. Despite his reticence, Rawsthorne was not afraid of solo display (most of his concertos are extremely demanding for the soloist and contain

[14] 'Rawsthorne's First Violin Concerto', *The Creel*, 3/1 (spring 1994), 7–28.

numerous passages of technical brilliance), but he seldom wrote a conventional cadenza, preferring to embody this element within the development of the material. This is one reason why he is such a satisfying concerto composer, since he intuitively understood, as Haydn did not, the need for brilliance and virtuosity, and how this could be assimilated into the music's logical progress rather than being reserved, in a kind of musical apartheid, for a long solo passage. Most of his concertos, therefore, simply do not require the large-scale solo cadenza. Here, however, he creates what is surely one of the finest of all concerto cadenzas, unfailingly musical and yet effortlessly incorporating technical challenge. It provides a mini-section of its own in which the material is developed still further, with its own rise and fall of emotion, replacing a recapitulation of the searching introduction with something that serves equally well to lead to a return of the 9/8 section, this time developed further and combining the two main themes to add to the intensity of the whole. After this, it is not necessary to do more than refer briefly to the second (3/4) tune (as usual, he avoids straightforward, complete recapitulation), before leading to a shattering climax on three brass chords, and closing the movement with quiet unison Gs.

The second movement is more overtly contrapuntal. There is an introduction, in which quick, nervous fragments on violin alternate with peremptory brass fanfares, followed by a fugue, whose subject is announced in the bassoons. Hans Keller thought the fugal exposition was 'like [a] none too valid excuse for dead end, or rather dead start',[15] but there is something immensely attractive about the sheer contrast of this complete change of mood, which is nevertheless another variation or development of the main theme. The movement looks like a rondo, with three slower episodes and an intermezzo section in 3/8, but the thematic integration is so complete that it has equally the feeling of a Rawsthornian sonata form in which each theme is developed before the announcement of the next. There is, however, a contrasting melodic idea which, though it turns out once again to be related to the principal material, sounds very much like a second subject group and forms the basis of the lighter 3/8 section (like a 'ghostly waltz', as Rawsthorne put it). In his Chopin article, Rawsthorne suggested that 'it is an important part of the composer's task to devise the various units of his structure in such a way that they sound like what they are. A bridge-passage must sound like a link, and not like important new material.' It is no use listening to this movement as if it were a conventional rondo, or a standard sonata movement, since it sets its own terms of reference.

---

[15] Concert review, *Music Review*, 9/3 (Aug. 1948).

The ending was altered for the final version of the work. Initially, it ended with forceful unison Gs and a final G major chord. Now, there is a quotation from Walton's *Belshazzar's Feast* (the chorus praising the various gods). This was simply a generous and affectionate tribute to the work's dedicatee, Rawsthorne's great fellow Lancastrian and friend. It is, however, not always convincing in performance, partly because he adds to the penultimate note an Ivesian discord before the conclusive major chord; it needs absolute conviction, perhaps even exaggeration, to bring it off successfully. Even admirers of the concerto tend to be uncertain about the aptness of such a closely integrated work finishing with something which is not really part of it. If the finale seems looser, repeated hearing reveals that it is just as tightly organized as the first movement.

The concerto as a whole ultimately leaves an unsatisfying impression, for all its beauty and variety. Perhaps this is due to its episodic nature, though everything flows very naturally; possibly there is one episode too many in the finale. Perhaps it is simply due to the length of time over which the work was sketched, and the number of times it must actually have been begun all over again (the initial poetic impulse behind it might have become vitiated by the passage of time). Perhaps it is due to the pervasive melancholy of the first movement. This is, after all, dominated by themes almost invariably descending at the end of each phrase. Colin Mason referred to the 'monotony' of Rawsthorne's music, and, while he betrays severe critical shortcomings (including constant reference to the Symphonic Studies as 'Symphonic Variations', which hardly gives one confidence), there is a case to answer in respect of some works, this concerto in particular. The monotony of style, he claims, derives from the use of augmented chords, which are devoid of tonal affiliation and therefore in the strictest sense 'atonal' (though Rawsthorne detested being described as an atonalist); thus, the music is essentially a series of melodic and harmonic decorations of chords that tend to sound alike.[16] A number of commentators over the years have regularly used the word 'grey' to describe Rawsthorne's harmonic style, and while there are many works of which that is the least appropriate description, there is indeed a certain sameness of tone about the slower invention throughout the concerto. It is possible, however, that it is the recurrent descending turn at the ends of most of the phrases that leads to this impression. Even in the finale, the fugue subject itself descends at the end of each phrase or sub-phrase, continuing the first movement's tendency while changing to an apparently more ebullient tone of voice.

[16] 'Alan Rawsthorne', *Musical Times*, 91 (Mar. 1950).

This tendency is not countered sufficiently, perhaps, by enough instances of a rising phrase. The fleeting touch of Elgarian 'nobilmente' in the first slow episode in the finale (Ex. 5.2(*a*)) brings expressive warmth, positive rather than melancholy, but is not maintained, the music reverting to the dying fall; a similar procedure occurs in the shorter final slow episode, recalling the same material but surrounding it with more straightforward bitonal chords of silvery beauty while the violin explores a slightly more open diatonic style for a moment (Ex. 5.2(*b*)). Here, however, the openness of the fourths in the violin line does bring a new quality to the music. A good deal of the livelier, rhythmic invention has a Waltonian aura about it, appropriately enough. The final Allegro Risoluto builds up excitement, the occasional hints of Waltonian extroversion enlarging Rawsthorne's horizons in some of the more vigorous passages of the movement (Ex. 5.2(*c*)). Mason praises Rawsthorne in this instance for having thoroughly absorbed this style and its implications, and consequently opening out his own.[17] There are, too, moments where he explores an extrovert manner in a way which owes nothing to Walton and everything to a more tonal, even traditionally violinistic way of looking at his material, often emphasizing the characteristic Neapolitan sixth, E♭. Had he perhaps opened out the melodic intervals a little more, or allowed his melodic lines to flower upwards more frequently, one wonders if the lasting impression would not have been of a fine work flawed by its inward-looking melancholy.

Mason also praised the 'crispness' of some of the chords in the finale of the Cello Sonata (1948) as indicating Rawsthorne's willingness to enlarge his harmonic world, but there are also other new elements in this work. Though Mason says that formal problems 'do not seem to have interested Rawsthorne much', several works (not least the Symphonic Studies and the First Violin Concerto, both of which are structurally adventurous) have indicated exactly the opposite.[18] The Cello Sonata's overall shape is unusual: the device of ending with the sombre, reflective opening section repeated as an epilogue is new, while the slow movement, fully developed though it is, becomes an equivalent to the introduction in its relationship with the finale (it derives from the same opening idea, too, which emphasizes the balance of the work). The coda to the whole work now takes its place as the world from which the sonata arises and into which it returns at the close, rather than being simply a thematic and/or formal device.

---

[17] 'Alan Rawsthorne (continued)', *Musical Times*, 91 (Apr. 1950).
[18] Ibid.

Ex. 5.2. Fist Violin Concerto, second movement: (*a*) from letter C; (*b*) from letter W; (*c*) 9 bars after letter E

(*a*)

(*b*)

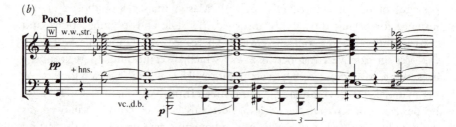

(*c*)

Duration 34"

The material of the opening differs at once from the material of the First Violin Concerto, in that every phrase rises (even the cello's first two-note phrase) (Ex. 5.3(*a*)), and when this material, played much faster, forms the surging first subject of the Allegro appassionato that follows, it retains this upward striving. The difference is marked: whereas the concerto's opening movement is melancholy, reflective, even (at times) almost passive, this is music of forward purpose even when slow. As one might expect from a composer who played both instruments, the writing is unfailingly idiomatic; indeed, much of the material stems from the character of the instruments (the cello's dark C-string sound and its plangent tenor register, for instance, are beautifully exploited). What is new, perhaps, is the directness of both the quick movements. The first, which follows an indecisive, meandering low cello solo at the end of the introduction, plunges straight into the matter at hand with passionate urgency, and explores some biting and ferocious alternating chords on the two instruments as part of the 'second subject', as one can for once legitimately call it (Ex. 5.3(*b*)). This Allegro is unusual in maintaining a high dynamic level for the whole of the exposition, only diminishing for rhapsodical meditation for the development.

The Adagio is prefaced by a piano introduction, recalling the first movement's introduction, and formally resembles a rondo more than anything else, complete with a somewhat more scherzando episode Poco più mosso before the return of the main cello tune. In the finale, the opening tune, bold and declamatory in character, is very decisive, once again plunging the movement straight into its purpose without hesitation—though as in Beethoven's 'Emperor' Concerto, this main theme is anticipated quietly in the piano at the

Ex. 5.3. Cello Sonata: (*a*) first movement, opening; (*b*) first movement, from letter D; (*c*) link from slow movement to finale

(*a*)

Ex. 5.3. *Continued*

(*b*)

(*c*)

close of the Adagio (Ex. 5.3(*c*)). These various links between the themes of
the different movements, sometimes by an extension of variation or meta-
morphosis technique, give the work an exceptional thematic integrity, helping
it to fulfil its passionate and expressive purpose. It is full of rich invention, emi-

nently satisfying to play, and since it is only about fourteen to fifteen minutes long it makes a very useful repertoire piece. In the epilogue, Rawsthorne uses an inverted version of the opening head-motif with exquisite effect, saving this device for just this moment. No audience could listen to the haunting final cadence, approaching a peaceful C major via a Neapolitan D♭ and A♭, without responding sympathetically to a moving conclusion so beautifully rounding off the work. It might almost be called 'Sonata-Ballade', for it satisfyingly fulfils both aspects (formal and narrative) of that title. Paul Hamburger happily commented, 'It is symbolic of the inspired precision of one of our greatest masters of form that this sonata starts with a 6-bar phrase (not even an 8-bar) . . . in which every note of the whole sonata is contained like a chicken in the egg',[19] and the combination of lyrical warmth, rhythmic dynamism, and tight formal control enables Rawsthorne to fulfil his aims completely.

The same year (1948) saw the composition of another outstanding chamber work, the Quartet for clarinet, violin, viola, and cello. Rawsthorne's fine understanding of instruments is again revealed by his instinctive choice of material for the instruments; the suave opening theme of the first movement (Moderato), begun without any preamble, can hardly be imagined on anything other than clarinet (Ex. 5.4(a)). The simple two-part counterpoint for clarinet and viola indicates that this work will give a higher priority to contrapuntal working than the Cello Sonata, but Herbert Howells warned against too much interpretation of the significance of this style ('the wisest and happiest of all listeners would be those accepting the interplay of two diversely-coloured and shaped melodic lines as a quiet concourse of sounds'),[20] and the dramatic contrast provided by the entry of the string chord in bar 8 is a genuine shock. A combination of A and B flat, this provides an essential element to be explored throughout the work, either explicitly as a harmony in the outer movements or split up into its component parts in the central slow movement. A third element, involving a dotted rhythm and a more urgent, impassioned treatment, follows this opening. The material for the whole work is thus presented in what is essentially a single continuous paragraph, containing rhythmic, harmonic, and tonal elements which can be explored and developed throughout—quite a different procedure from that followed in the introduction and Allegro of the Cello Sonata's first movement, or in its gradually evolving material. It should also be noted that the elements which go to make up the main theme are quite

[19] *Music Survey*, new series (winter 1950).
[20] 'A Note on Alan Rawsthorne', *Music and Letters*, 32 (Jan. 1951), 22.

different from those forming the ingredients of the equivalent theme in the First Violin Concerto's first movement: there the driving force was essentially the semitone, whereas here there is a wide range of intervals, including tones, semitones, sixths, fourths, and thirds, as well as a surprising but highly effective drop of two octaves plus a tone in bar 3. This is a very different lyrical style—less easy to sing, perhaps, but insistently memorable once familiar.

The first movement's shape is highly imaginative. It combines sonata form with ternary, in that the second part, a kind of development, is also a varied recapitulation of the exposition section, with the opening material returning to start it and the string chord from bar 8 interrupting at a corresponding point. When the third section, which would normally be the recapitulation, starts, the music stays closer to its original version than it did in the 'development', while being by no means the same, and once again the string chord's interruption is at the equivalent point. It is more a Sibelian rotation than a sonata form as such. Rawsthorne was known not to have been particularly fond

Ex. 5.4. Clarinet Quartet: (*a*) first movement, bars 1–8; (*b*) third movement, bars 1–9; (*c*) third movement, conclusion

(*a*)

(*b*)

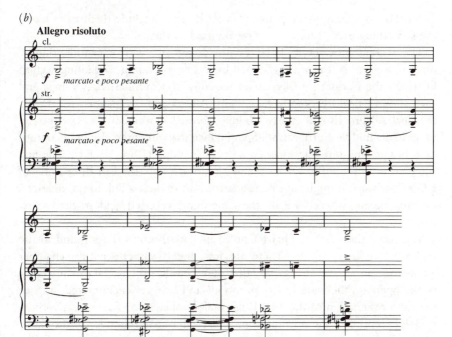

(*c*)

of Sibelius, but composers' personal tastes do not preclude them from learning something even from those most inimical to them.

The second movement, Poco Lento, is ternary, with a central, slightly quicker section for the strings framed by a slow, brooding, lamenting section in which the clarinet initially circles moodily in semitonal relationships and then allows lyrical freedom to take flight. After a pause, but not a real break, the final Allegro risoluto starts a highly unusual movement for Rawsthorne, more like a middle European stamping dance than anything else in his output (and brings him unusually close to Bartók) (Compact Disc, track 6). The first three notes of the finale's main theme (Ex. 5.4(*b*)) are the first three notes of a G minor scale; it might not be too fanciful to suggest a link to the quartet's opening theme, where G♭-F-E♭, the same figure reversed, appears in the first bar.

The place the Clarinet Quartet holds in Rawsthorne's output, and in the repertoire itself, is secure. There are few finer twentieth-century chamber works for clarinet and strings, whether one considers the lyrical expansiveness of the opening, the wide variety of moods and textures encountered in it, or the calm resignation of the final E flat major conclusion (Ex. 5.4(*c*)) with its nostalgic reprise of the opening tune and even a forte reminder of the skeleton of the important string chord. In every detail, it is deeply considered. The 'orchestration' is subtle and sensitive, witness the careful withholding of the clarinet's highest register until it is most needed, in the forceful, even barbaric dance rhythms of the finale. The same romantic fervour and rhythmic dynamism are present in the Piano Sonatina (1949), which combines great virtuosity with considerable intimacy of tone. William Mann commented, 'It is testimony to the power and integrity of Rawsthorne's mind that the consistent and continuous keyboard figuration hardly ever ceases to fulfil a musical purpose',[21] whereas Colin Mason found that 'the agreeable finger music . . . is really little more than the feverishly agitated and not at all melodic figuration of a few unrelated harmonies, essentially so static that no amount of figuration could ever give them more than a semblance of real movement'.[22]

The third movement, a kind of intermezzo marked 'Allegretto con malinconia', is marked 'attacca' to the finale, and at the first performance James Gibb performed the whole work without breaks, which gave A. E. F. Dickinson some problems: 'it was difficult to follow the movements because they came without any break: the second appeared to belong to the first, and after that anything might be anything. Performers are asked to give the lis-

---

[21] Mann, W., *Music Survey*, new series (autumn 1949).
[22] 'Alan Rawsthorne (continued)'.

tener a chance in future.'[23] This comment is breathtaking in its naïvety as well as its presumption, showing a complete lack of understanding of the tonal scheme as well as a failure to appreciate the clearly differentiated character of each movement. The link between third and fourth movements is effective because the third concludes with a fierce cadence in D minor followed immediately by a decisive move to C, the finale then commencing in B flat, a step-wise move in whole tones (the main theme of the finale explores a whole-tone scale, zigzagging in thirds). The work starts on B and hovers between B minor/major and C minor (see Ex. 5.5(*a*)), and the opening Allegro sostenuto e misterioso concludes with an apparent cadence using the opening four notes again and then shifting sideways to end on a D♭. The second movement ends equally ambiguously on an augmented triad (B♭–D–G♭). So the endings of first and second movements are as indeterminate or inconclusive as that of the third, and the case for playing the work without any conventional movement breaks is surely overwhelming. The sonatina ends decisively in B, though with typical humour (and reticence) Rawsthorne leaves it open as to whether minor or major.

In Dickinson's defence, it must be said that the harmonic movement is so fast and so ambiguous in all four movements that it is more difficult than usual to sense the tonal centre or easily to follow the argument. The slow movement is perhaps easiest because of its slow tempo and the reflective melancholy, which rises to intense passion in the central section; the feeling of the music is clearer and more direct, the customary false relations adding to what Wilfrid Mellers aptly describes as the 'elusive poignancy' of the music.[24] James Gibb suggests that the character of the opening Allegro sostenuto might have been inspired by Rawsthorne's fascination with the finale of Chopin's 'Funeral March' Sonata.[25] In the third movement, the elusive, even wayward character of the first movement is resumed, and only in the central section, with its almost Debussyan use of piano colouring and contrast between extreme registers, is there a more direct appeal to the senses (Ex. 5.5(*b*)). The brilliant finale is more like a modified sonata form with elements of the rondo, where not only is the main tune immediately accessible but the other ideas are also sharply differentiated. It is clearly inspired by the joy of writing supremely well for the instrument and exploiting its technical characteristics with a performer's understanding (Ex. 5.5(*c*)). It is perhaps significant that, in order to help interpreters understand better how to approach it, Rawsthorne peppers the score

[23] 'The Progress of Alan Rawsthorne', *Music Review*, 12 (1951), 87–104.
[24] 'Rawsthorne's Recent Developments', *Listener* (Nov. 1950).
[25] 'The Piano Music', Poulton iii. 60.

Ex. 5.5. Piano Sonatina: (*a*) opening; (*b*) third movement, central episode; (*c*) fourth movement, from p. 18, bar 16

(*a*)

Allegro sostenuto e misterioso

(*b*)

(c)

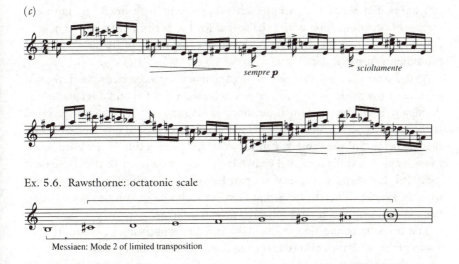

Ex. 5.6. Rawsthorne: octatonic scale

Messiaen: Mode 2 of limited transposition

with more interpretative instructions than usual. The score contains much use of words like 'agitato', 'lusingando', 'solenne e misterioso', 'espress. e molto cantabile', 'lontano', 'brusco', 'strepitoso', 'scioltamente', 'delicato', 'vigoroso', 'con bravura', and 'pomposo'.

Ex. 5.5(*a*) shows the first page of the sonatina, and Ex. 5.6 the octatonic scale which is clearly at the root of Rawsthorne's music. This scale is the same as Messiaen's second 'mode of limited transposition', and therefore can only be transposed three times: going up by semitones, one finds that starting on C or C♯ provides the notes missing from the one starting on B, but transposition to D simply repeats the notes of the scale, a minor third higher. It is, of course, a mode that automatically provides Rawsthorne with the minor and major thirds forming such an important part of his harmonic and tonal vocabulary. One might also mention the influence of Liszt and his division of the octave into two equal halves by the use of the tritone. Gibb points out that not only is the first movement monothematic, all material being derived from the opening theme, but also each movement has close links, either in the themes or in accompanying figures, with this tune. It is equally true, however, to say that this is partly a consequence of the use of this mode. It is not until bar 16 that it moves away from its first transposition, a change that is disguised by being enclosed within the continual flow of notes and is at the same time refreshing because it subtly enlarges the music's horizons. A similar effect is achieved in the recapitulation, where for the first time the music suddenly and dramatically resumes the opening material fortissimo; hitherto, it has been all half-lights and shadows chasing each other, rising only briefly to *mp* on a couple of occasions (one of the challenges for the performer in this work is to convey and sustain the mysterious character of so much of the first and third movements in particular).

At the same time as using this mode, the finale has a distinctly classical tonal scheme in the finale, with a first subject centred on B flat and a second on its dominant F. In the recapitulation, both are centred on B♮, which is revealed at the close to be the tonic of the whole work. The classical procedure of both themes being 'in' the same key in the recapitulation is thus maintained, even though this is a different tonal centre from that at the start of the movement itself. It is less surprising, therefore, that Rawsthorne's other outstanding work from 1949, the Concerto for String Orchestra, should be coloured by a strong neo-classical impulse, a true concerto grosso influence.

The baroque connection in this work is made explicit by the contrasting of a solo group with the main tutti only in the finale; elsewhere, with a few exceptions, the orchestra is used as a single unit. The scoring is largely functional, and highly effective as such, though there are two moments of sheer magic involving colouristic effects achieved simply from the sound of a string orchestra: in the first movement's Andante espressivo interlude before the recapitulation, where a violin solo revives the work's main theme from the slow introduction over a tremolando chord, and in the finale (Ex. 5.7(*d*)), where wide-spread sustained chords suspend activity for a brief moment so that the main rondo tune can creep back in two-part counterpoint and ease back into the dynamism that is its chief hallmark. Thematically the work is dominated by the theme of the first movement's two-bar introduction, Largo maestoso, which is marked to an unusual degree by fourths (Ex. 5.7(*a*)); the Molto allegro material which follows is wide-ranging and impassioned but essentially freer, almost rhapsodic in content. As the movement progresses it becomes clear that it is really the opening call-to-attention that is all-important, achieving through the work almost the status of a ritornello theme and appearing here before long in the bass (as it does several times during the concerto). A contrasting second subject (Ex. 5.7(*b*)) turns out to have a close relationship through its stepwise motion with the lugubrious first theme of the slow movement (Ex. 5.7(*c*)) and with elements also in the last movement. Equally strong melodic ties exist between the head-motif of the introduction and the main theme of the finale, through the extensive use of fourths, and there are other examples of thematic interrelationship (the way Rawsthorne derives extensive developmental passages from a dotted rhythm in the first quick section, for instance). What is most arresting about the concerto, though, is its emotional directness. Rawsthorne is anxious to define tonal centres clearly, so although augmented chords are still an integral part of the harmony there is more use of minor or major triads (often in first or second inversion) than usual. The glowing D major of the finale's Allegro piacevole theme, with its fourths and use of wider-ranging intervals, brings a sense of sunny freedom to a work which has been marked by passion and even tragedy. Its broad phrasing, too, adds to the feeling of resolution, contrasting with the turbulence and hesitation of many of the earlier ideas. The Lento is music not of melancholy but of deeper, more fundamental feeling, full of compassion and imbued with a sense of sorrow that is both personal and universal. Its main theme has the air of a funeral procession, with heavy tread, and though there are two episodes of

Ex. 5.7. Concerto for String Orchestra: (*a*) first 2 bars; (*b*) first movement, from letter B; (*c*) second movement, opening; (*d*) third movement, from 2nd bar of letter F

Ex. 5.7. *Continued*

(*d*)

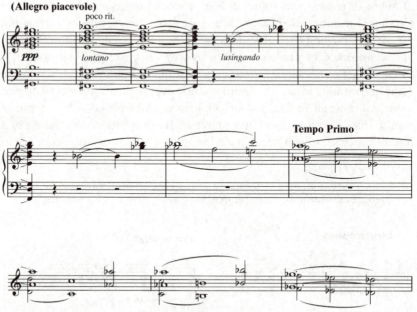

increasing emotional force, it is meditative lamenting that is the movement's principal mood.

In the finale, where the rondo form is exceptionally clear-cut, the appearance of a fugato adds to the contrapuntal vigour of the music's progress, but Rawsthorne also employs block chords and, in quieter sections, unusually long-breathed melodic lines to enrich the music's variety. It builds inexorably to the triumphant D major of the finish, a vital and positive conclusion attained through a good deal of orchestral virtuosity sometimes recalling the vigour of Vivaldi in particular. Howells referred to the 'straight-driving "Roman Road" progress of the last section' as an example of 'unfailing rhythmic continuity . . . the work of a man of decisive purpose who, within the larger continuity, can deploy fugatos, canonic elements, and even stretti by inversion, without obstructing progress',[26] and indeed Rawsthorne seems to delight in such contrapuntal sleight of hand as combining the fugato with a minor-key statement of the main theme in the bass. Donald Mitchell described the concerto as 'one of our civilisation's few civilised pieces',[27] and it is certainly an outstanding

---

[26] 'A Note on Alan Rawsthorne', 25.
[27] First performance review, *Music Review*, 10 (autumn 1949).

contribution to that extraordinarily rich repertoire of string orchestra music by British composers, who seem to have excelled in this particular medium. It is not surprising that, following its première and the first British performance (by Basil Cameron and the London Symphony Orchestra at the 1949 Proms), it was taken up elsewhere: Georges Tzipine was quick to programme it in Paris the following year, and it was one of the works Rawsthorne himself conducted in his Soviet trip in 1963. Its success depends, as so often with Rawsthorne, on sympathetic performance—above everything, it must not be too slow or ponderous.

The concerto was first performed by Gerard Schurmann (to whom it is dedicated) with the virtuoso Dutch String Orchestra on Radio Hilversum in June 1949, and later taken up by Sir Adrian Boult. The following year Boult gave the first performance of the First Symphony; Rawsthorne particularly liked Boult's performance of the symphony because, as he said, he treated it as if it were by Beethoven. The work, which was commissioned by the Royal Phil-harmonic Society, was eagerly anticipated; Rawsthorne, after all, was now a major established figure in Britain and, to some extent, abroad, and here was his first essay in one of the most important musical mediums, which he (like Brahms) had waited until his mid-forties before tackling. It was greeted with enthusiasm in most quarters. Hans Keller stated that it 'is the first symphony since Britten's 2nd String Quartet which at once faces and solves the modern sonata problem'.[28] He described it as 'a landmark in the development of our age's symphonic thought and shows a new stage in [Rawsthorne's] own devel-opment', and complained about the 'half-hearted response in those who like what they know: the new Rawsthorne perturbed, maybe even offended them'. Despite Colin Mason's strictures that Rawsthorne's almost obsessive use of augmented harmonies made sonata form impossible for him, it magnificently resolves this challenge. The quality of the work was immediately recognized, and performances followed quickly in both Britain and countries abroad, including Belgium and South Africa.

It is interesting to compare the ways in which Rawsthorne's works of this period begin. The Cello Sonata and Concerto for String Orchestra have slow introductions, quiet and substantial in the former, intense and very short in the latter. The Clarinet Quartet and Piano Sonatina both begin without pre-amble, gently and flowingly. The Allegro tempestuoso of the First Symphony, however, plunges straight into a world of darkness, violence, and turbulence, a dramatic opening which contains the germ of most of the symphony's themes

---

[28] First performance review, *Music Survey*, new series (Mar. 1951).

as well as immediately declaring its seriousness and vigour of purpose (Compact Disc, track 8). Though the four movements are, for once, separate, there are innumerable close thematic links between them. A quiet chordal build-up on the brass in the slow movement anticipates the opening of the finale, where a similar device is used to pile up loudly the notes that are then used melodically as the start of the Allegro tune (Ex. 5.9(*c*) below), and many of the secondary themes are dovetailed by anticipation in inner parts before their 'official' appearance. Rawsthorne gives the work a sense of continuity by, for example, closing the first movement on a quiet low G (the symphony's main tonal centre) so that the slow movement's powerful beginning on A♭-G is almost a melodic continuation as well as being a dramatic interruption, and the timpani's repeated Ds at the end of the scherzo form a dominant to the G at the start of the finale. There is both thematic and psychological integration at work throughout the symphony.

The powerful opening phrase itself (Ex. 5.8(*a*)) contains a number of crucial elements. The first chord is clearly G minor, but with its major seventh (F♯) added in the bass; this could be viewed as an augmented chord to which the G is added, but by this time Rawsthorne's strong use of a clear central tonality leads one to regard it as the minor triad with added seventh, and in any case that is what it *sounds* like. The top line is also important: the intervals of a third and a sixth link it with the openings of Brahms's Third Symphony and Stravinsky's Symphony in Three Movements, where these intervals are of vital importance throughout. The fourths which then take over the theme, and the downward and then upward sweep of the tune, are all important characteristics of his vocabulary.

The thematic integrity of the symphony is astonishing. The opening theme contains so many important elements (thirds, fourths, dotted rhythms, the first

Ex. 5.8. First Symphony, first movement: (*a*) opening; (*b*) from letter J; (*c*) from letter C

(*a*)

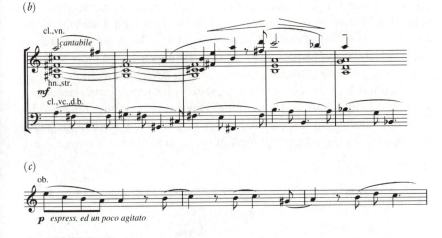

harmony with its semitonal relationship implied by the bass's F♯ against G minor) that it is hardly surprising that Rawsthorne can derive so much fresh inspiration from it as the symphony progresses. A woodwind tag punctuating the opening material assumes considerable importance during the development, clearly leading to the second subject on oboe (Ex. 5.8(c)) through its stepwise motion. At the opening of the slow movement (Ex. 5.9(a)), the rather Beethovenian recitative in the bass at the start, alternating with sombre horn chords, is marked by the use of fourths, which are strongly established in the symphony's second bar, while the chords themselves start with an F minor triad above E, the same semitonal clash with which the work opened (as did Vaughan Williams's Fourth Symphony). The second movement's main theme, on flute (Ex. 5.9(b)), is clearly a relative of the first movement's second subject, sharing with it a lonely, meandering air, though that is darkened in this Lento, which concerns itself with exploration of more sombre, even tragic, feelings. In the Allegro non troppo scherzo, in which Dyneley Hussey in *The Times* discerned a Beethovenian quality, the main section is marked by changing metres (5/8, 3/8, 2/8, and so on), but the main theme is a variation of the Lento's principal subject, and the contrasting 2/4 trio section is a variation of the woodwind tag from the first movement.

Rawsthorne in his own programme note describes the finale as 'more discursive than the rest of the Symphony'. It attempts to resolve the tensions expressed earlier with a more extrovert, even flamboyant, piece, and it is here, as in the finales of other works by Rawsthorne, that the problems occur (he used to say that Haydn was the only composer who invariably got his last movements exactly right). The material has links with earlier movements. The main Allegro risoluto theme itself (Ex. 5.9(*c*)) starts with a variant of the second and third bars of the work's beginning, but it opens out more diatonically, with the use of sequences to increase the impression of more straightforwardly tonal music. This is a movement full of attractive invention, with an occasional touch of Waltonian gusto, expressed with Rawsthorne's customary economy. Nothing goes on for too long. However, the relationship with the symphony's opening is not explored in depth, so that any sense of grappling once again (after the relative lightness of the scherzo) with the serious issues

Ex. 5.9. First Symphony: (*a*) second movement, opening; (*b*) second movement, from letter B; (*c*) finale, opening

(*a*)

(*b*)

(*c*)

raised in the first two movements is lacking. Furthermore, the agitation which so often bubbles beneath the surface in the opening movement is replaced by contrapuntal busy-ness rather than a resumption of the psychological complexity of the earlier music. Nor is there so much use of the march characteristics as in the earlier movements; march rhythms are almost as important to Rawsthorne as to Mahler, and often imbue his music with a heavy tread. In this work they are either prominent or at least a shadowy presence in the first three movements, including a doom-laden wind processional early in the Lento and an ambiguously cheerful trio tune in the scherzo. Their virtual disappearance in the finale separates it sharply from the rest of the work. The finale's introduction, almost minatory in its piling-up of the brass chord, seems in retrospect too heavy in view of the predominantly relaxed air of what follows, while the final G major cadence, because the argument of the symphony as a whole has not been fully re-engaged, seems somehow to be tacked on at the end. It was not until the Third Symphony that Rawsthorne was able to tackle the problem of the finale successfully in a major orchestral work (the Second Symphony, while both beautiful and masterly, stands apart from the others). This reservation about the First Symphony was shared by Hans Keller: 'the work offers masterly solutions of two of the three great symphonic problems, *i.e.* the sonata problem and the high task and test of the slow movement; whereas it does not seem to have overcome the third, *i.e.* the—ever since the Romantic age—painfully noticeable finale problem.'[29]

[29] First performance review, *Music Review*, 12 (May 1951).

This is the more disappointing as the overall tonal scheme is so beautifully worked out. The Allegro tempestuoso's G minor is firmly established several times, both with restatements of the opening theme and at other crucial moments, with a second subject in A minor (rather than the conventional dominant, D, which is reserved for much of the development). The slow movement is centred upon E minor, the dominant of A, but the F minor chord above a bass E in Ex. 5.9(a) gives a clue to the general direction since A♭, the third of F minor, becomes enharmonically G♯ to move the final chord to E major. This in turn becomes the dominant of the scherzo's A minor, with the march-like trio beginning in E minor; the first section is recapitulated (and inverted) in A minor once again, but the movement ends indeterminately, the timpani's repeated Ds sounding beneath an E flat minor chord on horns. The unequivocal G major of the finale is encountered throughout, though F sharp forms an important subsidiary tonality, while Rawsthorne's handling of shifting tonalities is carefully incorporated within the tonal structure. Other important subsidiary keys, both standing in a Neapolitan relationship to G, are A flat and E flat. It is a tonal scheme of great subtlety which not only works on its own terms but also expands linkage with the harmonic implications of the very first chord, an example of the skill with which Rawsthorne proves himself to be a real symphonist, able to put at the service of this demanding form all the experience he had gained in the handling of thematic material, harmonic pacing, and tonal shaping.

His orchestral style is both powerful and clear. It has genuine symphonic weight when needed, especially through the use of bass drum, tuba, and bassoons, along with cellos and double basses in octaves, but the texture, even when there is great activity, never becomes cluttered, and he avoids the besetting sin of some other British symphonists of the period of relying too much on a strong bass-line to carry the sound. On the other hand, as he has already shown in other works (notably the Symphonic Studies and Concerto for String Orchestra), he uses the bass instruments either to carry forward the development or to reintroduce main themes at important junctures in a way that demands the listener's full attention; it is no good listening to this in the conventional manner and expecting the top line to carry most of the main melodic interest. By contrast, the higher registers are used with immense skill, important expressive sections being solely in, say, upper strings, perhaps with a silvery sheen from added flutes, so that the texture never becomes over-reliant on middle or bass sounds. The slow movement in particular has some lovely, sweetly nostalgic high string writing, and block woodwinds are used effectively to lighten the texture in all three quicker movements. The lyrical restatement of the opening theme during the first movement's development, in violins and clarinets at half-speed, is extraordinarily spacious, with the cellos and basses initiating an accompanying ostinato with the first three notes of the theme. It is the spacing, leaving air between the bass, the middle harmony, and the top line, that creates the feeling of grandeur, of strength held momentarily in repose (Ex. 5.8(*b*)).

6

THE 1950s (1951–8)

IF the First Piano Concerto was Rawsthorne's definitive homage to the Baroque, with its toccata (the Capriccio), chaconne, and gigue (the Tarantella), the Second might be regarded as his tribute to Brahms, especially since it comes as perhaps the culminating point of his post-war romanticism. His relationship with Brahms is difficult to fathom. Some friends, such as Denis Matthews, thought he detested the music of Brahms, while others found his views varying from youthful enthusiasm to at least some degree of disregard. In the case of his Second Piano Concerto there are good grounds for thinking that, whether he liked Brahms's music or not, he had sufficient respect or even admiration to find his own source of inspiration in it.

The four-movement scheme, with the scherzo placed second, contrasts with the classical three-movement plan adopted in the First Concerto and immediately reminds one of the Brahms B flat Concerto (also his second). Rawsthorne's rationale for adopting this format was that it is 'difficult to pass immediately from a rather amiable first movement to a lyrical slow one . . . So, in this Concerto, a rather violent Scherzo is interpolated'[1]—much as, in the Brahms B flat Concerto, the demonic second movement is interposed between the epic/lyrical opening Allegro non troppo and the song-like third movement (Andante). The piano part contains far more Brahmsian bravura writing than any other of Rawsthorne's piano music, whether solo or chamber, with much use of octaves, sometimes filled in with the third or sixth, and there are a number of correlations between both the lyrical/decorative writing and the more virtuosic type of keyboard layout. The first movement has much of the airy lightness and grace that marks the joyous finale of the Brahms. Even more significant are the direct thematic relationships: there is a clear similarity between the scherzo movements of each work (see Ex. 6.1(*a*) and (*b*)), while both finales increase the tempo for the coda. A further kinship exists in the wide intervals which pervade the solo entries in the respective slow movements, even to the cadential turn of phrase at the top (Ex. 6.1(*c*));

---

[1] Composer's programme note.

Ex. 6.1. Brahms, Second Piano Concerto, and Rawsthorne, Second Piano Concerto:
(*a*) (*i*) Brahms, Scherzo, (*ii*) Rawsthorne, scherzo; (*b*) (*i*) Brahms, Scherzo, (*ii*)
Rawsthorne, scherzo; (*c*) (*i*) Brahms, Andante, (*ii*) Rawsthorne, Adagio semplice, from
letter C

(*a*) (*i*)   (*ii*)

(*b*) (*i*)

(*ii*)

(*c*) (*i*)   (*ii*)

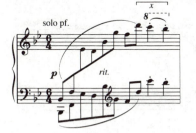

it is interesting that Rawsthorne gave this movement the Brahmsian title 'Intermezzo'.

This is not to accuse Rawsthorne of plagiarism but merely to point out what is simply a source of inspiration, whether subconscious or not. In any case, the concerto is unmistakably distinctive. The subtle incorporation of chamber textures into the fabric of what is ultimately a major virtuoso showpiece is beautifully accomplished within the overall balance of sound. Rawsthorne's skill as a composer of chamber music surely lies behind the lovely opening flute and piano duet (Ex. 6.2(*a*)), the flute stating the first part of a wonderfully con-

Ex. 6.2. Second Piano Concerto: (*a*) opening; (*b*) second movement, from 2 before D

(*a*)

(*b*)

structed, elaborately curling but still essentially simple melody, with the piano's flowing accompaniment providing a typically ambiguous harmonic colouring. The irregular phrase-lengths are beautifully judged, never predictable but always moving forward. Though there are important tutti passages, we are brought back to the world of chamber music, the wind ensemble this time, with the jaunty second subject initiated by a small group of wind instruments. There are many other chamber-like textures during the course of the work, such as little interjections from a group of wind or strings, as well as more clearly delineated moments of chamber writing (the slow movement's opening for wind instruments, for example, to which Walton paid tribute at the start of his Second Symphony's slow movement, or the delightful duet for clarinet and piano in the finale when the cheeky main theme returns almost shame-facedly). The piano writing is among the most supremely pianistic of the century—not surprising for an ex-pupil of Petri (whose remarkable command of tonal colouring must itself have influenced Rawsthorne's creative subconscious), but significant in that it was his habit to compose away from the keyboard, at a desk, using the piano only to check chords and other details. Yet even the accompanying figures at the start are most beautifully laid out for the instrument, both colouristically and technically.

The concerto was commissioned by the Arts Council for the 1951 Festival of Britain, at which it was premièred by Clifford Curzon and the London Symphony Orchestra, conducted by Sir Malcolm Sargent. It was an instant success, and the reason is not hard to find. It is rich in both virtuosity and poetry, which are perfectly balanced, and culminates in a riotously entertaining finale.

The flute tune provides useful cells for further development, being varied to provide apparently new material on occasion and discreetly referred to in other movements, and the overall tonal scheme, though seemingly traditional (F sharp is clearly the tonic, with a scherzo in B minor ending on F sharp, a slow movement starting on F sharp and ending in B major, and a finale most emphatically in F sharp), is full of Rawsthornian excursions from the main key, whose function of holding the tonality together is perceptible throughout. Even when a chord is ambiguous, as at the end of the scherzo, bass pizzicati reveal it to be F sharp major in essence. This makes it easier to follow than some of the earlier works at first hearing, and the use of pedal notes (or even what one might term pedal tonalities) similarly aids the listener. One should note the importance of the Neapolitan second (G), appearing almost nonchalantly at times (as towards the close of the first movement) and more overtly at others (as in the finale).

Formally, too, the concerto is apparently fairly conventional, though Rawsthorne's extraordinarily close handling of thematic relationships means that the usual structural terms are merely generalizations. The first movement, Allegro piacevole, is in a typically modified sonata form, with a greatly abbreviated recapitulation in which the second subject is omitted; the development of each of the main subjects occurs immediately after its statement, being incorporated thereby into the music's seemingly spontaneous flow of inspiration. The scherzo, avowedly a 'Rondo-like structure' (Rawsthorne's term), uses the main theme (cf. Ex. 6.1(a)) in augmentation and canon to provide an episode, which is resumed by the piano after a lighter treatment of the principal subject in perhaps the sunniest, most openly diatonic music to have occurred so far in his output (Ex. 6.2(b)). The slow movement is ternary, the central section being an E minor scherzando of airy charm, with outer sections possessed of exceptional meditative beauty, rising to an impassioned climax before the peaceful, bitter-sweet close. Rawsthorne's sleeve-note for the first recording (Decca, London 1956) states that this Adagio semplice 'has about it that nostalgic character so much disliked by the immobile intelligentsia of today, who confuse this quality with the emotional mess of the last century'. In the finale, after a brief brassy fanfare, the piano embarks on one of the cheekiest tunes in Rawsthorne's entire œuvre (Ex. 6.3(a)). During the progress of the rondo, it becomes apparent that virtually everything derives from this tune, which, suitably varied, provides the material for the episodes. The one new element is a majestic orchestral section in which a broadly sweeping melody combines with a vigorous, thoroughly characteristic countermelody to bring an epic element to the music (Ex. 6.3(b)). Some critics have objected that this grandeur is out of place, but it is undeniably both effective and exuberant, as if the composer is thoroughly enjoying his craft, and it communicates this enjoyment. Moreover, some of the finale is genuinely funny, though always to a musical purpose; one episode plays with slightly pompous dominant–tonic ostinatos in the cellos to profoundly humorous effect. Seldom was Rawsthorne in such an unbuttoned mood as in this finale. Its main tune is something of a stumbling-block for some commentators: its 'very simple, almost music-hall nature' (Rawsthorne's sleeve-note) is not to their taste, though the use of a popular source for concerto material should be regarded as acceptable here just as it is in Poulenc, Shostakovitch, or Arnold (not to mention Dufay and Palestrina in their masses!). However, it was definitely to the taste of audiences and performers alike. Clifford Curzon played the concerto in many countries, with numerous conductors, and other pianists took it up (not surprisingly, since the piano writing is masterly). It was performed in New York and at the Amsterdam Concertgebouw with Josef Krips, in Berlin by the Philharmonic with

Ex. 6.3. Second Piano Concerto, finale: (*a*) from bar 11; (*b*) tutti, from letter E

(*a*)

Ex. 6.3. *Continued*

(*b*)

Celibidache, with Beecham and Colin Horsley in London, and in Belgium and Australia, as well as being a repertoire work for many years in Britain. It retains a foothold on the repertoire, and one feels that, given the chance, it could well resume the place in public affection it once held; the music has lasted well. Several recordings contributed to its success, the first being by Curzon with the LSO and Sargent soon after the first performance, a recording of the utmost artistry demonstrating all Curzon's finest qualities of poetry and beautiful tonal colouring as well as conveying all the appropriate grandeur.

Alun Hoddinott summed it up well: 'this ebullient, extroverted work successfully and authoritatively coalesces a powerful and large-scale symphonic structure with direct tunefulness and thematic simplicity, a mixture that exerts the strongest appeal on differing levels.'[2] Though one might demur at the word 'simplicity' (the themes are deceptive), the indication of the work's richness of thought is well taken. It was generally greeted with enthusiasm. Paul Hamburger referred to the finale's main theme as having 'Self-confessed vulgarity . . . a bread-and-butter basis for the most complicated harmonic experiments, brilliantly solved, especially the horse play between F sharp and G tonalities of this movement'.[3] The following month, he eloquently summed up the work's quality: 'In sum, a great master has here brought about that perfect fusion of what Einstein calls the *galant* and the learned element which is the indispensable basis of good *concertante* music, in our day as much as in Mozart's.'[4]

Rawsthorne's reputation, after the *succès d'estime* of the First Symphony and the greater popular success of the Second Piano Concerto, stood high, and it is a great pity that Eric Blom, the editor of the 1954 edition of *Grove's Dictionary*, chose to ask Colin Mason to write the article about Rawsthorne. Mason, whose lack of understanding of Rawsthorne's music or antipathy towards it has already been demonstrated, wrote about this task to Alan Frank (12 January 1952):

As you may know, I am not completely sympathetic to Rawsthorne's music, but naturally I shall contrive to avoid suggesting this in my piece, which Blom wants to be factual, not critical, describing the style without attempting to judge it . . . You have probably heard that I'm now condemned to a fate worse than death, i.e. life in Manchester, if life it can be called.

An article presenting a more balanced view of Rawsthorne's music would more accurately have reflected his true stature, but Blom himself must be presumed, by his choice of writer, to have been out of sympathy. As a result, one important potential avenue of persuasive advocacy was closed off at a time when it would have greatly strengthened Rawsthorne's position.

Veronica Leigh's diary refers to the première of the Second Piano Concerto (17 June 1951): 'Lunch at [Great Pulteney Street, her home] with Alan till 4.0 p.m.—Excellent seats—Great success—Jessie's party after.' A visit to Battersea Pleasure Gardens with Jessie, Barbara, Alan, Edward Williams, and Marion Leigh followed the next day ('Fireworks & Big Dipper'). The diary reflects the changes that were being wrought in Alan's life, and his illnesses—

[2] 'Rawsthorne's Concertos', in 'BBC Music Review', *Listener* (31 Mar. 1966).
[3] Concert review, *Music Survey*, new series, 4 (Oct. 1951), 370.
[4] Concert review, *Music Review*, 12/4 (Nov. 1951).

'everyone seemed so different and changed' (18 June 1952), but Christmas was obviously fun: on Christmas Eve 'Dinner at Prada's with Alan. It was wonderful—he told stories.' In November 1955 he was 'thinking of letting his Baker St. flat', which a procession of friends and acquaintances used over a period of many years; he was still using it as a London base himself occasionally up to about 1961, though later he and Edward Williams took half-shares in a small apartment in Brewer Street. Veronica played to him Rawsthorne's Romantic Pieces for piano and the first movement of Beethoven's Op. 110 Sonata (15 November 1955), and he 'proceeded to teach me till 1 a.m.'. In March 1956, 'On the train (to Cambridge) I looked up . . . and saw Alan & his [second] wife, Isabel, progressing down the corridor so I dashed after them & we had a merry drink. Hated Isabel. She shrieked with laughter all the time and imitates Alan's mannerisms.' In May 1958, she revised her opinion of Isabel after making her first visit to their Essex home:

Alan's cottage is on a side road opposite a bright pink barn—actually 2 cottages knocked into one. You have to go out and in again from the sitting-room to dining room, taking care not to bump your head, especially after 3 glasses of sherry and ani-mated conversation. Isabel wanders in occasionally, waving paper & pencil, wearing black slacks & shrieking with laughter. I went for a walk up the road . . . then came back to play my viola to them, in their newly-built studio . . . [Alan] was emphatic that I *must* learn to present the piece & perform it, not just stand still & play so detachedly. He told the story of Leonard Hirsch playing [the] Bach Chaconne with his eyes shut & turning round gradually so that he ended up bowing to the wall . . . Next day, Isabel & I took the private (Jennings') bus to London. She was v. nice & I'm glad to find I like her.

One incident from Veronica's diary is characteristic of the bohemian world centred on Olwen Vaughan's French Club, where Veronica was working (13 February 1957):

French Club. To my joy, Alan came after hearing Walton 'cello concerto—with Edward Williams & Judy Swingler. I sat & drank with them & soon Olwen Vaughan called "Lodger" [Alan, who had a room there][5] from her table & the fun began. She became quite drunk & hung all over Alan & soon we discovered she had to catch a train to Nottingham for her father's funeral . . . When Olwen had to change into black, Alan & I helped her struggle into a tight skirt. Taxi to King's Cross . . . with Olwen alter-nately weeping & singing the Marseillaise. When we arrived Connie [French Club wait-ress] fell off the little seat when the driver opened the door. We left her & went to buy

---

[5] It is a delightful coincidence that, after his separation from Jessie in 1947, Rawsthorne lived for a while in Great Pulteney Street, where Haydn lived during his first London visit in 1791, and later occupied what was reputedly Chopin's room in St James's, at what was now the French Club.

a ticket. Olwen hid her purse, & when she produced it, Alan muttered, 'Yes, you *are* my favourite person' & we dragged her on to the platform.—cold & dreary—porters hauling mailbags & Olwen howling. We pretended to push the train, to make her laugh & then I gave Alan & Edward strong black coffee at home & I got to bed at 5 a.m.

The Soho of that period was described by Edward Williams, in his memorial address at Isabel's funeral in 1992, as 'a kind of cultural melting pot, a swirling meeting place of writers, poets, musicians, painters'.[6] One of the most famous 'hang-outs' was the Colony Room run by Muriel Belcher, a foul-mouthed and extraordinary character; among the denizens of her club was Francis Bacon, who painted a number of outstanding paintings of Isabel and was one of her closest friends.

Rawsthorne's output of concert music during the period 1947–51 had been considerable, especially considering the number of major film scores he produced. After the Second Piano Concerto, there was something of a hiatus: having produced eight substantial works in five years, he wrote only another five in the next seven years, before the Violin Sonata of 1958 seemed once again to release the floodgates of his inspiration. There were also, of course, a number of smaller works, but not all these are particularly successful. The *Coronation Overture*, written for the National Youth Orchestra in 1953 and performed by it in Britain and in Brussels, is one. Despite an attractive Handelian beginning in the manner of a French overture and some interesting contrapuntal development in the main quick section, it is regrettably lacking in real inspiration. It seems like an obligation rather than an inspiration, and both invention and orchestration are spread thinly. Rawsthorne began to show more interest in writing for choir, however, and the demands of this medium, in which he had only worked a little, may have contributed in the long term to the broadening of his style from 1958 on.

The first of this group of choral works to be written is the most substantial: *A Canticle of Man*, for baritone, chorus, flute, and strings (or piano, with which accompaniment it has often been successfully performed), commissioned for the 1952 Bryanston Summer School of Music. At twelve minutes, it is still relatively modest, a piece of vocal-instrumental chamber music rather than a massive statement, but there is no doubting the sincerity with which Rawsthorne sets Randall Swingler's fine, specially written text. (Swingler was by now married to Geraldine Peppin, whose daughter, Judith, later married another composer, Edward Williams, thus neatly squaring the circle of

---

[6] This memorial address, spoken in Thaxted Parish Church on 4 Feb. 1992, was printed in *The Creel*, 2/1 (spring 1992), 5–7.

friendship.) The work is a plea for peace, the only means through which mankind will reach maturity. The choral writing is effective, combining chordal work with interleaved counterpoint; the three baritone solos are expressive cantilenas, acting as a kind of ritornello. The use of the choir as an objective, questioning force, with the baritone giving a personal response, is also effective, while the handling of flute and strings is often sensitive. What vitiates against the complete success of the work is its episodic form, with frequent pauses closing off too many sections too firmly, as well as the failure to make the consolatory A major ending completely convincing. The dramatic climaxes, too, are not entirely convincing: one senses that they need rather bigger forces, instrumentally and chorally, to make their proper effect. What is perhaps more serious is that the Rawsthorne style descends into mannerism, possibly because of some remaining inhibition in writing for chorus. Melodic and harmonic turns of phrase familiar from other works no longer sound so fresh; the work as a whole seems slightly constricted, and the question of Rawsthorne's musical language, and how it can be developed and refreshed, is put before us by this work as by no others up to this point.

'Canzonet' was Rawsthorne's contribution to the choral collection 'A Garland for the Queen' (1953), designed as a contemporary equivalent of 'The Triumphs of Oriana' to mark the coronation of Queen Elizabeth II. The other composers represented, some by works which have become minor classics, were Bax, Lennox Berkeley, Bliss, Finzi ('White-Flowering Days'), Howells ('Inheritance'), Ireland, Rubbra, Tippett ('Dance, Clarion Air'), and Vaughan Williams ('Silence and Music'). Bernard Stevens describes Louis MacNeice's poem as 'a lyrical, almost Medieval, song of joy, in modern English but with a Latin refrain'.[7] Rawsthorne's setting is a delightful, gently lilting number, only two minutes in length, with a quiet but rich use of the choir's lower register and a free-floating soprano arabesque above (Ex. 6.4). It is interesting to note how easily Rawsthorne, regarded already as an instrumental specialist, adapted his style to take his place in the choral tradition without losing his individuality.

Three years later, Rawsthorne, together with the poet Randall Swingler, was commissioned to write *A Rose for Lidice*, in memory of the wartime destruction of the Czech mining town by the Nazis (Compact Disc, track 11). A note in the score says: 'The "Lidice Shall Live" Committee, first formed in Hanley, Staffs., organized the gift of a rose-garden which was opened in the rebuilt village in 1956', and simultaneous first performances took place in the Lidice

---

[7] 'The Choral Music', Poulton iii. 52.

Ex. 6.4. 'Canzonet', p. 3, bars 4–6

rose-garden and at a service in Thaxted.[8] The beautiful poem places the emphasis on the renewal of man's love through the symbol of the rose; hatred is mostly abjured, save in passing references to the Nazis' desire to 'Wipe out the name!' and to the 'murderer's heel' stamping 'on the eyes of children'. The consolatory tone of the work is summed up by the last line: 'Lidice hangs, a garland, round the cross of the world.' Unusually, Rawsthorne briefly employs spoken rhythms as well as wordless accompanying lines, and uses the name of the town almost as a ritual incantation at beginning and end. It is a hauntingly beautiful setting in which Rawsthorne is clearly more at ease with his typical harmonies than in 'Canzonet' in terms of choral layout (Ex. 6.5), and freer to unfold interweaving lines of counterpoint. The piece is a miniature perhaps, but it is both profound and touching, with strong links to the English choral tradition: some of the imitative, but never academic, counterpoint has a grace and naturalness that owns a relationship with great masters of the past like Byrd and Tallis.

Lidice's Thaxted première was given by Imogen Holst conducting the Purcell Singers, who also gave the première of the *Four Seasonal Songs* in a BBC broadcast in December the same year. They were originally entitled 'Four Part-Songs for Unaccompanied Choir', a title that Alan Frank (rightly) thought rather dull. They bring Rawsthorne fully into the mainstream of the English choral tradition, being settings of the kind of early seventeenth-century pastoral poems that composers of Warlock's generation particularly liked to set. Three of them are spring songs, the third alone dealing with autumn, and

[8] (OUP, 1962).

Ex. 6.5. *A Rose for Lidice*, from p. 5, bar 8

Rawsthorne's choral technique, while quite demanding, is both resourceful and virtuosic. He frequently divides some section of the choir in the central pair of songs, the outer ones being entirely in four parts, and there is great freshness in the writing. The first, 'Now the Earth, the Skies, the Air', is a vigorous setting in E flat (complete with key signature) contrasting lively counterpoint with block chordal passages (Ex. 6.6 gives a taste of its Handelian exuberance), and the second is marked by pealing imitative ostinato patterns like a carillon either above or below the slower lines in the other parts.

Ex. 6.6. *Four Seasonal Songs*, No. 1, opening

'Autumn' is more extended, utilizing male voices only to emphasize the change in tonal colouring; female voices begin the second strain and the full choir reaches a substantial climax, followed by a dying fall, on the words 'Leaving, worldling, of thine own | Neither fruit nor leaf behind thee.' The final song, 'Now the lusty Spring is seen', is a lilting 9/8 in an ultimately joyous A flat. The frequent key-changes during the last song in particular might make it difficult to sing, but Rawsthorne is careful to be as practical as possible in giving strong leads from one part to another. Only the received view of him as a purely instrumental composer can account for the almost complete neglect of these vocal works, which would be an ornament in any choral group's repertoire; *A Rose for Lidice*, in particular, is a small masterpiece.

Apart from the première of the Second Piano Concerto in June, and the earlier release of Basil Wright's film *Waters of Time* and later work on *Where No Vultures Fly*, 1951 also saw the first performance of one of the finest of the ancillary works of the period under discussion, and indeed one of the most beautiful of all his shorter orchestral works, the *Concertante pastorale* for flute, horn, and strings. The first performance was given by Gareth Morris and Dennis Brain with the New London Orchestra under Alec Sherman at Hampton Court Orangery in August, and there was some haste in the completion of the work, a late addition to the programme; indeed, the announcement of its inclusion in the season was printed on a separate slip and stapled to the season's brochure. The opening has already been quoted (Ex. P.1), and the autumnal tone so beautifully conveyed by the opening bars is sustained through the work. The mellow colouring delicately communicates the sense of nostalgia, even regret, and both in the handling of the strings, high at the start and low at the end, and in the fact that the second half of the work is a gradual dying fall, the most intense climax occurring only after about seventy-two bars (out of 236), Rawsthorne ensures that it is the reflective mood that dominates. Thematic integration is extremely subtle: though the form is basically ternary, there is a false recapitulation in the middle (with the tune in the flute instead of horn), and subsidiary accompanying figuration forms the basis of newer material in the next episode while being at the same time derived from a little figure in the main theme itself. There is little actually new in style or technique, though the work's feeling is unique in his output, but one impassioned flute phrase is important in its anticipation of the kind of dramatic recitative-like melodic line Rawsthorne was to employ frequently a decade later (Ex. 6.7(*a*)). The conclusion is lovely, low Cs on the flute with wide-spread string chords mostly in C major around it; Rawsthorne asked Morris what the lowest note was on the flute and rewarded him by giving him a whole series of quiet, long Cs, difficult to play because of the breath control needed. It may or may not have been a private joke by the composer, but the effect is magical.

Ex. 6.7. (*a*) *Concertante pastorale*, from letter D; (*b*) Four Romantic Pieces for piano, No. 2, bars 3–6

(*a*)

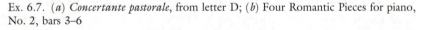

The Four Romantic Pieces for piano, written for Frank Merrick's 70th birthday and first performed by him in the Wigmore Hall in March 1953, are charming and beautifully written for the piano. The title gives the clue: this is piano music using an approach familiar from Romantic music, notably Chopin, Liszt, and even Brahms, and the melodic and harmonic invention, while as usual entirely individual, derives from this tradition. This is particularly true of the second piece, in F sharp major; one is reminded by this expressive and graceful music that Rawsthorne numbered Mendelssohn among composers he admired (Ex. 6.7(*b*)). The first piece is notable for a powerful Allegro molto transformation of the theme of the introduction, closely related to the opening of the Cello Sonata, and the third is a perky scherzando. The final piece is a grandiose, statuesque harmonic statement, quietening as it goes and unusually blunt in its bitonality (which is always implicit in Rawsthorne's harmonic schemes, but seldom so clearly stated as here). It hovers between a pedal note C and its Neapolitan second, D♭, before ending peacefully in C major. Like his other piano works, the Romantic Pieces have appealed to pianists, and their direct quality makes them among the easiest to follow for an audience unfamiliar with his idiom, though they lack the concentrated intellectual or emotional fire of the Bagatelles, Sonatina, or Ballade. Merrick played them in Norway soon after the première, and among other performances one may note Arthur Loesser's American première in New York in 1959.

One of the most important of Rawsthorne's steady output of major film scores during the 1950s was for the 1953 film by Adrian de Potier and Basil Wright *The Drawings of Leonardo da Vinci*, with a commentary by Michael Ayrton read by Laurence Olivier, C. Day Lewis reading Leonardo's own texts. Scored for flute, trumpet, violin, cello, and piano, the music was reviewed by Hans Keller in the *Musical Times*. His introductory remarks touch on an important topic:

If Alan Rawsthorne had written a concert piece playing twenty minutes and forty seconds, its first public performance would have been a major event, not only from the musical, but also from the journalistic standpoint. But since he wrote a film score of that length instead, the cultural press, musical or general, has not so much as noticed its existence.[9]

Keller drew attention to the overall sonata-ternary form of the score, in which there are clear exposition, development, and recapitulation sections spread through the six separate parts of the score and utilizing, with utmost discretion, numerous contrapuntal and developmental devices. The score is unusually onomatopoeic at moments—suggesting a splendid scratchy cat, for instance,

---

[9] Vol. 97 (Jan. 1956), 29.

some characteristically evocative water music, and a powerful storm. But this is never gratuitous, and is always integrated thematically, within an underlying tonal scheme hovering around C and C sharp. There are interesting links with other works, from the Cello Sonata to a phrase which echoes the opening theme of the First Symphony and anticipates that for the 1961 Concerto for Ten Instruments. Above all, the score memorably evokes the sense of time passing, the consideration centuries later of an earlier art of timeless quality.

The sequence of feature film scores during this period, up to his last (*Floods of Fear*) in 1958, was started by a film that was, ecologically and socially, well ahead of its time. *Where No Vultures Fly*, directed by Harry Watt, was chosen for the Royal Film Performance in 1951, going on general release early the following year, and it proved immensely popular, so much so that in 1953 the same team produced a sequel, *West of Zanzibar*. *Vultures*, the story of which concerned the establishment of an African national park and the attempt to drive out the ivory poachers, required less music than some of the previous films, and demanded less of the composer, in that it was a straightforward adventure story, however didactic its purpose, and so lacked the psychological or atmospheric dimensions that had earlier drawn such evocative scores. Rawsthorne, however, conjured up an almost frightening piece of music for the vultures, and a main title cue of considerable dramatic power. This was one of the films on which Gerard Schurmann assisted Rawsthorne, and he has always been concerned to stress the debt he owes to Alan's support and encouragement. *West of Zanzibar* was a simpler adventure story, with a relatively conventional score, much of which is obscured by the sound effects. Though entertaining, *West of Zanzibar* did not cause such a stir as *Vultures*, which was a seminal work in encouraging people to think in terms of the conservation of animals rather than the destruction of them and their habitat. Perhaps it was even the first ecological feature film.

The Cruel Sea, directed by Charles Frend, was released in 1952 and proved not only another box-office hit but an outstanding war film, in which (exceptionally for the time) the Captain, played by Jack Hawkins, expressed horror at what war forced him to do. The film, taking its cue from Nicholas Monsarrat's novel, expressed respect for the enemy, rather than blind hatred. It was not, for all its stiff upper lip (which trembled from time to time), simply a jingoistic exercise, and deserves proper reassessment. Rawsthorne's score was particularly fine. Gone are the scintillating colours of the Second Piano Concerto or the autumnal tints of the *Concertante pastorale*: he vividly communicates the surging greyness of the heaving seas, the tense monotony of the seemingly endless waiting, and the dramatic explosions of action. There are moments of compassion for the victims of war, enriching a film which, despite opportunities to do so, never becomes sentimental. Once again, several tense sequences are without music; one is reminded especially of Michael Powell's wartime film *One of our Aircraft is Missing*, which managed to do very well without any music at all. In a desolate, nocturnal scene, with the survivors of a submarine attack drifting in the ocean recalling sounds and voices from their shore lives, Rawsthorne's music, spare and austere, is unusually Debussyan without losing any of his special identity; Philip Lane has successfully reconstructed from the soundtrack (the manuscript having being lost) a Prelude and Nocturne which present the film's main themes, including this particularly moving section (Compact Disc, track 10). It is inevitable that in any sizeable film with a good deal of music (*The Cruel Sea* lasts just over two hours), monothematicism would be a solution to the challenge of writing so much in a short time, and Rawsthorne perhaps a shade overdoes the use of the main title theme. However, it is a pity that he felt there was little or nothing that could effectively be exploited in concert form: Philip Lane's collation demonstrates that this is unfair to what is overall a magnificent achievement.

Another war film with naval connections is *The Man who Never Was*, directed by Ronald Neame and released in 1955. This is less satisfactory, partly because of some wooden acting and scripting (despite the fact that the screenplay was by Nigel Balchin); for some reason, it lacks the necessary electricity. Based on the true story of 'Operation Mincemeat', a wartime hoax designed to mislead the German military command in the Mediterranean theatre, it elicits from Rawsthorne a score which is suitably mysterious, and, especially in the atmospheric prologue, full of foreboding. It is interesting that so many of his films should feature water, usually the sea, and include music for piano solo, in this case an amiable doodling in roughly the style of the Four Romantic Pieces. He uses 'Deutschland über alles' to underscore the German military scenes, a very obvious and Hollywoodian technique, indicating perhaps a loss of concentration on his part, since it is such a cliché of film music, but he does at least bring considerable imagination to it. In some instances, he subtly works the German tune in among the various threads of his own music. He also underscores the Irish spy's message-sending with Morse code figuration in the woodwind made into a melodic, as well as rhythmic, device. There is not a great deal of music in the film, and it is not, as a whole, a score with the distinction of some of his earlier ones.

Lease of Life, directed by Charles Frend in 1954, was a more intimate, personal drama, the story of a poverty-stricken Yorkshire parson finding fulfilment

just at the time when he is diagnosed as having heart disease. It is articulate
and touching, very well acted (except for a rather too doe-eyed Robert Donat),
and unusually realistic in its portrayal of a music student's life, a subject normally treated by film-makers (and writers) with as much realism as life on Mars.
It gives Rawsthorne another opportunity to use piano music, not only his own
original material but also classical repertoire. Oddly enough, one of the main
motifs of the score, heard here in the orchestra, is a version of the theme from
his earlier Theme and Four Studies for piano. One special feature of
Rawsthorne's film music in general is particularly applicable to this sensitive
score: his use of classical forms such as the miniature rondo for the credit titles
brings with it a sense of potential variation through the film, and he uses this
to take part in the emotional development of the action, foreshadowing it
subtly so that when, for instance, the parson suffers his first heart attack, we
are already prepared for it and sympathize the more deeply with him. The
music, as it were, integrates with the action to become almost one of the characters. It is an ability that marks Rawsthorne at his best as one of the greatest
film composers.

Rawsthorne's life during the 1950s was unsettled, in many ways. The death
of Constant Lambert in 1951 was a serious blow. Denis ApIvor has stated that
the only time he saw Rawsthorne in tears was on the day of Lambert's funeral.[10]
Alan's move to the country, however, was eminently happy, as was his life with
Isabel, Lambert's widow. It is extraordinary that, after a life as varied and
romantic as hers, Isabel should happily have settled to country life so easily.
She was born Isabel Nicholas, changing her name by deed poll to Epstein when
she became the sculptor's model (and mistress). Her first husband was the war
correspondent Sefton Delmer, with whom she lived in Paris, during which time
she had intense affairs with Derain, Picasso, and Giacometti (with whom she
also lived for a time). Constant Lambert was her second husband, Rawsthorne
her third. She was a painter of exceptional accomplishment. In 1984, Barbara
Rawsthorne wrote to Isabel (at the latter's request for a note of reminiscences
of his life in Little Sampford):

I remember when, in 1953, Alan told me you and he had found a cottage in the country
and were going to live there I was delighted.

It seemed to me he had been living a somewhat nomadic life for some time; it had
not been a good time for him for many reasons, and I felt that to live in the country
would give him a great deal. For years he had wanted to do so, and I think that to
make this move at this point was the best thing he ever did, the time was ripe and the

---

[10] 'Biographical Essays', Poulton ii. 44–6.

locality perfect . . . in order to [contact him] I generally had to telephone round to all his friends in London to see whether they knew where he was!

Life at Sudbury Cottage *did* give him a great deal, and over the years it gave him serenity. He liked doing little jobs in his own home, and no longer qualified for the nickname 'Useless' given to him by student friends in his student days during holidays on the Norfolk Broads. He got on well with the local population and liked to know all that was going on in the village . . . he was a great one for gossip wasn't he? . . . I have so many happy memories of being there at Sudbury Cottage with you and Alan, and I associate laughter always with those times—I don't mean only the laughter that one can hear, but the quiet sort that one feels inside one.

The *Cambridge Evening News*, in an obituary tribute, gave a vivid description of life at the cottage: 'A warm and lived-in home, full of cats and cushions and salivation from the kitchen smells. The piano with the hospitable bottles upon its top, the huge logs in the open hearth, the clutter of books, and sheet-music, and manuscript. And talk, which was rich, effortless and seemingly endless, like some long and leisurely game of tennis upon a vicarage lawn.' (One is tempted to remark that some of Isabel's language might have surprised a vicarage, however.)

Alan's move to the country, taking him out of the detrimental (if convivial) round of drinking establishments, was of prime importance in re-establishing his creative and emotional equilibrium: he described it to James Gibb as 'my escape to reality'. The years in Essex, however, started with a setback, a serious haemorrhage in December 1953, and he spent that month in University College Hospital. The following year he and Jessie were divorced, having been separated for several years, and in 1955 he married Isabel. In view of the fact that Alan's drinking was a major cause, if not *the* major cause, of his illness, marriage to another heavy drinker might seem to have been unwise (it certainly appalled Walton), but there is absolutely no doubt that they loved each other deeply and continued to do so. Little of their corrrespondence has survived, and almost nothing from this period, but in one incomplete (and therefore undatable) letter, begging her to live with him, he wrote of his determination to win her: 'in the end the Hound of Heaven has nothing on me.' There were other serious illnesses, especially in 1961, after which he was forbidden alcohol (for three years), and an attack of pneumonia in April 1971 before the haemorrhage which killed him in July of that year. Despite the international spread of performances of his music, he refrained from much travel, and indeed only crossed the Atlantic once, in 1954 to lecture at the Toronto Conservatory Summer School. The New York office of OUP reported back to headquarters in London (13 August 1954) that he was a 'great success in

Canada . . . [his pupils and others in the Summer School] greatly enjoyed working with him', though they were understandably a little confused at his failure to use the trip to call in on New York. This might be put down to antipathy to America and things American, but it seems much more likely that he really disliked extensive travel away from home and could not, in any case, be bothered to take part in the personal appearances and self-promotion that are such an important part of a composer's career. He was the last person in the world to promote himself, and would probably have disliked anything that smacked of this activity.

After a few fairly unproductive years, 1954–5 saw the presentation of three major works, a decided increase in important creativity. The 1954 works were a setting for speaker and orchestra of six of T. S. Eliot's poems in *Old Possum's Book of Practical Cats*, commissioned by the Edinburgh Festival, and the second of his 'official' (i.e. numbered) string quartets, first performed at the Cheltenham Festival that year by the Griller Quartet; the ballet *Madame Chrysanthème* followed in 1955. *Practical Cats* and the Second Quartet in particular have a great deal to offer; indeed, the quartet remains one of the finest of his chamber works and was a strong favourite of Rawsthorne's among his own compositions. Its four movements are all characteristic forms, and the language seems not to be radically different from earlier music, but comparison with the First String Quartet shows how far he had travelled musically, and he now found a way of refreshing his idiom, partly through the sheer intensity of thought and concentration of means. Though most carefully wrought, with all his mastery of thematic integration, it has great formal control yet rhapsodic freedom of expression, as well as considerable variety of melodic and rhythmic types. The tunes themselves, too, are direct and evocative, however concentrated their working may be. The first movement, like that of the Concerto for String Orchestra, starts with a slow, two-bar chordal phrase containing several important musical cells, followed by an Allegro agitato imbued with something akin to the warm expansiveness and underlying urgency of the opening of Brahms's C minor String Quartet (Ex. 6.8(*a*)). The dotted rhythm of bar 1 of the introduction becomes, in diminution, a vital element of the main theme, and it forms an important part of the second subject (Ex. 6.8(*b*)), which has a touch of Ravel's Piano Trio about it and whose more relaxed manner is given an underlying agitation by the continuation of the 7/4 metre which dominates the movement (an unusual time signature for Rawsthorne, and one which encouraged him to longer melodic spans). Rawsthorne obeys classical convention by placing the second subject in the dominant (G) and the recapitulation of both first and second subjects in the tonic (C). Typically, the first subject is developed somewhat before the second is introduced, this in turn being developed with much organically derived polyphony prior to the recapitulation which makes the briefest of references to the second subject before the movements ends quietly with an apparently new phrase on first violin.

Ex. 6.8. Second String Quartet, first movement: (*a*) opening; (*b*) from letter B

This new phrase reveals itself as the opening theme of the second movement, laid out chordally in a way which recalls the opening of the quartet
texturally and marked 'Allegro appassionato sempre molto rubato', a clear indication of both its character and the element of rhapsodic freedom anticipated.
It is an impassioned theme whose outline is basically descending, and its
quicker tempo alternates with a melancholy Adagio appassionato based on a
meditative viola tune, the two themes being developed in combination to lead
to a return of the first section. The slower viola tune resumes, with a new countermelody, and the movement closes with a short reprise of the first theme, at
the slower tempo. It is an unusual scheme, the two main themes associated
with different tempos but also developing with each other, and it is the slower
speed that finally wins the day. The parallel with the second movement of
Brahms's A major Violin Sonata is interesting: here too there are two tempos,
varying the same basic material in this case, but they are more sharply differentiated, and the quicker one returns to finish Brahms's movement. It is interesting that it was the second movement that was written first: in a pencil sketch
for a programme note, Rawsthorne wrote that he then 'proceeded, as it were,
in both directions therefrom'. The third movement he described as 'a rather
aloof, subdued dance, emerging out of the shadows and disappearing again',
and its ghostly waltz-like atmosphere, fragile in the delicacy of its precisely
judged scoring, is maintained almost throughout, with only one episode of
this brief rondo-like structure being marked 'forte' (and then it is muted). The
ritornello main theme, characterized particularly by fourths, is referred to only
briefly on its first reappearance, and on its final one (Ex. 6.9(a)) is divided
hesitantly between viola and first violin; the instruments are all muted throughout this deceptively simple, charming movement.

The finale is perhaps the most striking movement of all, a theme and three
variations in which the theme is related to the quartet's opening bars and the
slow movement's waltz theme (Compact Disc, track 9). It is hardly fair to call
it merely a theme, since it already develops into a variation as it progresses;
indeed, this procedure recalls the third movement of Webern's Variations for
Piano. The theme leads naturally into the first variation; the dovetailing of each
variation into the next is so beautifully managed that the music presents a seamless flow of music, quite the opposite of the episodic effect normally achieved
in this form. The gradual intensification of counterpoint adds to the sense of
growth and development, through the second variation's rhythmical and
contrapuntal complexities (Ex. 6.9(b)) to the remarkable, almost late-
Beethovenian final variation. Here, liquid demisemiquavers in one or two parts
flow around rhapsodic, lyrical phrases (Ex. 6.9(c) shows the cello and then
the viola varying the theme). The final climax is quite brief, but a massive

Ex. 6.9. Second String Quartet: (*a*) third movement, from p. 17, bar 1; (*b*) fourth movement, from letter A; (*c*) fourth movement, from p. 22, bar 4

(*a*)

(*b*)

Ex. 6.9. *Continued*

(*c*)

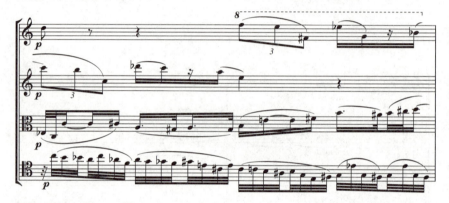

one would have burst the bounds of an essentially self-contained quartet. After this has died down, all four instruments play an ascending figure of demisemiquavers together, pianissimo, the work ending with a quiet coda recalling the opening of the theme, high chords above a cello phrase ('the cello adding a note of interrogation below')[11] that concludes with a falling third, repeated (G-E), which was soon to become a familiar figure in later years. One of the most original features of this fine movement is that a fairly complex theme is gradually simplified as it proceeds, while the polyphonic development of its ideas becomes simultaneously more complex.

The final variation recalls nothing so much as the flickering third movement of Berg's *Lyric Suite*, while Ex. 6.9(*b*) similarly reminds one of the kind of inventive dexterity in Berg's earlier String Quartet. There are, too, unusually

---

[11] Composer's sketched programme note.

strong reminiscences of Bartók's quartets (especially the second) from time to time, at least on a superficial glance. But there is nothing like either composer in the actual sound of the music. Any such influences have been absorbed into the musical bloodstream, while there are also some new elements, both melodic and structural; the marvellous, uninterrupted flow of the finale is in particular a fine achievement. The tonal scheme seems almost to have a Nielsenish progressive tonality. From the C of the first movement, with much emphasis on its dominant G (which is, of course, the minor third of E minor) and the slip down to B minor at the end, the music proceeds through an increasing emphasis on B minor in second and third movements (the latter commencing in a kind of B flat) as well as the finale's theme, to close peacefully in what seems an inevitable E minor, as if this key were the aim right from the start. The final chord brings another link with Berg, being similar to the final chord in the first movement of his String Quartet. This by itself would not be important, but it underlines one's feeling that, however different the underlying method, Rawsthorne's mature style owes almost as much to Berg as to Bartók, texturally and polyphonically as well as harmonically. The ghost of the waltz which runs through Rawsthorne's career and assumes great importance in the post-1950s is another link, pervading so much of Berg's music as it does. Another important aspect of the overall shape of the quartet is that each movement is basically slower than its predecessor. The hint of a new spareness of thought both extends his range and looks forward to some aspects of his last period. Many critics, while full of praise for the quartet's technique and enlargement of Rawsthorne's vision, felt it to be elusive, even enigmatic. Michael Kennedy, in the *Daily Telegraph* (13 July 1954) summed it up well, however: 'This is a work of deep inner strength, serious but not sombre, and predominantly lyrical.' Though composers are not always good judges of their own work, Rawsthorne was surely correct in estimating this quartet so highly; it remains one of the finest from any British composer.

Practical Cats, a vivid expression of Rawsthorne's enormous affection for these delightful creatures, is a completely different kind of piece. It was commissioned for a children's concert at the 1954 Edinburgh Festival, and therein lies the problem: the work, however charming, is quite unsuited for children. There are innumerable musical jokes scattered around the score, such as a little clarinet and side-drum fanfare for the 'Beetle's Tattoo' and a delicious flute and clarinet 'Three Cheers', both for 'The Gumbie Cat', delicately interpolated into the texture. These are much too discreet for any other than the reasonably sophisticated listener, and in 'Gus: The Theatre Cat' there are innumerable musical references which need to be fully appreciated (the Waltonian 'seaside' piccolo motif, for instance, or the splendidly melodramatic climax for the introduction of 'Firefrorefiddle, the Fiend of the Fell'). The work as a whole contains an enormous number of musical jokes or references. 'Bustopher Jones' is given quite a few of these: a grandiose, rather imperial version of the overture's main theme to emphasize his pomp, with a strong reminder of 'Abide with me' at the end of the orchestral introduction (though this also links thematically with the whole-tone phrase taking such an important part in the overture's melodies), and a brief but clear reference to 'Land of Hope and Glory'. Rawsthorne's experience of writing film music, when from time to time the suggestion of a well-known tune of one kind or another is a useful part of the craft, must have come in very handy for this work. The tune for 'The Song of the Jellicles' turns 'Boys and Girls come out to play' into a jig-like version of the overture's main theme. The matter of the whole work, indeed, derives from this very short orchestral piece.

The overture runs for only just two minutes, yet it teems with brilliant ideas, a little masterpiece of orchestral virtuosity. Every instrument has a brief solo, and the recapitulation, when the opening of the main theme is given to solo flute accompanied only by a sustained note on two horns, the orchestra bursting in vigorously with the rest of the tune, is both exciting and very funny. Some (but by no means all) of the main themes of the overture (and thus the work) are given in Ex. 6.10: (i) is the main tune, which is stated above a pompous tonic–dominant oom-pah bass, (ii) the next phase of the tune, given initially in chords, (iii) a contrasting second theme in first violins, and (iv) a lyrical oboe tune, acting as a third subject but also a slower version of (i). It is worth noting that the sequence of notes asterisked in (i) (E-D-C) occurs a tone higher at the end of (ii), where it outlines the end of a descending whole-tone scale passage; these notes form an important cadential motif throughout the work, notably for the words 'Three different names' in 'The Naming of Cats'. The development of this array of brief tunes makes for a fully formed sonata movement, a dazzling display of compositional dexterity; one is convinced that the overture would make an ideal encore piece for any touring orchestra.

The characterization of the different cats is admirably sharp and affectionate, partly through the kind of musical references already discussed and partly through the variation of the main cells of the work. An appropriate atmosphere of mystery surrounds 'The Naming of Cats', with some lovely preening phrases in the woodwind (Ex. 6.11(a)). The amiable 'Gumbie Cat', a kind of variation with two alternating tempos, is personified by sweetly lyrical but ambiguous major/minor thirds and sixths, while 'Gus''s down-market rakish-

Ex. 6.10. *Practical Cats*: overture, main themes

ness is given suitably sleazy expression. Rawsthorne gives him accompanying figures which vary cells from the overture (Ex. 6.11(*b*)). A tender siciliano for 'Old Deuteronomy', imbued with the delicate compassion at Rawsthorne's command, and the exuberant 'Song of the Jellicles' bring the work to a close. The final cadence consists of contrary-motion scales, a device first encountered at the end of the Second Piano Concerto, where it was fully prepared and completely fresh. It is still acceptable here, but it was to become a distinct

Ex. 6.11. *Practical Cats*: (*a*) from 'The Naming of Cats'; (*b*) from 'Gus, the Theatre Cat'

handicap in later works, where it sometimes seems that Rawsthorne relied on it to provide an ending when he could not think of anything else.

The career of *Practical Cats* has been more intermittent than it deserves. The initial reception was mixed, owing largely to the feeling that it was essentially too sophisticated for children's concerts, though the inventiveness of the music was appreciated. There is also the problem of combining speech with music; Rawsthorne's solution was simply to note down the verbal rhythms, without pitch. There were a number of performances after the first, notably the USA première conducted by Milton Katims in Seattle (a plan for him to record it with Peter Ustinov narrating unfortunately fell through) and a further performance of excerpts at a Philadelphia Orchestra children's concert in 1966 (what an audience of American high-school children thought of Eliot and

Rawsthorne one cannot imagine), and in 1971 a reduced orchestration by Bryan Fairfax was given by him with his orchestra, Polyphonia, Spike Milligan narrating. The work is best known through the recording by Robert Donat, with the composer conducting the Philharmonia Orchestra, but some of the tempos are a little sluggish (though the overture is sprightly enough) and Donat, sadly, was audibly struggling with the asthma from which he died, so the performance, for all its considerable merits, does not do the work full justice. It is a pity that so entertaining a work, highly suitable for an adult audience in the right context, should be so overlooked. It is a pity, too, that two such disparate but contemporaneous works as this and the Second Quartet should be equally overlooked, for *Practical Cats* was a real advance in terms of broadening his style and directing it to a new purpose.

The same was true of *Madame Chrysanthème* of the following year. The ballet, at forty minutes or so, is one of Rawsthorne's two longest works (*Carmen vitale* is the other), but for whatever reason not one of his most successful. Undoubtedly, the ravages of ill health earlier in the 1950s, and the phenomenal amount of music he had produced during the previous decade (bearing in mind that he was an extremely slow and careful worker), as well as the various personal upheavals, were detrimental to his concentration; but *Practical Cats* showed that his humour and sensitivity were intact. What was not, perhaps, was his ability sharply to bring out dramatic character, certainly so far as human beings were concerned (he had little trouble with the cats of the previous year), for the characterization is one of the disappointments of the ballet. It was written for the Sadler's Wells company and first performed at the Royal Opera House, Covent Garden, with choreography by Frederick Ashton and costumes and designs by Isabel (whom Rawsthorne married that same year). In five scenes, it is adapted from the book by Pierre Loti that also inspired the story, play, and opera *Madame Butterfly*. Arriving in Nagasaki on a French warship, a young sailor, Pierre, falls in love with a young woman, Chrysanthème, and after agreeing a price with her parents, the two are married to the accompaniment of a procession of lanterns. Pierre's ship is ordered to sail, and Chrysanthème tries vainly to persuade him to stay, giving him a bouquet of chrysanthemums and begging him to return for one last goodbye. He does so, only to be bitterly disappointed to find her counting her financial blessings from the transaction. He departs, disillusioned by her mercenary spirit.

Chrysanthème is really the opposite of Butterfly, who in roughly comparable circumstances is less pragmatic. One would have expected Rawsthorne's bitter-sweet melancholic mood to have ideally suited her, and he does portray

her with a good deal of sympathy, charm, and fragility. But the characterization of the remaining dramatis personae is less vivid: there is not really time
for them to develop, but neither Pierre nor the more important ancillary characters come alive in the music. Nor does the main romantic *pas de deux* live
up to the challenge (Ex. 6.12(*a*)), with its conventional turns of phrase and
lack of positive warmth. For all the richness of scoring at the climax, and a
melancholy suited to the doom-laden nature of the story, it is, indeed, less full-
blooded and convincing than the brief romantic cues in films like *Saraband
for Dead Lovers* and *Pandora and the Flying Dutchman*. There are also some
faintly clumsy joins between sections of the score, and though there is a lively
dance for the arrival of the ship, a more ceremonial treatment of the same tune
for the entry of Pierre and his friend Yves is a generalized reference rather than
a revealing piece of characterization. Overall, there is insufficient differentia-
tion between the various characters.

There are, however, some delicious touches of wit, including the shortest
possible quote (a single, immediately identifiable chord from Mendelssohn's
'Wedding March'), and Scene 4, beginning with the Procession of Lanterns,
contains a number of short and highly effective dances that Rawsthorne later
formed into a suite. It is a pity that Chrysanthème's solo dance is too wayward
and unstructured to form part of the suite, but a vigorous Sword Dance in
7/8 (with a processional trio section) and a lively Hornpipe are particularly
successful. So too are Rawsthorne's characteristic methods of integrating the
thematic material by the use of particular intervals. The opening of the Pro-

Ex. 6.12. *Madame Chrysanthème: pas de deux* (Scene 4); (*b*) Procession with Lanterns;
(*c*) the first two Japanese ladies; (*d*) from the Procession with Lanterns

(*a*)

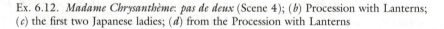

cession (Ex. 6.12(*b*)) has an accompaniment which exploits a phrase (marked *x*) already heard earlier in the ballet in a lively version and recurring as a melody for the entry of the three Japanese ladies in Scene 2 (Ex. 6.12(*c*) gives the first two, the second inverting the tune). Perhaps the most imaginative stroke of all lies in the scoring for an orchestra with triple flutes and trumpets, two each of bassoons and horns, one oboe, piano, celesta, harp, percussion, and strings, plus the inspired addition of a simple, folk-like solo for wordless mezzo-soprano at beginning and end. Possibly the most beautiful music comes in the dance for the Mousmès and in the Procession, where the opening theme is piled up chordally in canon (Ex. 6.12(*d*)).

Rawsthorne was even more last-minute in the completion of this score than usual, and called upon the help of composer friends such as Gerard Schurmann and Denis ApIvor to complete the orchestration. He made a basic error in cre-ating a relatively lightly scored piece but not ensuring that Ashton and the dancers appreciated how delicate the scoring was. As a result, the dancers could not clearly hear the quieter portions of the music, nor could the audience appreciate them fully over the inevitable stage noise. This must certainly have contributed to its relatively mixed reception, though it is fair to add that Alan Frank was able to write about the New York première that OUP's 'New York Manager, Mr. Dowling, reports that [it] was a big success with the audience. He took Stokowski with him, who genuinely liked it.' When the ballet suite was unveiled at the Proms in 1957, the selection contained the Procession with Lanterns, Sword Dance, Hornpipe, and 'Les Mousmès', at the close of which the main theme from the Procession is recalled. Unfortunately, and to general criticism, a quick coda of some ten bars, derived from a slower phrase introducing the Procession, was tacked on to give the suite a rousing finish; instead, it reduces the whole thing to a much more mundane level. It was an extraordinary misjudgement by a composer of such experience. It should surely have been possible to invent a more convincing finish. The rest of it is delightful, revealing that the essential style of the whole score has a genuinely balletic quality that makes one regret all the more the thinness of so much of the inspiration.

The following year, 1956, saw the first performance of Rawsthorne's Second Violin Concerto, which was originally planned to last about sixteen minutes with the title 'Concertante for Violin and Orchestra' (not the sort of title which encourages soloists to take a piece seriously). After the revisions following the première, the duration was about twenty-six minutes. The first performance itself was singularly unsuccessful. The conductor has been blamed for being unsympathetic, but Rawsthorne's extensive revisions to the finale suggest that he had not been able to define his thoughts with his customary clarity. In the finale, a Theme and Variations, he added an extra variation, and he also made a number of cuts in the first movement and had several attempts at getting the end of the slow movement right. Though he often made slight changes fol-lowing a première, this work had more extensive alterations than almost any other of his compositions. In the circumstances, it was not surprising that substantial changes had been made during the First Violin Concerto's creation; it is more worrying that even more alteration should have been needed to the Second before it reached its proper shape. The reception of it was decidedly cool, many critics expressing disappointment. Arthur Jacobs described it thus: 'The music did not sing. This was the cold Rawsthorne of the String Quartet No. 2 instead of the appealing and lyrical composer of the Second Piano Concerto',[12] a view which implies that the composer should have repeated himself, which is odd, when he was so often criticized for apparently doing just that. Several writers found a lack of singing quality in the concerto, yet it is full of lengthy melodic lines, and one wonders whether they went to it with preconceived expectations and were unable to adjust their parameters. Hugh Ottaway did find much to admire: 'The maturity of composition, the wonderfully imaginative textures, the warm, unaffected treatment of the solo instrument, the firm control over great harmonic mobility—these are immediately striking and often moving'; however, doubtless inspired by the slow movement's bleakness, he found the music's emotional world 'tending always towards a desperate introspection'.[13] Gerard Schurmann puts the blame fairly and squarely on the performance, which

was frankly rather a disaster. Very few realized the difference between the score and what they heard of this wonderful work. Its subtle lyricism and polished refinement make it superior, in my view, to the first concerto for the instrument. A little care is needed here and there over the balance of some 'forte' brass passages, especially when they occur in the proximity of prominent solo violin entries and exits, but the combination of polytonal melodic invention and rich harmonic ambiguity looks forward tantalizingly to the superb Violin Sonata of 1958.[14]

It is clearly a distinct advance in subtlety of large-scale construction, with a remarkable change in some aspects of the musical language, however familiar some turns of phrase might be. Sebastian Forbes makes an important point:

With the benefit of hindsight, it is convenient for us to observe that such a work would have to have made a decisive and immediate impact if it was not to be lost in the turmoil and excitement of a new aesthetic for British music introduced by William Glock a few years later. An unsuccessful première created, in this instance, a situation from which recovery would inevitably be an uphill struggle.[15]

[12] *Hallé* magazine (Dec. 1956).
[13] *Musical Times*, 97 (Dec. 1956), 653–4.
[14] 'Recollections of a Long Friendship', Poulton i, 6.
[15] 'Forgotten Treasure?—Rawsthorne's Second Violin Concerto Newly Considered', *The Creel*, 2/1 (spring 1992), 9–26.

He also points out that, in the context of the 1956–7 BBC Symphony Orchestra programmes, this new concerto 'would have felt truly new and contemporary', yet within a few years Berio, Boulez, Stockhausen, and Maderna would
be the major overseas figures promoted by the musical establishment. With
the rise of the so-called Manchester School and their brilliant contemporaries
such as Richard Rodney Bennett and Thea Musgrave, Rawsthorne would very
quickly cease to be a major force in British new music. (It is ironic that this
should particularly have happened when he began to produce a series of
supremely rewarding new works from 1958 onwards, and it is enormous credit
to him that he was able to rise to this challenge and extend his own language
without denying his musical integrity.)

The Second Violin Concerto distinguishes itself from the lyric-dramatic First
at the outset of the opening Allegretto (Compact Disc, track 12): there is no
introduction setting forth germinal ideas and close intervallic relationships.
Here, the solo violin commences a smooth cantabile melodic line, without pre-
amble but with a genuinely singing quality. A whole chapter could easily be
written about the opening few bars (Ex. 6.13(*a*)), with all the possibilities they
contain. Clearly, tribute is being paid to the opening of Prokofiev's Second
Violin Concerto, but the register is an octave higher, and Rawsthorne's procedure is quite different. He outlines triads of E minor and A flat major, and
then proceeds, via E flat, to outline an A major chord. Among the implications of this process is the fact that A♭, enharmonically spelt as G♯, is the third
of the tonic relative major (E); the device of using a single note, with its different enharmonic spellings, to pivot between two keys is familiar from Haydn,
Schubert, and Sibelius, among many others, but is a new element in
Rawsthorne's technique, at least in the extent to which it starts to pervade this
work. One striking feature, implicit in the opening six notes, is a strong use
of bitonal harmonies, which are seldom brought so firmly to the foreground
as in this work (Ex. 6.13(*b*) gives one of the first-movement climaxes, with the
chords pulling each other in opposite directions). The opening bitonal possibilities, to limit oneself to the most obvious, include E minor/A flat, A flat/E
flat, and E flat/A major, bringing the tritone into play as a possible feature.
This potential is soon given expression by the first orchestral chord, a quiet
combination of E minor and B flat major (a tritone apart, one must note) with
the bass-line reinforcing the B flat tonality. The outline of the theme itself is
clear and memorable, so that even when it is inverted it remains instantly recognizable, and of course its nature is such that it could also be used serially as
a kind of eight-note row (Rawsthorne was a great admirer of Stravinsky's *Agon*,
which briefly uses a six-note row, while the Septet of 1953 employs an eight-

note series). Thematic derivations from the opening tune are numerous. The
first interval, a falling minor third, provides the impetus for a subsidiary theme
when the key shifts down a semitone to E flat soon after the start, and the
descending semitone A♭-G in the opening solo is the basis for the second
subject proper (if that is the correct term in a work where, even by
Rawsthorne's standards, thematic material and development are consistently
intermingled). The ancillary motifs in the woodwind at the start also form

Ex. 6.13. Second Violin Concerto, first movement: (*a*) opening; (*b*) tutti, from 8
before letter J

(*a*)

(*b*)

useful material; indeed, the clarinet phrase starts with the same semitonal descent (Ab-G) already noted. So what appears on the surface an almost casual flow of easy lyricism turns out to be a complex web of relationships between melodic cells with harmonic and tonal implications.

This Allegretto achieves an exceptional balance between musical argument and a soloistic concerto style. Schönberg's term 'developing variation' sums up one of the most important facets of Rawsthorne's compositional technique, which is brought to especially concentrated fruition in this movement (and readying him for the complex thematic workings of his later period). Referring, in his famous article 'Brahms the Progressive', to an important cell in Beethoven's Op. 95 Quartet, Schönberg also says: 'its reappearances, its reincarnation in other themes can . . . be caused subconsciously; the mind of a composer is dominated by every detail of his idea, the consequences of which accordingly will show up involuntarily and unexpectedly.'[16] There are relationships between the Allegretto and the other movements, too, for though the tonality (A) of the slow movement is the dominant of the Allegretto's E, it is also a key strongly implied by the violin's opening phrase (Ex. 6.13(a)), and in turn, the accompanying figure of the finale's theme derives from material heard originally in the slow movement. The shaping of the Allegretto is supremely well ordered, the three main climaxes having differing degrees of intensity, with the first (illustrated in Ex. 6.13(b)) being by far the longest and most sustained. It achieves the status of an important orchestral developmental section as well as simply a climax, the soloist's succeeding entry continuing the intensity and carrying the emotional development of the music forward. The fact that the other two climaxes carry successively less weight, the last being the shortest and abruptly cut off to leave only a quiet coda, has the effect of gradually withdrawing the work's emotional world from a public statement to a more internalized expression, preparing the way for the remarkable slow movement.

The Poco Lento is possessed of a bitter darkness that is exceptional even for Rawsthorne, and it faces unblinkingly the frozen anguish that is starkly revealed. Whereas the soloist set the Allegretto in motion unaccompanied, here it is the orchestra that presents the material, in a lengthy exposition. The main elements are a harsh call to attention in the brass (A minor, moving to A flat) and a quiet, uneasy rocking figure in strings that sounds like an accompaniment in search of a tune. These searching, almost fragmentary ideas form the basis of most of the movement (Ex. 6.14 gives the second phase of this section,

---

[16] *Style and Idea*, ed. L. Stein (London, 1975), 398–441.

PLATE 1. Deardengate House, Haslingden (now demolished) *c.*1907, with the Rawsthorne family pictured outside.

PLATE 2. Family group: Hubert and Janet Rawsthorne with Barbara and Alan, *c.*1909.

PLATE 3. Alan Rawsthorne *c*.1909.

PLATE 4. Alan Rawsthorne aged 27.

PLATE 5. Sergeant Rawsthorne, Muir Mathieson, and William Alwyn at the recording session for Alwyn's music for 'The True Glory', Scala Theatre, London 1945.

PLATE 6. The composer in London, early 1940s.

PLATE 7. Alan and Isabel Rawsthorne in her studio at Little Sampford, 1967.

PLATE 8. Alan and Jessie Rawsthorne at the time of their marriage in 1934.

PLATE 9. Alan Rawsthorne and Alan Bush in Armenia, 1963.

PLATE 10. The composer with the harpist Marisa Robles, late 1968.

Ex. 6.14. Second Violin Concerto, second movement, from bar 10

when woodwind solos have their own more melodic version of the brass phrase). When the violin enters, it is with a declamatory treatment of the tune, handled with such freedom that it becomes almost like an accompanied cadenza. A long-breathed theme and accompaniment seems to be forming itself, with a hint of consolation, to be disrupted by the only solo cadenza-like passage in the whole work and a very brief recapitulation of the main ideas. The hint of consolation, however, has the effect of implying a wider emotional world, so the step from this Arctic close to the lovely, more open atmosphere of the final Allegro moderato is a natural one.

The overall tonal scheme of the concerto appears fairly simple, the three movements being centred on E minor, A minor (with no hint of A major to relieve the bleakness), and E minor/major. There are frequent references to Neapolitan relationships (e.g. the opening harmony of variation 3 in the finale is an A minor triad plus the note F). The first movement, however, is more complex, though the tonal procedures it employs are echoed elsewhere in the work, including much use of Neapolitan tonal relationships (both the sixth

and the second) as transitional areas and the use of particular keys to mark
important moments (several vital junctures are in D minor, for instance, including a magical false recapitulation before the real one). E minor, though the
tonic key, is used quite sparingly, and then usually for the most important
moments of all, emphasizing its prime importance: its first substantial reappearance after the start is at the point of maximum intensity, after the first and
longest orchestral climax, when the violin grasps the movement once more and
takes control of its direction, and it returns to dominate the brief recapitulation and coda. There are phrases in the codas of both first and second movements that anticipate important motifs in the later Violin Sonata (a rising
three-note scale figure, and a falling minor third) and link the two works
together, as well as relating other thematic materials (the falling minor third
is the mainspring for important tunes in both the Allegretto and the Poco
Lento).

The tonal shift in the main theme of the first movement from E minor to
A flat also colours the beginning of the finale's theme (Ex. 6.15). This charming tune, as deceptively casual as the very opening of the concerto, is inverted
for a full orchestral statement (bar 15 of Ex. 6.15) which gives it a completely

Ex. 6.15. Second Violin Concerto, finale, bars 1–18

different, somewhat darker atmosphere. There is, indeed, some doubt as to whether this inversion is not already a variation rather than part of the theme, but it feels like an integral part of it, rather than something developing away from it. The variations which follow mostly derive from the violin's original version of the theme, though they are developmental by nature, not merely decorative, and unfold in such a way that it is sometimes difficult to decide how many there actually are. Some major lines of demarcation exist, however, and must be regarded as markers enabling one to discern the principal variations, though an argument could be made for there being seven rather than five of them. The A minor inversion of the tune, now in the top line of the orchestra, recurs after eleven bars rather than fifteen (Rawsthorne never believed in straightforward repetition) and flows seamlessly into variation 1, in which the theme is in the bass with fragments, some of them in diminution, used as decoration above; the arabesques are, therefore, fully integrated into the argument rather than merely ornamental. Then the violin, with a display of sheer virtuosity rare in this work, begins to attack the theme with vigour. Variation 2, in 5/8 time ('Vigoroso e poco drammaticamente'), has pounding low chords above which the soloist uses the theme melodically but with intensity, rising from the lowest notes of the instrument to a high G. The music descends to the third variation, a 3/8 scherzando interpolated after the first performance and serving to diminish the tension more satisfactorily than the rather abrupt original transition (Ex. 6.16(a)). The theme this time appears

Ex. 6.16. Second Violin Concerto, finale: (a) third variation; (b) fourth variation; (c) from fifth variation

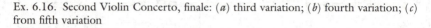

(b)

Andante tranquillo ♪ = c. 138

Duration 3'33"

directly only after ten bars defining the character of this new section, and is derived from the tune to some extent but concentrates on E minor and its Neapolitan second, F, rather than the initial tonal sequence of E–A flat. The scoring is mostly light and spare, the violin line lively and alert, in a variation whose airiness makes a perfect foil to the heart of the movement, variation 4, in which changing metres and a beautifully singing melodic variation of the theme are given a rich setting by accompanying harmonies and fragments of wind counter-melody (Ex. 6.16(*b*)). A gradual accelerando leads to the fifth variation, in which high spirits and exuberance are on display, the preponderance of major chords emphasizing the positive character of this final section (Ex. 6.16(*c*)).

It is this closing variation that gives cause for concern. As occasionally before, Rawsthorne's difficulty with the last-movement problem leads him to try and banish the clouds prevalent from time to time in the work (especially throughout the slow movement) by introducing extrovert high jinks that do not necessarily ring true. The proportions, even after revision, are not convincing: the section still seems too short. There is, however, an additional factor. The original metronome marking for this final variation was $\downarrow$. = 92 (and therefore $\downarrow$ = 138), which seems reasonable, as it is fast enough for the slightly pompous humour to communicate properly. The revised full score has no metronome marking, while in the published violin and piano score it is $\downarrow$ = 92, at which tempo this whole section becomes ludicrously pedantic (see Ex. 6.16(c) if played at the slower speeds). This last must surely be a misprint. The faster tempo works better, given a really excellent performance (some of the scoring is uncharacteristically muddled), though possibly a slightly slower mark (say, 132) would result in less of a scramble.

One of the striking features of the concerto is the strong sense of narrative, the unfolding of a story, that is begun in each movement without any preface. The first and last movements start gently, the central Poco Lento with a dramatic fanfare (using the Scotch snap rhythm), but in each case the music, however formally organized it may appear to be, pursues its course with a natural spontaneity that, for the most part, seems almost improvised. The extraordinary degree to which so many elements are developed and interrelated is the art which conceals art. Sebastian Forbes states his conviction that 'in harmony and in structure, Rawsthorne probably derived greater satisfaction from his music *feeling right* than from whether any pre-compositional devices were fulfilled', and this is a view that can only be supported by sympathetic listening.[17] In his combination of instinct with technical complexity, Rawsthorne again showed his kinship with Brahms. Schönberg's term 'musical prose' summed up what he saw as Brahms's approach to generating thematic lines through flexibility. He also noted that, along with this essentially narrative-like approach, the close integration of accompanying figures with the essential intervals and other features of the basic thematic material was another important feature of Brahms's technique. Rawsthorne's compositional methods have much in common with these aspects of Brahms's methods. A lesser composer might well have reduced the opening twelve bars of the Allegretto to a single line, perhaps on solo violin, with or without some accompanying figure; Rawsthorne's subtlety lies in the division of the material

---

[17] 'Forgotten Treasure?'

between soloist and selected orchestral solos (oboe, clarinet, flute) with some notes sustained, thus emphasizing some of the harmonic implications and also the hierarchy of importance among the main material and subsidiary cells.

The orchestration is mostly superb. The use of harp is particularly subtle and pervasive, and the handling of percussion immensely telling, with minatory beating on the timpani in the Allegretto, sepulchral tenor drum and xylophone tappings in the Poco Lento, and quiet washes of suspended cymbal throughout the work. The strings, often muted, add a silvery sheen to many of the chords, especially in the first movement, and it is notable how careful Rawsthorne is to employ the different registers of the instruments for expressive effect—for instance, the Poco Lento's extremely intense use of high strings and woodwind for an anguished cry of bitterness. This concerto, despite the reservations about its close and the fact that it needs listeners to meet it halfway before it will reveal its secrets, is a most remarkable and resourceful work. It is surely significant that Rawsthorne took so much trouble over its revision, and that the changes were so substantial; he must have known that it was a work of special quality and have determined after the première that the potential of its ideas should be properly realized. It is this, too, that leads one to persevere in trying to understand the apparently unsatisfactory ending: after so much labour on his part, in a work where so much else has the quality of unstrained inevitability, one cannot escape the conclusion that it must be right, after all. Rawsthorne knew that the expansion of his musical language, with its potential for future development, needed particularly conscientious work to allow the subtle play of his instinctive imagination full and adequate expression.

The first performance after the première, and therefore the first to incorporate the revisions and give the work as we now know it, was not until January 1963, with Manoug Parikian, George Hurst, and the BBC Northern Orchestra (now the BBC Philharmonic) in Chester Cathedral. It therefore came during Rawsthorne's most fecund period, and despite the allurements of the new modernism, it is a surprise that it received little attention; possibly, while the newer works were beginning to be appreciated with some relish, his works from the mid-1950s were lumped together and relegated to a corner of critical attention.

Rawsthorne's last feature film was Charles Crichton's *Floods of Fear* (1958), a gripping if rather lurid melodrama set amid torrential floods. It gives little musical opportunity, since the characters and situations are fairly stereotyped, except for a good deal of turbulent flood music (water again!) which is accomplished and exciting. It is a pity that this relatively undistinguished, though highly atmospheric, film completed his work in features: it never allows the music to become part of the characters in the way some of the earlier ones had done. After this, he wrote for a few shorter films and for television up to 1965, but with the renewal of his energy in concert music in the Violin Sonata and Second Symphony, it was perhaps beneficial that his concentration was not so seriously disrupted by film work during this period in the way it must have been during the 1950s. This must surely account for the disappointing nature of the Overture *Hallé*, written for the 1958 centenary of the Hallé Orchestra and first performed by the orchestra with Sir John Barbirolli in February 1958. Rawsthorne's original title was 'Prelude for Orchestra', to which Barbirolli objected (with good reason). He eventually accepted the inevitable, and in a letter to Alan Frank (14 January 1958) wrote: 'Well, well, I would settle for "Overture: Hallé". I only thought that my piece is a little less formal than the word "Overture" now suggests. The title will also be confused with the town in Saxony, of ancient traditions, and will doubtless be construed as a tribute to Gen. Goering.'

It is a curiously unsatisfying work, with a lengthy slow section after two false starts (a device familiar from *Cortèges*) that hints at the desire to work on a larger canvas. The main body of the piece is quick, however. Unfortunately, with the exception of a dainty and balletic third subject, the main themes are undistinguished reworkings of Rawsthorne style rather than freshly minted tunes, and the various treatments of them are fairly pedestrian—though one section, combining the three themes after the manner of one of Barbirolli's favourite repertoire pieces (Wagner's overture to *Die Meistersinger*), is more imaginative, and just before the close there is an intriguing passage in which the trombones, rising by step, push the tonality of the chords above them similarly upwards by step, a procedure akin to that found in a number of Beethoven's works (and, in more recent years, in Robert Simpson's symphonies and quartets). The final C major cadence, however, is thoroughly unconvincing, and the lugubrious nature of the lengthy slow section is not completely dispelled by the rather automatic high jinks following it. In short, it is a work that seems unsure of its purpose, obeying without conviction the dictates of its official *raison d'être* (a tribute) without following through its inner inclination to explore a more serious, even intellectual arena. It is strange that so indeterminate, almost hesitant a work should immediately precede the completion of one of Rawsthorne's greatest works, the Violin Sonata, and a new creative period in which much of his richest and most rewarding music was produced.

7

RENEWAL (1958–63)

IN his 1962 radio interview with Malcolm Rayment, Rawsthorne said:

I think that the music of Walton is of very great importance . . . I cannot see the complaint of critics that he continues to write the same sort of things that he has written before because I can't see why he shouldn't. I cannot imagine, for example, Haydn sitting down to write his hundredth symphony and saying, now I really must look out that I haven't written this sort of thing in my ninety-ninth. It seems to me rather an impoverished sort of critical view.

He warmed to the critical theme: 'I think they frequently seem to treat music rather as though it were a new waistline. The critics are sort of Christian Diors of the profession, and they are very anxious that one should be right up to the minute . . . In fact, to join the avant-garde I should think perhaps you should have a stiff medical.' With his own Violin Sonata, completed in April 1958, Rawsthorne himself made a stylistic leap forward, a greater one, perhaps, than any his friend Walton made during his mature career. Michael Kennedy, in his *History of the Royal Manchester College of Music*, referred to a review he had written of a Rawsthorne 60th birthday concert at the college in 1965: 'In the violin sonata the hand of a master is everywhere apparent.'[1]

It was written for Josef Szigeti, though there is no record of his having ever played it. Indeed, J. O. Ward, of the New York OUP office, wrote to Alan Frank on 30 January 1959, apropos the interest Joseph Fuchs was showing in the work, 'I agree very strongly with you that it is pointless to hold out for Szigeti (I think I told you that his proposal is for us to arrange and finance a recital!)'. It is shocking to find that, even in April 1958, Szigeti had no agent (though one gathers his playing was not what it had been) and was trying to fix concerts for himself. He was somewhat miffed to find that the first performance had taken place during 1959 in a BBC studio broadcast by Manoug Parikian and Lamar Crowson (who soon recorded it on long-playing record for Argo), though as Alan Frank pointed out when advising Rawsthorne how to respond to a letter from Szigeti, 'since the work has been

---

[1] (Manchester, 1971), 162.

published for some time, there is no means of preventing a public performance anywhere'.[2]

There is hardly a richer or more complex work in Rawsthorne's output, yet the surface of the music is elegance personified, except for some rough humour in the Scherzo. The four movements are linked by common material, essentially a discussion between D minor/major and E flat minor (F♯, or G♭, being a pivot between D major and E flat minor). This argument affects every aspect of the work, harmony, tonality, and melody. It appears in the first bar as a clash of harmonies in the piano, building up a chord with a phrase that ends with a fourth (B♭-E♭) and a falling third (E♭-C), the latter being an especially important melodic ingredient in the work. The answering violin phrase outlines, with unusual octave displacements, a cluster of semitones (A, B♭, B♮, C); this is another feature of the work's invention but is also linked to the basic harmonic argument (the key-clash contains D, E flat, F, and F sharp, so that of that group of semitones only the E is missing), and it also ends with the falling minor third (C-A) (Ex. 7.1(a)). The second phrase of the opening extends the ideas a fraction, pushing the last piano note from C down to C♭ and allowing violin and piano both to imply that the fourths will be used lyrically as the work progresses. The piano part in bar 7 is an inversion of the B♭-E♭-C figure from bar 1, while the violin's downward whole-tone phrase allows the G♭ to force the piano's F downwards in the manner of a baroque suspension. The final violin phrase of the introduction clearly shows that the Scotch snap is more of a Hungarian snap, with a Bartókian phrase presumably in tribute to Szigeti's Hungarian heritage. The Allegro non troppo itself then commences with a variation of the opening piano figure, treated melodically and in the same key to make the derivation immediately apparent, though after two bars Rawsthorne starts to move away. Characteristically, he develops this material as the first section progresses, along with a subsidiary theme in B based more straightforwardly on major/minor false relations, so that when an apparent second subject appears (Ex. 7.1(b)) it is the sound of a sonorous G-string timbre and the use of the piano harmonies in a more colouristic way, rather than the tune itself (initiated by a variation of the two opening piano phrases), which gives it the character of a new idea. Throughout the movement there are innumerable little melodic phrases, derived directly or indirectly from the main cells, which are instantly memorable, while the final climax is built up through a most exciting crescendo on the piano. The movement closes with a recapitulation of the introduction, extended by a bar to reiterate quietly the crucial D minor/E flat minor harmony.

---

[2] Letter, 2 Sept. 1959.

The importance of the semitone is emphasized by the Allegretto second movement, a hauntingly beautiful, ghostly waltz, in which the instruments enter in the opposite order from the first movement. The violin enters with a sad, circling melody moving over its first phrase from A♯ down to A (and back

Ex. 7.1. Violin Sonata, first movement: (*a*) opening; (*b*) from 2 bars before letter D

(*a*)

Ex. 7.1. *Continued*

(*b*)

from A to B♭ at the end of the second phrase), after which the piano's descending decoration shifts from D minor to C sharp; one calls it D minor rather than the F minor/major suggested by the first few notes simply because the D minor chord from the end of the first movement is still reverberating in our imagination (Ex. 7.2(*a*)). Formally this is a free rondo, with the semitonal relationships clarified when the last appearance of the ritornello theme is outlined in augmentation before it resumes its initial motion (Ex. 7.2(*b*)). The tonality ranges widely, but it is D minor (with important use of keys a semitone either side of it, and its subdominant, G minor, and dominant, A minor) that forms the tonic; the final phrase discreetly reminds one of E flat minor, the piano right hand closing on a B♭ (Ex. 7.2(*c*)). The texture of the music is delicate, reticent, even fragmentary at times, with the violin muted throughout to emphasize the veiled sadness. There are moments of passion, but the muted violin keeps them within expressive bounds. It is an extraordinarily original piece, composed, like the first movement, with the utmost economy of means yet with amazing richness of melodic and colouristic detail.

In the first movement, Rawsthorne juxtaposes triplets in the piano with quadruplets on violin. The third movement, a Toccata aptly marked 'Allegro di bravura' (Compact Disc, track 13), exploits this argument still further, with

Ex. 7.2. Violin Sonata, second movement: (*a*) opening; (*b*) from letter E; (*c*) ending

(*a*)

(*b*)

(*c*)

the main section of another rondo-like structure characterized by a triplet tune in the violin (reminiscent of the finale of Prokofiev's Second Violin Concerto) over a torrent of semiquavers in the piano right hand, the whole supported and given immense exuberance by a polka accompaniment in the left hand (Ex. 7.3(*a*)). The instruments exchange these ideas in varying ways, often retaining the rhythmic conflict, as the Toccata progresses. A swaggering second subject, sounding like a new theme, turns out to be a variation of the violin's opening triplet tune expressed in the polka rhythm, a typical example of Rawsthorne's technique of utilizing accompanying figures to inspire thematic material. The first movement is again recalled with a powerful restatement of the sonata's opening piano and violin phrases (Ex. 7.3(*b*)) before the main theme returns to close the Toccata in a burst of fireworks, including two brief cadenza-like flourishes for the violin above sustained piano chords and a final brilliant scale, simultaneously D major (descending) in the piano and E flat major (ascending, finishing on a D) in the violin. These major scales are symptomatic of a generally greater exploitation of major-key implications in this movement compared with the others.

Ex. 7.3. Violin Sonata, third movement: (*a*) bars 8–12; (*b*) from letter E

(*a*)

(*b*)

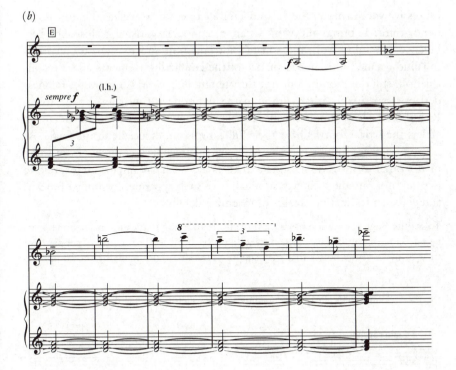

After this scintillating and exhilarating scherzo, which is extremely virtuosic for both players, the final Epilogue (Adagio rapsodico) provides a haven of peace and tranquillity. The opening two bars (Ex. 7.4(*a*)) outline the work's first piano flourish, using both instruments (the violin taking the more melodic fragments, the piano reducing the D minor/E flat minor to an impressionistic wash of colour). The central part of the Epilogue is devoted to a serenely lyrical violin tune, accompanied by restless but subdued harmonic shiftings in the piano (Ex. 7.4(*b*)). The theme is the fullest expression of the melodic use of the interval of a fourth, always implicit as an integral part of the work from the start but until this point not allowed to flower in its own right. It is also a melody clearly showing a new range of resources in Rawsthorne's lyrical armoury: such a wide-ranging tune using such a clear diatonic style and such a wide variety of intervals is unlike anything that came from his pen even ten years earlier. The final section is an expansion of the sonata's introduction, closing with a lovely reminder that D is the foundation of the work, E flat minor its inseparable companion (Ex. 7.4(*c*)), and joining them by using D major and the F♯/G♭ they have in common. This closing line utilizes a rising phrase from E♭ to G♭ that was first seen as a new item in Rawsthorne's

expressive vocabulary in the Second Violin Concerto, as well as the now rising
minor third. It brings the work to an exceptionally satisfying close, the turbulence stemming from the sonata's introduction and its dramatic clash of
tonalities calmed into an acceptance of the conflicting elements and a recon-
ciliation, still questioning but not threatening. The work's expressive richness
derives from the fact that, although the semitone is the main driving force,
Rawsthorne allows simple tonality equal prominence where needed, and above
all lets the lyrical fourths have their full expression, especially in the finale. As
a result, is never sounds constricted by narrow technical confines. I can think
of no other British violin sonata that essays such an important expressive
journey, nor one that achieves so much with such apparent economy of means
and yet such fascinating wealth of inventive detail.

To me the English tradition has been broken . . . In trying to pick up this national heritage I think that in certain cases mistakes have been made. That is to say people have
tried to make vague noises that they suppose resemble those made by the composers

Ex. 7.4. Violin Sonata, finale: (*a*) opening; (*b*) from letter B; (*c*) ending

(*a*)

(b)

Pochiss. più mosso, quasi Adagietto ♩ = 58

(c)

of the 17th and earlier centuries. To me their spirit involves a good deal of cosmopolitanism and certainly a great deal of adventure and that I think is the sort of thing that has been seized upon by Tippett for example, a composer whom I greatly admire, rather more than the followers of the folkey business.[3]

This remark is particularly interesting, coming as it did at the time when he was making his closest connection to the English vocal-choral tradition, in *Carmen vitale* for soprano, chorus, and orchestra (1963) and the *Medieval Diptych* for baritone and orchestra, written the previous year. There were strong signs of this forthcoming *rapprochement* in the Second Symphony (1959), commissioned by the Feeney Trust for the City of Birmingham Symphony Orchestra, who gave the first performance under Meredith Davies in September 1959. April Cantelo was the soprano soloist in the last movement, a setting of a poem by Henry Howard, Earl of Surrey (1516–47) concerned with the coming of spring. Rawsthorne's literary tastes were wide, but he had always shown a fondness from his earliest days for English pastoral poetry, and this choice was entirely characteristic.

The symphony exploits a dual tonality as does the Violin Sonata, but this time the key-centres are a major third (or diminished fourth) apart, being E and A flat. The very fact that this sound is at the heart of the work implies not only a diatonic basis for the music, but also a sense of major-key dominance which, if not carried through rigorously, does at least colour the sound of the work and give it an open, lyrical warmth far removed from the turbulence of the First Symphony. It does not try to tackle the issues raised by the earlier work, but instead forms an affectionate homage by the composer to the countryside in which he now, so happily, lived, and to the changing seasons. It is hardly programme music, even if the finale is a song—but neither, as Peter Evans puts it in his article on the composer in *The New Grove* (fortunately Rawsthorne had a more sympathetic commentator this time), is there any 'relapse into an amorphous modal rhapsodizing', even if some of the material is distinctly folk-like. This last is especially true of the third movement, a 'Country Dance' based on an extremely cheeky theme (already quoted as Ex. 3.1(*c*)) accompanied by bitonal harmonies.

Curiously enough, Colin Mason, who had earlier proved so unsympathetic, had by this time apparently found a way of appreciating Rawsthorne's music. He had been full of praise for the Violin Sonata, and now, in his review of the first performance of the Second Symphony (*Guardian*), he was exceptionally positive about the new work. He even liked the 'Country Dance': 'the popular

[3] BBC radio interview with Malcolm Rayment for series 'The Composer Speaks', recorded 24 May 1962.

hit of the work—rather like the last movement in the Second Piano Concerto, only better. It is a rondo, with a witty, subtly made, and irresistibly catchy tune that is probably Rawsthorne's most brilliantly musical invention ever.' The movement has, alas, not so far made the work popular (though there have been a number of performances, including an American première in New York in 1962 conducted by John Barnett with the National Orchestral Association, the Russian performances conducted by the composer, and two recordings), but one hopes a time will come when people are ready to appreciate its gracious simplicity. The 'Country Dance' moves towards a full statement of the tune only gradually, with fragments of it above shifting bitonal harmonies as if one is approaching the country fair from afar with the noises of revelry in the distance, and though the trio section is straightforward, the effortless deployment of canonic devices in both this and the central section of the equally straightforward slow second movement provides added richness. It should be noted that the bitonal harmonies at the start alternate between chords a third apart and chords a semitone apart: G flat-B flat, G-A flat, E flat-G, and G-A flat, all major. The revelry of the 'Country Dance' is at times genuinely comical; indeed, one is tempted to say that it has something in common with Shakespeare's rustics. At bottom, this scherzo is both humorous and *about* humour. The English, as is well known (they often say so themselves), are renowned for their sense of humour, but when it comes to music they seem strangely reluctant to laugh—yet this movement is, occasionally, an invitation to laugh. Its placing, as the third movement, is precisely judged, which makes it all the more surprising that Rawsthorne originally envisaged it as the start of the work.

The slow second movement is ternary, though with an introduction that turns out to be an initial part of the first subject group and not merely a preface, and a middle section in which a lugubriously jog-trotting tune (another, slower country dance, perhaps) hovering between A minor and A major is stated three times, once as a single line, once in two-part canon, and finally, most forcefully, in three-part canon. As Mason wrote, this central section 'is retrospectively lit up and given new interest by the beautifully made return to the earlier material', the music turning a corner, as it were, and using the intensity built up in the trio section by leading naturally into a dramatic restatement of the recitative-like main theme. The most important elements in the main theme, which is really a group of cells (see Ex. 7.6(*a*) below), are the opening horn cantilena, leading to a chord of open fifths and a hovering semitonal figure wavering between A minor and major, and the two-part recitative on flute, oboe, and first and second violins. The open-fifth harmony is an important extension of Rawsthorne's liking for fifths to underpin his chromatic style, a method he used increasingly during the 1950s to anchor the shifting tonalities above and make the progress of the music easier to assimilate. All this material exists, either directly or in embryo, in the very opening of the first movement (Ex. 7.5): the semitonal hovering (violins), the bitonal chord combining E minor and A flat major (remembering that A flat and E *major* would have G♯, or A♭, as the pivotal note in common), or, in the first subject itself, the close relationship between the wonderfully lyrical tune's upward swing and

Ex. 7.5. Second Symphony (*Pastoral*), first movement, bars 1–16

the opening of the slow movement's horn cantilena. Note also the subtle, shifting phrase structure, never quite predictable but always satisfying, as well as the fact that the first phrase of the melody contains the triads of E minor, A flat major (spelt as G sharp), and B major, a device which permeates the harmonic colouring of the movement and indeed affects the whole work.

This Allegro piacevole is full of delightful invention. The first subject group moves almost at once to a second phase (at letter A) exploiting the whole-tone scale and devoted largely to thirds and sixths (nearly always major thirds, one notices); this again is beautifully judged so that the little shifts in the phrase-lengths sustain the attention, and the moments of dramatic power or intellectual play (such as further use of canons) are integrated into the overall context without exploding beyond its boundaries. The sonata-form structure is handled imaginatively, this time doing away with a definite second subject. For once, however, there is a fairly extensive development, starting after a climax and a resounding horn phrase in F sharp (half-way between E and A flat), at the point where one would normally expect a second subject to start. The main material is reduced merely to hesitant fragments—deconstructed, almost, since it is reduced to its component parts (chords, fragments of melody, rhapsodic woodwind solos, and so on)—before the development proper manages to resume the onward momentum. The movement ends simply, but most beautifully, with an E major chord on low strings, and three A flat major horn chords quietly dissenting.

It is the finale that presents the most unconventional idea, a slow epilogue setting the poem by Henry Howard. Rawsthorne's manuscript programme note describes it thus:

It is derived from the material of the first movement, on which it meditates with the help of a soprano . . . a setting of a poem by Henry Howard . . . which he calls 'Description of Spring, Wherein each thing renews, save only the Lover.' However, it was not this melancholy state of affairs which caused me to think that the poem would make a suitable conclusion to my composition. It was the beautiful alliterative verse, the close observation, and the general expression of the pleasures of life in the country.

However, there is a melancholy aspect to it; the last lines of the poem reveal an underlying, almost Hardyesque ambiguity:

> And thus I see among these pleasant things
> Each care decays, and yet my sorrow springs.

Rawsthorne, with the subtle mix of emotions he could convey and the delicacy of his utterance, was born to set this poem, which proves the ideal choice for a reflective finale to a work such as this. Colin Mason was full of praise: 'it works as a convincing finale by sheer force of surprise as much as by any demonstrable musical relationship to what has been heard before. It is a self-contained and beautifully shaped song (with a da capo characteristically con-densed to a few bars) that could easily have a successful separate existence, and with a piano accompaniment will probably do so' (a pious hope that remains unfulfilled). The scoring is exceptionally delicate, quite often with just a solo oboe or trumpet in duet with the voice, and the song, delightfully subtle in its word-setting (see Ex. 7.6(*b*)), is framed by the silvery chords with which the symphony began (this time with E major rather than minor). The final cadence (E major with the gently dissenting A flat major from the horns, as at the close of the Allegro piacevole, leaving the E major alone at the last) (see Ex. 9.7 below) has a rare and magical autumnal beauty. In his expression of Arcadian peace and self-fulfilment, Rawsthorne is nevertheless aware of the shadows over Arcadia and the inexorable progress of time.

Ex. 7.6. Second Symphony (*Pastoral*): (*a*) second movement, bars 1–11; (*b*) finale, from 3rd bar of letter B

(*a*)

(*b*)

In his manuscript programme note, Rawsthorne revealed that

I have many doubts as to whether this piece is really a symphony, and at one time I decided . . . to call it a 'Symphonic Suite'. It is, I think, symphonic in style, but perhaps has not quite the right shape for a symphony. After being a nuisance to my publishers and others while considering the matter, I decided to call it a 'Pastoral Symphony' . . . it is good to try to find a title from which the listener can form some idea of the kind of thing which he is about to hear.

Robert Simpson's requirement for a true symphony was that it should 'travel'. Rawsthorne's *Pastoral* does not really travel anywhere; rather, it contemplates four abstract scenes of pastoral inspiration. Yet the manipulation of the material is undeniably symphonic, and to call it merely a 'Symphonic Suite' would have done gross injustice to its innate qualities of unity and development. Above all, the shape *is* satisfying in a thoroughly symphonic way: there is a sense that, when the opening chords return at the end, they have somehow been changed by the various things they have observed or caused. There is much below the surface, as in all Rawsthorne's best works: one might cite the undercurrents beneath the apparently calm, lazy surface of Debussy's *Prélude à l'après-midi d'un faune* as a parallel. It is dangerous to overstate the case, especially for such an apparently modest work as this, but it has lasting qualities, as well as an expressive, reflective value for the listener prepared to forgo prejudice. The symphony startled listeners at the time, largely because of received opinions about the composer to which the anonymous reviewer in *The Times* gave expression (29 September 1959): 'Alan Rawsthorne, until now, has been the most urban of English composers . . . [this symphony] unexpectedly exhales the calm and invigoration of pastoral life.' The same reviewer also noted that the work has 'a sincerity that strikes below the surface of the emotions to fundamental, intense passion'. The pastorality is different from that of Vaughan Williams in his *Pastoral Symphony* (which uses a pastoral atmosphere to create a kind of war requiem), and closer perhaps to that of Beethoven (an expression of feeling rather than a tone-painting). Just as this work was brought to public life, William Glock, at the BBC, was initiating a revolution in our musical life; a work like this, as delicate as a flower, was hardly likely to flourish under the new modernist regime. Fortunately, Rawsthorne had enough character and force of personality to be able to play his part in this tougher compositional world (with works like the Quintet for piano and wind and the astonishing Third Symphony) without either abandoning his own compositional identity or losing the added expressive riches which the *Pastoral Symphony* and Violin Sonata had brought to his music.

Following the *Pastoral Symphony*, orchestral music continued to be a regular feature of Rawsthorne's output. *Improvisations on a Theme by Constant Lambert* (1960) was commissioned for the Northern Sinfonia, with whose conductor Michael Hall they gave the first performance in January 1961. The scoring is for roughly classical orchestra (double woodwind, four horns, two trumpets, timpani, and strings), and the theme upon which it is based derives from the opening of Lambert's last work, the ballet *Tiresias*, which Rawsthorne, among others, had helped to orchestrate; the failure of the ballet was a last, devastating blow to the ailing Lambert. The dedication of *Improvisations* is to Isabel, Constant's widow and now Alan's wife. *Improvisations* is a good title: this is too informal, even rhapsodic, to be a set of variations. It was extremely unusual for Rawsthorne to base one work on a theme by someone else: not since the 1936 *Studies on a Theme by Bach* for string trio had he done so.

The *Pastoral Symphony* is echoed by some of the invention. After a brief, forceful prefatory Allegro risoluto announcing the theme (a series of seven notes, with the fourth, third, and second then repeated to complete a ten-note phrase), the music slows to a Poco lento and an almost static section in which the opening chord, built in serial fashion out of the notes of the theme, audibly relates to the silvery world of the symphony's first chord, though this time there is a darker, gloomier atmosphere. Serial terminology is even used in Rawsthorne's programme note: referring to a violin solo in this improvisation, he says it 'plays a phrase which is a retrograde (or backward) version of the seven notes of the theme. This will supply the material for section five.' Clearly, there are to be his customary close relationships between the various transformations of the theme, as well as hints of a move towards an acceptance of serial methods; the latter looks forward to the Quintet for piano and wind and, even more, to the Third Symphony, which adopt something of these methods quite consciously but entirely idiosyncratically. There is nothing dogmatic or automatic about the way he comes to use them. Equally, his is a usage quite different from that of Walton, Britten, or Shostakovich. Rawsthorne used serial methods, as he had used a more open diatonicism in the Second Symphony, to expand his language.

Though much of the work employs devices familiar from elsewhere, there are some powerful moments. Two such occur in the third and fourth improvisations. In the third, a running passage in the cellos is provided with a tune of distinctly march-like tread above it, which is allowed to reach a vigorous climax. This section is cut short, the fourth intruding with a more passionate intensity. The ending of *Improvisations* employs, as in the *Pastoral Symphony*, A flat major horn chords over the tonic major harmony, C in the case of this newer work, but it seems a gesture placed deliberately rather than arising naturally out of the content of the music. The final section itself, to be sure, is a lovely altered reprise of the first Poco lento, but it cannot carry the whole work, and nor do the slow sections, for all their beauty. This is a likeable work, but its gestures sometimes run out of steam. It is as if the contrast between the large-scale nature of some of the ideas and the small scale of the orchestra and scope of the work, lasting only some twelve minutes or so, were impossible to reconcile.

Improvisations was well received at the time, and achieved a recording in the USA by Boris Brott and the Northern Sinfonia, who also recorded the next, more completely successful, work for chamber orchestra, the Divertimento of

1962. This is one of the Rawsthorne's happiest orchestral inspirations. Harry Blech and his London Mozart Players (for whom it was written) used it as standard repertoire on a number of tours including one of Germany, and it received performances by numerous orchestras in Britain and abroad as well as two recordings. Its success lies in the seriousness of purpose with which Rawsthorne tackles such an amiable task as writing a present for a friend from student days (Blech). Both first and last movements (a Rondo and Jig respectively) have sombre episodes, that in the Rondo being a particularly characteristic example of a new kind of almost static dependence on narrow harmonic movement back and forth (Ex. 7.7(*a*)) above which fragments of melody float somewhat indeterminately. It contrasts with the utterly delightful, sunny lyricism of the main tune, and with the strenuous contrapuntal treatment of a relatively new, striding theme in a later episode, where toughness of thought comes over without distracting from the essentially good-natured warmth of the Rondo as a whole. The strenuousness of some of the first movement is echoed in the final Jig, also (very roughly) a rondo form, in which lively string writing is driven hard by upward-thrusting horn and woodwind phrases. This is a cousin, but a much more forceful, even aggressive one, to the Second Symphony's 'Country Dance', and the main theme itself is made out of a series of short phrases rather than a single tune. The simplicity is in the effect, which is easy to follow, rather than in the matter, which is full of sly rhythmic disruptions, especially the contrast between 6/8 and 3/4. The high spirits return, after a reflective episode, with a final flourish. Both outer movements end with scales in contrary motion, rather more satisfactorily in the Jig, a touch mundanely at the end of the Rondo, but this is the only slight blot on an otherwise splendidly alert work, whose heart lies in the touching Lullaby forming the central movement. The tenderness of its bitonal harmony and hesitant lyricism, is shown in Ex. 7.7(*b*), the third phase of the main theme, where the string ostinato, rotating chords of A–E–B and C major, provides a touching background for the oboe's plaintive line, the use of the two oboes at the end being particularly effective. Rawsthorne's instrumentation is, as always, acutely sensitive to the timbre of the instruments in each register: his use of solo string trio (two violins and cello) to reintroduce the main theme in the Rondo for one of the ritornello sections is particularly effective, and oboe and horn solos are perfectly judged. The divertimento is, in its own way, a little masterpiece, whose success is hardly surprising. It has a delightful combination of effortless charm, high intellectual endeavour, and, above all, splendid tunes.

There was no commission fee for the divertimento, which was written purely as a favour, but a complaint was made about having to pay hire fees for the

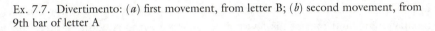

Ex. 7.7. Divertimento: (*a*) first movement, from letter B; (*b*) second movement, from 9th bar of letter A

orchestral material. Rawsthorne wrote, wrily, to Alan Frank on 17 March 1962: 'As to the £3.15.0 for hiring the parts—well, I should think he can afford it, to help keep his poor old friend off the dole . . . I should just send in the bill as usual . . . , and let him rejoice that the score does not include eight horns and a chorus.' Needless to say, this debate had no effect on their great friendship: Blech continued to programme the divertimento, and in 1976 took the *Concertante pastorale* on a tour of Germany. Rawsthorne's substantial flow of performances and recordings in Britain and abroad enabled him to earn his keep, but he was never well off and continued to support Isabel and himself by composing incidental music from time to time, writing some for documentary films and one of his few mature scores for the straight theatre, the Stratford production of *Hamlet*. During the period 1959–61, however, there was a relative paucity of concert works, perhaps because of his physical state. Having achieved domestic happiness, he was beginning once again to suffer ill health due to his drinking, and in 1961, shortly after the Cheltenham Festival première of the Concerto for Ten Instruments commissioned by the festival, he once again fell seriously ill with a haemorrhage.

Referring to Rawsthorne's illnesses, Gordon Green wrote that they were

related to the character of the man. He loved people. Rich and poor, young and old, wise and foolish, saint and sinner—all found in him vast reserves of admiration, geniality, sympathy or compassion to meet their needs. He was broad-minded in the sense of all-embracing, a man with whom one could both share a triumph and confess disgrace . . . the mature man was entirely devoid of class-consciousnesss. He was naturally drawn to the English pub; his misfortune was that he could never really get drunk. When companions realized that they had taken more than enough he was not even mildly lit up, and inevitably he drank more than he should. Though he had an extraordinary capacity for remaining sober, this was, of course, not matched by an equal capacity for resisting the physical effects of alcohol.[4]

After the illness of 1961,

he was told that he must forgo alcohol and he abstained for three years. When, after those three years, he was told he might drink wine he confined his drinking to wine for the rest of his life, doubtless taking more of it than was wise, for, good patient though he might be, it was not in his nature to play the timid invalid; within limits, he preferred to live his life and take his punishment.[5]

Undoubtedly, the three-year abstinence gave Rawsthorne renewed creative energy, but his imagination had already been fired up again by the Violin Sonata in 1958, and he had then entered the richest and most productive decade of his life. Isabel herself, of course, was a heavy drinker, and it cannot have been easy for Rawsthorne to abjure liquor in those circumstances, though he had always been able to draw on reserves of quiet determination. There is no doubt that, despite spectacular rows, the couple were exceptionally happy together. When Isabel was on an extended trip to Africa (which gave a new richness and variety to her paintings), he wrote to her in Nigeria (19 February 1961): 'Dearest Girl—I love you to distraction. I think of you all the time', closing the letter 'to you I send—well, words fail. Immer noch dein [an

[4] 'Alan Rawsthorne—2 (Brief Record of a Friendship)', *Composer*, 43 (spring 1972).
[5] Ibid.

emphatic version of "still yours", and probably a quotation]'. He also made sure that his closest friends were well aware of their mutual devotion, assuring them that he had never been so happy. This emotional security must have been a major factor in enabling him to renew his career to such purpose, and to produce such a magnificent stream of works in this period.

The Concerto for Ten Instruments (1961) is an assured and even powerful ensemble work. Its four movements are particularly notable for the resourceful handling of the instruments, a wind quintet plus string quintet including double bass, contrasting almost orchestral tutti passages against solos, sometimes with accompaniment, sometimes in counterpoint. In the final Lento sostenuto, the crux of the argument is presented first by woodwind quartet (thus omitting the horn) and then by string quartet (omitting the double bass), an intriguing way of reaching and then quitting the final resolution of the ideas. Tonally the work is unusual for its emphasis on B flat as the first movement's tonic followed by C, G, and, for the epilogue, B flat once again, though this time it is far from clearly defined, and the work closes with a chord of C minor and B flat major combined (triads already contained in the Preludio's opening violin solo and the chord derived from it) but inflected by a stopped horn phrase closing with the E♮ that is left hanging in the air (Ex. 7.8(c)). It is as if he wanted to deconstruct not simply the musical material itself but the essential tonality, which he seems to emphasize quite heavily in the Preludio so that its return at the start of the epilogue can lead to a more meaningful questioning at the end.

The opening Preludio starts with neo-classical alertness, emphasizing that the title ' Concerto', in the old concertante sense, signifies a solo spotlight on the instruments as the music progresses (Ex. 7.8(a)). In the central section, where Rawsthorne is once again reducing the material to its bare bones, the influence of serial methods emerges in some unusually bold and prominent octave displacements. This is also true at the close of the Preludio, where he builds a chord from the notes of the opening violin solo in true serial fashion (Ex. 7.8(b)); this chord returns, pianissimo, to open the final Lento. The second movement, Andante poco doloroso, is substantial, with unusually long-breathed melodic lines and an equally unusual sustaining of accompanying harmonies for long periods. It has a beautiful central section in which the tune is stated in the cello and bass under mysterious, almost Holstian harmonic decoration, followed surprisingly by a completely new section marked by dotted rhythms à la French overture. The scherzo, Allegro molto ritmico, is driven by a repeated 2/4–5/8 rhythmic structure, with a trio again using dotted rhythms to produce a perky little march tune. There is nothing particularly

Ex. 7.8. Concerto for Ten Instruments: (*a*) Preludio, bars 1–3; (*b*) Preludio, last 5 bars; (*c*) finale, ending

(*a*)

(*b*)

(*c*)

unusual about this, except for a strange and mysterious interlude before the scherzo returns, but it is attractive, and beautifully scored. The concerto hovers on the verge of being among Rawsthorne's finest chamber works; in the last resort, it perhaps lacks the sheer memorability that would make it indispensable to the repertoire, but it is so musicianly, and so enjoyable, that it deserves the considerable success it has had, including a first American performance in Fredonia in 1964 and use as part of the score for a ballet, *Cage of God*, produced by the Cologne Ballet in 1971, by the Lausanne Municipal Ballet, and, in Britain, by Western Theatre Ballet (the Theme and Variations for two violins was also used for the ballet). Above all, it is the contrast between the mystery of the slow movements and the neo-classical freshness of the first movement that is most attractive.

In 1962, Rawsthorne suddenly began to pour out a succession of major works. Apart from the Divertimento, there are the *Medieval Diptych*, *Lament for a Sparrow*, and two chamber works, the Quintet for piano and wind instruments (completed early in 1963) and the Piano Trio. The last was commissioned by the City of London Festival for the Menuhin–Cassadó–Kentner Trio and originally (rather clumsily) entitled *Concertante a tre*; Rawsthorne wisely revised the title before releasing the work. The original title gives a clue to the nature of the piece. Both this and its predecessor, the Concerto for Ten Instruments, deal with similar matters of balance and instrumental relationship. 'Concertante' had always, of course, been a favourite concept: the baroque concerto grosso is never far from his thoughts, even in full orchestral works. In the Concerto for Ten Instruments, the contrast between the string and wind groups is so clear that he could allow the exploitation of soloistic and/or group spotlights to develop the material. In the Piano Trio, there is a different challenge. While the title indicates precisely what the piece is, it no longer suggests the concertante style of which there remains a vestige, through the contrast of piano material with string music. They are either separated or allowed to sound simultaneously and balance against each other, and there is much contrast between strong tutti passages (the main theme itself, for example, announced in powerful unison octaves) and more soloistic writing.

Played without a break, the trio falls into three movements, Introduction, Capriccio, and Theme and Variations, though the Capriccio is also particularly dependent on variation techniques to form the various thematic elements. The trio is not entirely convincing: the quiet ending, though undeniably beautiful, is a bit too pat. Furthermore, many of the devices Rawsthorne uses are so familiar that they seem almost to have been assembled from ready-made parts, like a kind of Rawsthorne do-it-yourself composition kit. One says 'almost', for there is still something immensely attractive about the ideas, the strength with which they are worked, and the vigour of the characterization. The Introduction, for instance, is memorably bleak, especially once the piano has reached the bass clef, suggesting the kind of desolation that has been much imitated by Shostakovich's successors. The main theme of the Capriccio is announced brusquely after the Introduction has paused on a multi-tonal piano chord (Ex.

7.9(*a*)) which recurs at the very end of the work as a rising violin line (Ex. 7.10(*b*) below). Rawsthorne's own programme notes reveal that 'much of the music is based on a phrase of six notes, with its inversion. This is used to fashion both melody and harmony, in various manipulations, and is often only hinted at or present merely by implication.' It is also anticipated embryonically at the very start of the trio: the strings move outwards from their third note (C♯) to an open fifth, A–E (the first two notes), with the piano introducing a kind of incipient commentary, a four-note scale introducing another melodic element that is also to play a substantial part in the work's progress. The Capriccio itself, after the decisive announcement of the work's head-motif, pursues a path of highly contrasting sections, some dominated by an infectious 5/8 rhythm building considerable excitement, some full of romantic bravura, notably in piano solos looking back to the solo writing of the Second Piano Concerto in keyboard style, and some more severe. There is, for instance, a passage for the two strings alone of almost purely harmonic nature, another deconstruction, as it were, of the music's basic material down to one chordal process, elongated into a whole section of its own (at which point it has become clear that this movement is more like a set of variations than the sonata-rondo it seemed

Ex. 7.9. Piano Trio: (*a*) from 5 bars before letter B (*b*) Capriccio, from letter K

(*b*)

to be). Immediately after this, the cello begins a fugue, using complex cross-rhythms; the piano entry, also moving across the basic 4/4 metre, makes performance very tricky. There is an almost Jacobean fantasy about the metrical dislocations and canonic devices at this point: the music does not sound in the least like pastiche, nor indeed does it reveal any connection in terms of the sound, but the technique is a distinct link with English music of a much earlier period (Ex. 7.9(*b*)).

The join to the Theme and Variations is provided by hesitant string passages and piano interruptions, first of the main theme and then (by an anticipation) of the Theme. Once the strings have moved from C♯ to an open fifth A–E (as at the start of the trio), the piano is able to announce the Theme, in simple octaves. This was a surprise to Rawsthornians at the time, since such a folk-like, almost medieval tune was unlike virtually anything else in his previous output, but its antecedents exist in tiny phrases in earlier pieces, as well as in his lifelong liking for whole-tone phrases (Ex. 7.10(*a*)). The entry of this tune, so simple and diatonic after the chromatic and rhythmic high jinks of the Capriccio, is singularly moving, as if another world had suddenly opened up magically in front of one's eyes. The shifting metre creates an uneasy undertone and, at the same time, emphasizes the almost plainchant-like phraseology. It prepares the way significantly for the medieval-inspired vocal works that were to come. The variations themselves are fairly conventional, though highly enjoyable, culminating in a vigorously contrapuntal exercise followed by a gradual descent to the work's coda. The move from C♯ to A–E at the opening clearly outlines the A major tonality of the work, so this is a logical harmony on which to end (Ex. 7.10(*b*)), coloured as it is by the subtly different piano chords before the rising violin line, and by the use of the falling Neapolitan second (B♭), a typical device for arriving cadentially at the final tonic chord. Rawsthorne's own suggestion that these might be called meditations instead of variations is significant, revealing the freedom with which he approached the working of the material: indeed, the variations, running smoothly into one another until the sudden arrival at the busy counterpoint of the Allegro con brio, are more seamless and less contrasted than the various episodes in the Capriccio. Piano trios are reputedly difficult to write, and certainly there are not so many good ones that a work of this quality should be ignored. Nor, it is fair to say, has it been completely neglected: performances took place in Berlin and elsewhere soon after the first performance, and it continues to be performed from time to time.

In June 1962, the month before the Piano Trio was unveiled, *Lament for a Sparrow* received its first performance. It was commissioned by OUP, along with works by other OUP composers, and first performed by the Elizabethan Singers under Louis Halsey. It is a pity that, unlike Rawsthorne's later carol 'The Oxen' (written for the OUP printed collection *Carols of Today*), they did not record it, because it is a lovely, delicate setting for chorus and harp of Catullus's 'Lugete, O Veneres Cupidinesque', a lament on the death of the beloved's pet sparrow, imbued with a sense of loss and nostalgia perfectly suited to this aspect of Rawsthorne's musical character. Unlike the wonderful setting of Skelton's 'Lament for Philip Sparrow' in Vaughan Williams's *Five Tudor Portraits*, this does not assume the qualities of a universal requiem: it remains within a more modest, intimate world, and is a lament for the transitory nature of life on earth. Rawsthorne's orchestral harp writing had always been highly effective. Here, he displays an acute awareness of the harp's ability to convey immediately a particular, other-worldly atmosphere, never lapsing

Ex. 7.10. Piano Trio: (*a*) Theme and Variations, Theme (for piano); (*b*) conclusion

(*a*)

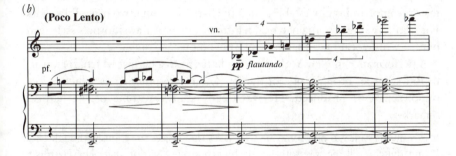

(*b*)

into conventional impressionistic devices. The deployment of the choir reflects his liking for concertante use of solos and tutti, with effective use of solo tenor, division of some of the parts, and, in particular, separation into female voices for one section followed by male voices for the descent into the shadows of death. The lamenting, too, is clear-eyed, given the natural melancholy of some of Rawsthorne's characteristic turns of phrase; there is nothing self-indulgent about it. Nor is there any pastiche, or any suggestion of medievalism or of deliberate archaism. The word-setting is delightful, subtle, and never over-pictorial: witness the setting of 'circumsiliens modo huc modo illuc | ad solam dominam usque pipiabat' ('hopping about, now this side, now that, and chirp-ing just to her alone') (Ex. 7.11). The harp part decorating 'circumsiliens' is not merely decorative, since the harmonic colouring given by the sharpened fourth (F) permeates the whole piece, as does the diatonic nature of the chords in the next two bars. The piece is rich both in block chordal writing and expres-sive contrapuntal work, and sustains a level of poised beauty from first bar to last, the final (Neapolitan-inflected) cadence from D flat to F, neither major nor minor in either case, being an especially satisfying resolution of the F major/minor ambiguity established in the harp's opening two bars of the work. Furthermore, the essentially lyrical nature of much of Rawsthorne's style leads him to write vocal lines that are both melodious and singable.

A performance in New York elicited a letter from a harpist which, forwarded to Rawsthorne, brought one of the few lengthy responses this reluctant cor-respondent ever produced. He was clearly stung by some of the harpist's remarks:

It is really very nice to find someone who takes the subject so seriously, though I fear I can't quite go all the way with him in his rapturous assertion that 'The Harp is to

Ex. 7.11. *Lament for a Sparrow*, from pp. 10–11

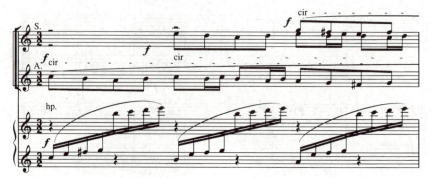

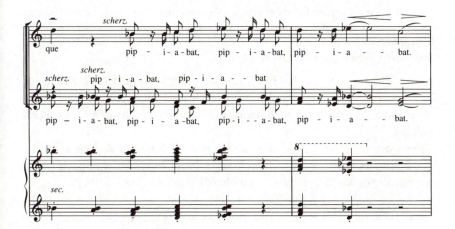

music What music is to Life.' Perhaps he means that, in the end, everything is a question of wire-pulling. He seems in some doubt as to when to stop the sound of his instrument. The general principle is that when I write notes I expect sounds, and when I write rests I expect silence, broken though it may be, in the case of harps, by the vicious kicks of the player crashing his gears in preparation for the next passage, or furiously tuning his upper strings.[6]

It was unlike him to be quite so acid—but it reveals just how sensitive he was about his own extremely professional approach to his craft, and any aspersions which might be cast against it. He goes on to address some of the technical questions with unanswerable logic and authority.

Lament for a Sparrow marked a return to vocal music (specifically, in this case, choral music) after a considerable gap following the little group of choral pieces composed during the mid-1950s. *Medieval Diptych*, for baritone and orchestra, is even more significant, being Rawsthorne's first substantial work for voice and orchestra since the early *The Enemy Speaks*. He chose to return to medieval texts for the first time since the lost Chamber Cantata of 1937, maintaining his tendency to choose either from living poets with whom he could work directly (Swingler, MacNeice, Rodgers) or from writers of a much earlier period with whom he felt a particularly close sympathy. The *Diptych* was commissioned by the BBC for the Proms, and first performed in August 1962 by Peter Glossop, with a long-standing and devoted Rawsthornian, Norman del Mar, conducting the BBC Symphony Orchestra. In his programme note, the composer states:

I have called this composition a 'Diptych' because the texts, particularly the first, are so pictorially evocative. Both are concerned with the Virgin Mary; the first as Mater Dolorosa, bewailing the tragedy of the dead Christ on her lap, and the second, in more cheerful vein, praising God for her existence. 'We must thank God for the Fall of Adam,' says this poem, 'since but for this event Mary would never have become Queen of Heaven, and that would be a pity'—a medieval way of looking on the bright side of things which is both attractive and touching.

At the close, after resounding, repeated cries from the baritone of 'Deo Gracias', there is an outburst of orchestral high jinks which vividly conveys what Rawsthorne later described as 'a certain ferocity in most medieval rejoicing'.[7]

The work is particularly significant for the use Rawsthorne makes of distinctly Schönbergian devices, though these have always been implicit in his own method of working anyway. Now there is a definite, and deliberate, incor-

---

[6] Letter to Alan Frank, 29 Jan. 1963.
[7] See his introduction to *Carmen vitale*, *Radio Times* (Oct. 1963), quoted in Ch. 8 below.

poration of some aspects of serial technique into his own vocabulary. The orchestral introduction not merely sets the mood of foreboding, but also introduces the eight-note tone-row for the first song (Ex. 7.12(*a*)). The first four notes, in cello solo with octave displacements, usually appear in the same order throughout the song; the second group of notes (Db-Eb-C-Bb) tend to be less rigidly handled, though the subsidiary theme they produce punctuates the work with a sobbing cry (whether quiet or loud) that acts as both an expressive device and a thematic link. This slow part of the introduction also introduces immediately the two main themes, in embryo, the second group of notes becoming important as a secondary subject (begun in bar 4), though it never flowers into life as a fully-fledged theme in its own right but acts more as an important comment from time to time. The only other material in the movement is a march-like tune which suddenly emerges as an orchestral interlude between the second and third of the three verses, leading to an eruptive, percussive climax (anticipating even more dramatic outbursts in the Third Symphony). Otherwise, all the melodic lines relate to this basic material, as do the

Ex. 7.12. *Medieval Diptych*: (*a*) bars 1–8; (*b*) first movement, from first vocal entry; (*c*) second movement, opening; (*d*) second movement, vocal entry

(*a*)

Ex. 7.12. *Continued*

(*b*)

Bar. solo
poco affret.

Più mosso

mf

Sud - den - ly   a - - fraid____   half

wa - king   half____   sleep - ing____

(*c*)

bn.,vc.   1   2   3   1   2   3   4   5   6   7   6

p

8   9   10   11   12   12   4   12

(*d*)

Bar. solo
p

A - dam lay i - bound - den,   boun-den in   a   bond;____   Four_ thou-sand

win - ter thought he not too   long,____   thought he not too   long;____

p

harmonies: bar 3, for instance, reveals that the harmony of two superimposed
major thirds stems directly from the first four notes of the theme, while the
first entry of the voice, setting the scene vocally after the orchestra has established the basic atmosphere of menace and dread, outlines the note-set directly
and clearly (Ex. 7.12(*b*)). The essential integrity of the material is very strong,
and is seldom diffused for long. The second movement also begins with a serial
idea, this time a real twelve-note row, with some repetition of the first four
notes and the sixth (Ex. 7.12(*c*)). Its relation to the ballad-like baritone entry
with 'Adam lay i-bounden' is clear (Ex. 7.12(*d*)), though this time the serial
element is less rigorously pursued than in the first song, the melodic develop-

ment being freer and less reliant on a close relationship with intervallic or tonal elements in the harmonies. The material is shared and developed between soloist and orchestra more equally than in the first song, though some ideas were exchanged there too. There are also occasional cross-references to the first movement (a phrase associated with the woman seated, 'dismayed', also occurs in the second song, for instance).

The structure of the work follows that of the words, relating the verbal refrains to musical phrases with the same purpose, though in one case in the first movement the orchestra takes what was previously a vocal line. There is a degree of imbalance in its proportions, which makes the second movement (at less than half the length of the first) not entirely satisfying as a peroration. Possibly Rawsthorne wanted a short quick section in the first movement's introduction not only to state the eight-note 'serial' theme most directly (which it does, in trombones) but also to link with the brassy and percussive conclusion of the second movement, using texture as the balancing device—but the prevailing atmosphere of the first song is so slow and dark (even extending to a quotation from the *Dies irae* on the word 'thwerting'), and the second so direct and folk-like, that the connection, if intended, does not communicate to the listener. For all that, it is a gripping work, with an unexpectedly direct dramatic power in both songs and a real sense of human sympathy.

The overall tonal scheme of the whole work is most interesting. Tim Mottershead maintains with much supporting evidence that the work is firmly rooted in E,[8] which makes its conclusion a semitone higher in F very surprising, both on paper and in performance. Taking the first movement alone, one has a strong sense that E underlies it, with A minor as a logical subordinate key-centre; others, of course, appear at various times, including touches of F and C. He points out, however, that 'the original four note cell will fit only into the scale of A harmonic minor', which suggests that an alternative view might be that E is a kind of gigantic, and repeated, dominant upbeat into A minor. Though the opening of the second song indicates E minor, the entry of the vocal line (also E minor) is accompanied by a strong suggestion of C major, shifting to a kind of C minor (7.12(*d*))—yet the vocal line persists in alternating between E minor and E flat minor. E becomes less fixed as a tonal centre as the song proceeds, with the vocal part ending emphatically in C after an A minor flourish, and F is touched upon quite significantly a couple of times during the movement. The choice of F to finish the work, therefore, is not quite so startling as it appears, since its dominant (C) has been increasingly

[8] 'Medieval Diptych', *The Creel*, 3/2 (spring 1995), 19–31.

marked during the work, and the relative minor of C (A minor) has been of such importance throughout. In addition, of course, the very opening chord (bar 3 of Ex. 7.12(*a*)) superimposes E major and F major; one recalls that Rawsthorne enjoys not only Neapolitan key-relationships, but also the semitonal slip upwards (as from a leading-note to a tonic), as well as semitonal slips downwards from the Neapolitan second to the tonic. One can also note that the subsidiary motif in bar 4 is, at this point, in B flat minor, the subdominant minor of F. Perhaps in the end the *Diptych* is a subtle play on tonality. If the final F major chord still sounds surprising, it must be because Rawsthorne has not sufficiently prepared one in advance, though it is fair to add that not all listeners find it as much of a shock. Perhaps the innocent ear absorbs more than the closer listener.

The orchestration, for full orchestra without violins or violas, is carefully organized so that the sound of the massive tutti is reserved for a few important moments, and there is much chamber-like texturing, as well as subtle exploitation of instruments such as alto flute, bass clarinet, untuned percussion (single but highly effective strokes on gong or suspended cymbal, for instance), and solo strings. (The American première was not until 1972, when the work was given at Oberlin College *with piano accompaniment*; it is difficult to imagine how this could have been very satisfactory, since Rawsthorne's orchestral writing is so carefully conceived in terms of the instruments.) The vocal writing is also effective, with a freedom between syllabic setting and extended melismas on significant words ('life', 'weeping', and 'singen', for instance) that is a far cry from the restricted style of so many of the unpublished early songs. It is also quite dramatic in its approach to the word-setting: there is a feel for situation and character which differentiates between compassion for the mother in the first song and bluff heartiness in the second. At one point in the first movement, Rawsthorne added a footnote in the score: 'the voice part should follow its own declamation rather than the bar lines in the orchestra'; this shows a willingness to experiment with the relationship between voice and orchestra, though in this case the experiment is of doubtful success, since the vocal part is still so anchored to the tonality in the orchestra that anything more than the slightest separation would be destructive, one feels. What is most striking is Rawsthorne's instinctive understanding of the medieval psyche, which was to be explored at greater depth in *Carmen vitale*.

Over the last eight years or so, Rawsthorne had widened his musical style through various devices. Trying orchestra plus narrator (*Practical Cats*), ballet, a new enlarged diatonicism and a more directly bitonal harmonic style, the introduction of almost medieval simplicity for some of his thematic invention, a new emphasis on longer melodic lines and the use of a wider range of intervals, longer sustaining of tonal bases or underlying harmonies—all these things had enriched his language, taking him away from over-reliance simply on shifting tonality *per se* or on augmented harmonies, while never reducing the personal nature of his musical vocabulary. At the same time, the gradual approach towards a genuine integration of serial elements within his own style, much as Haydn adopted and made his own the fashionable trends of his day, enriched his music still further and made available to him a new reservoir of technical devices with which to achieve his musical aims. He had, in the same period, enlarged his style by becoming more openly diatonic in some works and more intensely chromatic (through the serial-style organization of his material) in others, while remaining recognizably the same musical person. The two extremes, already co-existing comfortably, were combined in one of the finest of all his chamber works, the Quintet for piano and wind instruments commissioned by the BBC and first performed in the spring of 1963.

The third movement, a flickering scherzo (almost a perpetuum mobile in which the winds occasionally take over the continuous flow from the piano), is the first genuinely serial piece from Rawsthorne's pen. There is no doubt that the opening piano scurryings are a twelve-note row, nor that the succeeding figuration is fairly strictly derived from it (the horn theme, for instance, is the retrograde version of the row, in its original transposition) (Ex. 7.13(*c*)). Even what sounds like a hint of a trio theme in the middle section, still accompanied by scurrying piano figuration and given a new character by the use of dotted rhythms, can be related strictly to the row. The composer himself makes no mention of serial technique in his programme note, possibly owing to a fear of drawing too much attention to it. Yet it never sounds in the slightest like anybody but Rawsthorne, with perhaps a new, indefinable element—which can as easily be put down to the perpetual motion, something he had never exploited before, as to the influence of Schönbergian methods. This is, however, not the only movement to have serial leanings, though they are not so rigorously pursued elsewhere. The amiable 6/8 main theme of the first movement uses a nine-note row which is developed thematically during the course of the movement, and is often split into its component parts. It is gradually assembled during the slow introduction (Ex. 7.13(*a*)), its first phrase being put together by the piano in bars 9–10. A few bars later, the piano plays an inverted version of it, showing that serial influence exists as early as the quintet's introduction, and though the main Allegro non assai is not strictly serial, the material is mostly closely related to some part or other of this theme. A similar process is undergone in the introduction to the fourth and final movement, with a decidedly serial handling of a horn theme which returns later during the main body of the movement for one of the episodes, though the main part of the movement is based on one of the few genuinely Bartókian themes in Rawsthorne's output (Ex. 7.13(*d*)), contrary-

Ex. 7.13. Quintet for piano and wind instruments: (*a*) opening; (*b*) second movement, from letter C (piano part only); (*c*) third movement, opening; (*d*) finale, from letter B

(*a*)

(*b*)

(*c*)

Allegro non troppo, poco misterioso ♩ = ca. 138

(*d*)

Allegro risoluto ♩ = ca. 168

Duration 10'20"

motion scales. But these, it comes as no surprise to learn, are anticipated by phrases in the first two movements, so they are not completely new.

The structures of the work are not new, either, but by now Rawsthorne has so defined his priorities that recapitulations, when not necessary, simply do not exist as such, and the establishment of key-centres is as strong or as elusive as it needs to be. The first movement's recapitulation is merely a slower reminiscence of the first subject before a final flourish, which reaffirms the B minor tonic only on the very last note (as does the scherzo), and the dark, even tragic slow movement (placed second) reduces the recapitulation of its first subject by shortening it slightly and leaving only vestiges of the rocking piano figure that accompanied its exposition. The slow movement is a remarkable achievement, ranging from a semitonal first subject accompanied by bitonal six-note chords, through a lugubrious march-like theme accompanied by an unusually persistent B minor harmonic structure in the piano and then developed by the piano with exquisite tenderness, to a powerful passage in which, from extremely quiet and complex chords developing the previous harmonies still further (Ex. 7.13(*b*)), the music quite suddenly rises to an impassioned and rhetorical climax, marked by double-dotted rhythms and an extreme rise and fall of the individual melodic lines, often quite quickly as in a cadenza. The cadenza idea is revived with the introduction to the finale, where the thematic material it is assembling, albeit with a serial aspect, is stated in what amounts to a written-out recitative passage for ensemble, dividing into different combinations of instruments. Elsewhere, the music reveals an enormous harmonic range, from the complex chords of the slow movement to simple repeated major chords under a quiet reworking of the finale's main theme. At this point, Rawsthorne even puts down a series of straightforward dominant sevenths (though not in root position) in the piano, something quite outside his normal harmonic world but witty and apt.

Rawsthorne's exceptional ear for sonority has, one ventures to suggest, never been so supremely honed as in the music of this period. In his manuscript note for this work, he said that the wind instruments 'in such an ensemble as this create a challenge, in that they are all individualists who do not automatically unite to produce a homogeneous tissue of sound, as do the instruments of the string quartet usually employed in a piano quintet. So one aim in composing this piece was to try to turn these fascinating idiosyncracies to good account.' This is modest in the extreme, for the balancing between piano and ensemble, either as a group or with individual solos, is perfectly judged, and moreover seems utterly effortless. Despite the dark purple gloom of night that seems to envelop much of the music, there are gleams of light, and considerable wit; the scherzo is in its way a perfect example of what one might call 'serious wit', and in the finale there are delighted wind gurglings after the piano's subsidiary subject crosses over the established metre, quietly putting a cat among the pigeons. There is not a bar of padding in the work. When a chord or a note is held alone for a complete bar, it is because the moment of rest is required by the formal balance of the whole piece. And surely, no work using a small wind ensemble such as this has such a bewitching beginning, so perfectly judged in terms of the sound of each instrument and their relationships with each other (Ex. 7.13(a)); this is an exotic, enchanted world, reminiscent of the best of French wind writing rather than anything in the English or German traditions.

8

PERSONAL STATEMENTS
(1963–6)

RAWSTHORNE's critical reputation was perhaps never higher than at this time. He had accomplished a substantial broadening of his musical language, had renewed himself so that new works usually accomplished their aims with freshness of purpose and inspiration, and had made what in hindsight seems an inevitable and logical accommodation with serial technique, in a quite unselfconscious fashion. It was a different achievement from Britten's in *The Turn of the Screw*, where a composer one might have thought completely antipathetic to serial technique succeeded triumphantly in using it both as a technical and psychological means of fulfilling his operatic vision; Rawsthorne's chromatic style, after all, was more likely to lead him in this direction. But his absorption of what was likely to be most useful from the modernist spirit of the times was widely appreciated. With his next work, *Carmen vitale* ('Song of Life'), he quite deliberately chose to make a contribution to a genre that was seen by some to be outmoded (even more than the symphony), the English oratorio tradition. Admittedly, he called it a 'Choral Suite', hardly a very impressive title, but it is as much an oratorio as many other choral and orchestral offerings, and it represents his art at its peak. The urgency of its theme, together with its modernity in reaching back through the centuries to find a message all too relevant today, enables Rawsthorne to achieve his deepest, most personal statement, and as such it is one of his greatest works. It is a pity it was generally assessed according to fashionable opinion of the genre rather than on its own terms, for no work demonstrates more clearly just how far he had travelled.

Wilfrid Mellers, however, did appreciate its qualities and significance. Placing Rawsthorne, who had once been seen to derive his style from central European sources, 'unambiguously' among the British, he said that the

chromaticised diatonicism is consistent with the idiom of the instrumental works with which he made his reputation in the 'thirties. At the same time the piece clearly has some relationship to the post-Handelian choral tradition, and at a deeper level to the great days of England's past. The texts are medieval; so are some of the melismatic vocal techniques and the use of a plainsong cantus firmus. The melodically related triads are an extension of the renaissance device of false relation; the forms favour the baroque conventions of polyphonic fantasia, contrapuntal fugue, and ground bass chaconne. Yet the writing for solo voice is probably more 'advanced' in its chromaticism than any of Rawsthorne's earlier work; past and present are fused, as are the English and European traditions . . . it is . . . not only the biggest but also the deepest work he has given us for a long time. [It is actually his longest, at forty-five minutes.] It is not afraid of its theme, which is Man's birth, life, and death; it even makes some approach towards justifying God's ways to man—and this, for a twentieth-century artist, is a bold theme indeed.[1]

Introducing the work in *Radio Times* in October 1963, Rawsthorne wrote:

The texts used in this composition are by unknown lyrical poets of the Middle Ages. I find the thought and imagery of this period very sympathetic for musical setting. To the modern reader the words seem to stand forth with renewed vigour; and they seem more vivid for being so directly categorical. In the first Aria, for example, only one noun has a descriptive adjective directly attached to it. Consequently one feels that music can make a real contribution, if only adjectivally, [in which he is being unduly self-effacing] and eventually the words weave themselves easily into a complex musical structure.

I have made use of the beautiful chant 'Ut queant laxis' in various ways. Tenors and basses sing it at the outset, the phrases alternating between them. The work then proceeds in the following order: Fantasia (Chorus), Aria, Choral fanfare and orchestral fugue, Aria, Chaconne (Orchestra), Chorus, Aria, and final Chorus. The latter is in the nature of a warning.

Before us lies a world of happiness which we now have the means of entering. But the choice is ours, immediately and irrevocably, whether we achieve this world and become part of it, or turn our backs upon it, bringing about the inevitable catastrophe. Thus it may appear that the Chorus's cry of 'Now is well!' is not quite so carefree as it might be. Anyway, there was a certain ferocity in most medieval rejoicing.

These admirable summaries of the work also sum up its theme, in language as direct and elegant as the texts themselves. What they cannot do, however, is convey its subtlety, or the complexity of its emotional world. Rawsthorne achieves a marvellous balance between vividly conveying the warning, on the one hand, and celebrating both misery and joy (in other words, humanity), on the other. What is so astonishing about the work, his own personal testament, is that he was capable of making so formidable a statement when all through his life he had fought shy of public utterance. His music always had a strong emotional world, but until then it was often kept under the surface,

---

[1] 'Rawsthorne and the English Tradition', *Listener* (10 Oct. 1963).

so that one has to meet it half-way to begin to realize what that world is. *Carmen vitale* is no less controlled, no less subtle in its interplay of emotions, but the overall impact of it is massive—all the threads of his work drawn together in one visionary unity. It needs to be added that Rawsthorne had prepared the way for this work during the development of his style over the previous seven or eight years. The serial aspects of his thinking, however personal and free, contrasting with the explorations in the opposite direction (including the simple plainchant-like melody of the Piano Trio), had given him a reservoir of means which could be put towards almost any expressive ends that he wished.

The plainchant, a hymn to St John (Ex. 8.1), is used extensively throughout the work, most of the choral writing being derived from it. Rawsthorne used it for its atmosphere of devotional neutrality, rather than for the meaning of its words. Mellers suggests that he also chose it 'because each phrase begins on an ascending degree of the scale, so that it was traditionally the basis of the ut-re-mi type of fantasia: a manifestation of divine-seeming contrapuntal oneness beyond personal passion. Rawsthorne's ut-re-mi fancy is both choral and orchestral, the modality being gradually chromaticised while purity is pre-

Ex. 8.1. *Carmen vitale*, Fantasia, choral entry

served by the luminous, crystalline orchestration.'[2] It should be stressed that the modal manner of the chant is set in a diatonic, triadic harmonic ambience, containing elements (open fifths and fourths, for instance) that connect directly with the medieval style of the chant, and other elements (implications of bitonality, intervals of sevenths or ninths) which can also connect it equally directly with the world of Rawsthornian harmony. Its handling in the opening number expands into florid, Bachian counterpoint culminating in two exuberant, elaborate settings of the phrase 'Sancte Joannes'. Throughout the work, Rawsthorne uses the chant not only to provide the chorus with singable, often stepwise lines, but also to emphasize the contrast with the more angular melodies given to the soprano soloist, and thus the contrast between the personal voice of the solo and the more objective, observing voice of the chorus. (This is particularly effective in the first Aria, 'I am a Child', at the solo phrase 'When I am dead', to which the chorus comments 'When she is dead', the eerie atmosphere being enhanced by the rhythmic structure of the canonic choral writing as well as the subtle orchestration.) When Rawsthorne wishes to give the chorus a disjunct line to sing, as at the start of the final chorus, he simply divides the notes of the line and gives one note to each voice in turn, a pointillist technique resulting from the need to be as practical as possible in giving the singers their pitches. The chant informs the writing for orchestra, too, providing little motifs which inflect the music; it is anticipated by solo trumpet and then horn in the brief, mysterious orchestral introduction before its first choral statement (the phrases of which are given in Ex. 8.1), and pervades the texture either overtly or discreetly at many junctures.

The three Arias, of which only the first contains a choral part, present personal views of the relationship between life and death. In the first of the two Parts, the Aria is 'an impassioned melismatic outcry concerning man's birth into a world of woe, and his ultimate destiny as "wormes ware"' (Mellers).[3] The first movement of Part II, 'O Death, rock me asleep', reverses the process: here, instead of a birth-song aware of ultimate death, we have a resigned farewell to life that is also a lullaby. In the third Aria, 'I have set my heart so high', the soloist sings positively, with soaring, virtuosic melismas, of the love of God which renews the joy of life. In all these songs, the soprano lines are wide-ranging, the intervals conveying the anguish of the first two Arias, with a great cry of 'Christ help mine soul' in the first Aria (Ex. 8.2(a)), and the exuberant leaping optimism of the third, where the orchestral harmonies have

[2] 'Rawsthorne and the English Tradition'.
[3] Ibid.

a more diatonic basis that helps to reinforce the air of confident jubilation (Ex. 8.2(*b*)). The Handelian sequences reinforce the exultant grandeur of the melisma. There is even a touch of Purcell, in the dying fall on the fourfold repetition of 'I die' at the close of 'O Death'. In the final Chorus, the soprano solo reappears, presenting what Rawsthorne, in a handwritten note in the

Ex. 8.2. *Carmen vitale*: (*a*) Aria 'I am a Child'; (*b*) Aria 'I have set my heart'

(*a*)

RNCM archives, described as 'one of the oldest and most effective antitheses in the world—the relation of an individual to a crowd'.

The Choruses inhabit a more impersonal world. In Part I, they comment on the soprano's Aria and contain two settings of the plainchant: in the opening Fantasia, where it is developed into quite an elaborate setting, and at the beginning of the third movement, Chorus and Fugue, where it is divided between a 'Small Chorus', presenting quiet phrases of the chant (Andante) with some divisions into chordal writing, and a 'Main Chorus', which interrupts these proceedings Allegro and fortissimo with anticipations of the vigorous fugue subject to come. At the close of the purely orchestral Fugue, the Chorus re-enters with the fugue subject (a straightforward variation of the chant) in augmentation, to close Part I on a massive, dissonant chord (Ex. 8.3(a)). It is not until the very end of the work that this final cadence is resolved (see Ex. 8.5(b) below): its fierce but inconclusive blaze of sound reverberates through the whole of Part II until this resolution. The two choruses in Part II present an important contrast. 'A litel child there is ibore' concerns the Christ child, born for man's redemption, so that birth is now positive and affirmative. The setting is sweet and lyrical, rising to what Bernard Stevens

Ex. 8.3. *Carmen vitale*: (a) Fugue, last 4 bars; (b) 'Now is well', from fig. 70

(a)

(b)

Si -then it is well, well— we do,— For there is none but one of two,—

Hea - ven to get or hea - ven for - go;—

In tempo, ma meno mosso ♩ = ca. 56

Oth - - er me - - ne none——

Ex. 8.3. *Continued*

described as Pérotin-like ecstasy on the words 'Gloria tibi domine',[4] with much use of almost modal triadic motion. In the final Chorus, 'Now is well', telling of the triumph of Christ over the foul fiend, it is the soprano solo that declaims the warning: 'there is none but one of two, | Heaven to get or heaven forgo', upon which wordless female voices enter as the soprano expounds the choice (Ex. 8.3(*b*)); the inner choral part (top altos) echoes fragments of the plain-chant, reminding us subtly once again of the balance between the objective and the subjective views of mankind's fate.

The final Chorus is exultant, the leaping, running orchestral part reinforcing the chorus's massively triumphant song of praise. In both outer sections, the sopranos' top note gradually moves from G, through G♯, to A; that this process is effective a second time is due to the fact that, having moved quickly to G♯, they move back again to G, which remains for a while the top note of the melodic outline. When A is finally re-established, it has already been signalled as an aim to be worked towards; the sense of triumph is all the more potent for the ambiguity underlining it in the final cadence (a somewhat similar tonal procedure is encompassed in the third and final movement of Webern's Variations for Piano, Op. 27). Norman Kay assessed the final chorus thus:

the composer wanted to introduce the minatory note that is part and parcel of all medieval jubilation. To do this, he deliberately plays the words against the music. While the chorus sings 'Now is well and all things aright', the music, though strong, perches in a warning manner on that most uncomfortable of intervals, the tritone. What might

---

[4] 'The Choral Music', Poulton iii. 52.

have been a united shout of confidence becomes a much more contemporary matter of individual question and thought.[5]

The choral writing throughout is eminently practical, not least because the various melodic lines clearly have their own tonal centres, reinforced by the orchestration, which frequently provides useful cues to aid intonation. It is a demanding sing, but the division between soloist, chorus, and orchestra is such that there is time to relax and prepare for the next substantial number and to build up stamina for the great final Chorus.

The two purely (or largely) orchestral numbers, one in each Part, are both characteristic Rawsthorne archetypes. The subject of the Fugue (Ex. 8.4(a)) is dynamic and vigorous, scored with all the excitement and invention at the composer's command. He deploys all the contrapuntal devices available to him (augmentation, inversion, canon, stretto, and the like) with enormous gusto, but the attempt to unite all the elements in a positive paean of praise by this contrapuntal working is undercut by the Chorus's final cadence, however, and the resolution is left to Part II. This also contains the orchestral Chaconne, in which the theme (Ex. 8.4(b)), related to an inner phrase from the first Aria, adopts the same procedure as the Chaconne in the First Piano Concerto, combining what is basically a descending outline with a rise of a semitone in actual tonality for each variation from G up to B. It then develops semitone cells from the chaconne theme over D and then C♯ pedals, and resumes more straightforward treatment of the ground bass, using it as a melody and drawing attention to its countersubject from the first variation, the suspensions flowering into expansive overlapping melodic lines. After a powerful climax, the countersubject is recalled, along with some of the sighing octave phrases that have been an important feature of this movement. It ends quietly and inconclusively with a reminder in the bass of the plainchant and a shift in the accompanying harmony from E major to E minor, the G being forced down from sharp to natural by an A♯ above it creating a suspension. Above the resultant harmony, an E flat minor plainchant phrase prepares us for the open fifths opening the next chorus, 'A litel child'. One of the most striking features of the Chaconne is that it inhabits something of the tragic, doom-laden world of the Sarabande from Busoni's *Doktor Faust*. Rawsthorne uses these two orchestral staging posts to mark the progress from misery to hope, the Fugue's ebullience proving temporary as it turns to dissonance with its final chord, the Chaconne redressing the balance with a peaceful, questioning conclusion, hinting at consolation after the intensity of its variations.

[5] *Observer* (20 Oct. 1963).

Ex. 8.4. *Carmen vitale*: (*a*) Part I, Fugue subject; (*b*) Part II, orchestral Chaconne, first 11 bars

The orchestration of *Carmen vitale* is extraordinarily resourceful, ranging from the massive sonorities and earthy vigour of the Fugue to the most delicate instrumentation. 'A litel child', for instance, is accompanied only by woodwinds, horns, timpani, percussion, and harp (no strings or heavy brass), emphasizing, especially through the use of the cor anglais, the medieval quality of the carol without the need to resort to any kind of musical pastiche. It is noteworthy how often Rawsthorne is able to resort to chamber-music textures, using just a few instruments, to achieve the effects he wants, saving the bigger sounds for the most appropriate moments. Perhaps the most remarkable number is 'O Death', where bell sounds proliferate, mostly produced not by the tubular bells (which have only two significant notes) but by the most im-

aginative combination of instrumental timbres, an enormous amount of atmosphere being created by extensive use of solo piano, whose rocking accompanimental phrases give an unearthly, uniquely timeless quality to the sound.
It was an inspired stroke to use the piano in this way; I know of no other
orchestral writing which does precisely this. The funereal atmosphere of this
song is reinforced by fragments of a ghostly march tune, first heard in the voice
and later transferred to muted trumpet, oboe, and tenor drum—just a single
phrase, but extraordinarily and eerily evocative. Similarly, the compassion, and
the hint of passing beyond sorrow, for the words 'cease now the passing bell;
I Rung is my doleful knell' are beautifully conveyed by a descending harp scale
over an A flat major cluster and a shift to the warmer string sound for a D
minor ninth chord on 'Rung' (Ex. 8.5(a)), with the sounds perfectly calculated to convey the subtle mix of emotions by contrasting with the bell-sounds
and skeletal keyboard chords prevalent up to this point. The balance between
orchestra and voices is carefully managed throughout, so that the final cadence
(a typical use of Neapolitan notes), marked by a great horn cry, reaches one

Ex. 8.5. *Carmen vitale*, Part II: (*a*) Aria 'O Death', from 8th bar of fig. 44; (*b*) last 6
bars

Ex. 8.5. *Continued*

(*b*)

of the few massed tuttis in the entire work to great effect (Ex. 8.5(*b*)). The last note is an open fifth D–A, but the note before it is F♮, so that the effect is to hint at D minor rather than major, a suitably ambiguous ending but another blazing chord. Just as Britten's *The Turn of the Screw* ends with an inspired use of A major to convey tragedy, Rawsthorne's D minor is a rare use of a minor key to suggest resolution and triumph—assuming, that is, that mankind chooses heaven rather than forgoing it. Only a composer with great confidence can ask us this question in the midst of an expression of triumph. As Mellers says, 'Rawsthorne's splendidly ambiguous triumph-song is relevant to us all . . . the voice of God, when it finally blazes in a fortissimo version of *Ut queant laxis*, is resonantly potent, yet riddled with false relations. In these spiritually parsimonious days we should be grateful for so sturdily affirmative yet so meticulously honest a score.'[6]

The first performance of *Carmen vitale* was at a BBC Symphony Orchestra concert in October 1963, conducted by Norman del Mar, with Heather Harper superb as the soloist. During the preceding weeks, Rawsthorne had been in Soviet Russia. Rawsthorne's travels abroad were surprisingly limited. Apart from the 1954 visit to Canada and frequent visits to Holland, his European travel was restricted mostly to a few trips to France, Italy, Spain, Germany, and Eastern European countries. One trip, to Bulgaria, included a visit to the cave where Orpheus was reputed to have gone in search of Eurydice. His major journey in the 1960s was to Soviet Russia: he and Alan Bush went there as representatives of the Composers' Guild to conduct their own works (the Russian record company Melodiya issued recordings from these performances, Rawsthorne's works being the Concerto for String Orchestra and the second Symphony, with the finale sung in Russian). He wrote to Isabel from Moscow (23 September 1963):

A slightly numb feeling is wearing off very slowly. From Heath Row [*sic*] to Socialist Realism in 3 hours 20 minutes needs a moment or two to recover. It is about an hour longer than from Sampford to King's Cross. We were met in style as we descended from the aeroplane, by cheerful care-free faces, and the news that we must immediately press on to Armenia, where we are due to give a concert later in the week. The name of the capital of Armenia escapes me at the moment, but it is something like Erewhon; no doubt you could look it up on a map. So thither we go to-morrow morning and start rehearsing. Perhaps they will play on gourds and rams' horns . . . I have eaten a meal of bortsch and some boiled sturgeon. I have walked right round the Kremlin in the dark, a journey of about a mile. Our concert in Moscow is on the third of October, with the Moscow State Orchestra. We have five rehearsals and a sub-conductor to do the dirty work.

In an article on his Russian trip in the *Sunday Times*, he declared himself astonished at the wealth of cultural activity in Armenia:

There are, I believe, about 3 million people in Armenia, and about 600,000 in Erevan, which is to all intents and purposes a new city. Yet they can fill a good-sized concert-hall with people who are sufficiently interested and curious to come and listen to two strange Englishmen conducting their probably quite unknown music—listen, indeed, with great attention and subsequent enthusiasm.

---

[6] 'Rawsthorne and the English Tradition'.

Their State Orchestra, with which we worked, is a splendid body of musicians, and gives regular concerts which are supplemented by visiting orchestras, chamber-music groups and so forth. There is an opera-house in full swing. The Armenian branch of the Union of Soviet Composers is housed in a building (a building, be it remarked, not half a room in an office-block) of five or six floors, with recording rooms, rooms for making music, rooms for being sociable, rooms for office work, and the like. This is flanked by blocks of flats, in which composers can live. 'Do they not quarrel?' I asked, but immediately saw the foolishness of my question, for composers can quarrel quite happily even if they live in different towns or even countries . . . I have dwelt upon the visit to Erevan because this kind of cultural life in a small state will probably never have been considered possible by most English people, or indeed considered at all . . . Unfortunately there didn't seem much time to discuss the musical situation as I should have liked, particularly with the younger men. There are many points I should like to have raised, some of them fundamental. For instance, in the U.S.S.R. there seems to be an official tendency towards the view that all art is didactic. I cannot agree with this notion. People do not in fact visit the incomparable Hermitage in order to study sociology.

Again, composers appear to seek to make their points in an idiom which is completely familiar to their public, whereas a greater impact would often be created by methods that are new and therefore arresting. They should have greater trust in their public. For myself, I have a rooted mistrust of all Governments, and a dislike of orthodoxies.[7]

During the next two years, 1964 and 1965, Rawsthorne produced four concert works a year, as well as incidental music for a short film (*Messenger of the Mountains*) in 1964, and a television production of *A Tale of Two Cities*, an interesting score that might be worth a short suite, in 1965, while during 1966–8 he composed three concert pieces a year—a remarkably sustained and energetic period of creativity, much of it on a large scale. Not all of these compositions were of the highest standard, and not all were published—but it might be expecting too much to anticipate, for instance, that all the works of 1964 could maintain the supremely high level of the Third Symphony and the *Elegiac Rhapsody*. It is, however, surprising that he showed so little insight into the brass band medium when he wrote his Suite for the National Youth Brass Band of Scotland, to a commission from the Scottish Amateur Music Association. The Overture of this work begins with a positively Handelian flourish, similar to the opening of the *Coronation Overture* and used again later in the *Overture for Farnham*. When the tempo quickens, there is some contrapuntal working of promisingly arabesque-like phrases, but without a great deal of conviction. It is in the second movement, Lament, that Rawsthorne's normally sure hand with instrumental texture most seriously slips. Perhaps his beloved

---

[7] 'The Composer in the USSR' (13 Oct. 1963).

augmented chords, which pop up with more frequency when he is less inspired (just as the Alberti bass does when Haydn is tired), simply do not sound well on brass band. The sound is ungrateful, and the attempts at 'local colour' (i.e. the use of the Scotch snap), while undoubtedly well meant, ring hollow. Things improve with the final two movements, a somewhat Prokofievian Romance in which traditional band style is emulated with the aid of a slightly music-hall euphonium solo, and a March with straightforward and engaging content as well as a splendidly alert ending. These two movements, possibly because they are written in a more conventional brass band style and avoid augmented harmony to a greater extent, are considerably more idiomatic than the first two. One is tempted to wonder why a composer whose brass writing for orchestra is so splendid, and who was after all a Lancastrian, should clearly have found brass band such an unsuitable medium for his own style.

Of 'He does not die', a Hilaire Belloc setting for mixed voices and two pianos written in 1964 for George Watson's College, Edinburgh, Alan Frank wrote from OUP to Rawsthorne (31 December 1964):

I was able to hear the broadcast . . . I think that it sounded well for the occasion for which it was written but, quite honestly, I have to say that we don't see much prospect for its future use either by schools or adult choirs. Oddly enough, if you don't mind my saying this, I didn't feel the setting sounded, for the most part, like you.

He would only publish, though preferably for piano duet rather than two pianos, if the composer was really keen; presumably he was not, for it never appeared in print. This is rather a pity, since, though not possessed of the most personal of Rawsthorne characteristics, it is a vigorous and effective little piece, looking forward to the Concerto for Two Pianos in some of its keyboard writing (see Ex. 8.6) and skilfully laid out for both voices and instruments. The B flat major tonality, emphasized by the key signature, is unusually sustained, and this was perhaps what led Frank to regard it as uncharacteristic, though there are enough melodic and harmonic fingerprints to leave one in no doubt as to the composer's identity. The subject of the poem, that one's influence on one's environment is what gains one immortality, presents the artist as hero, blessed by nature at the close of the work in a pleasant, peaceful B flat major. The opening vocal phrase outlines its simple, diatonic nature, showing the fourth to be as generative an interval as the third. It might be more practical to provide a piano duet transcription of it, because although not a major addition to the Rawsthorne œuvre, it is an eminently singable, communicative little piece, with plenty of rhythmic vigour of a fairly conventional kind in the quicker sections and some delightful interplay between the vocal melismas and the keyboard activity.

EX. 8.6. 'He does not die', bars 1–3

Two other choral works remain from this period, the first a four-part unaccompanied setting of Hardy's 'The Oxen' for the OUP anthology of specially
composed works *Carols of Today*, much of which was also recorded. This had
already been set beautifully by Vaughan Williams as a baritone solo in his great
Christmas work *Hodie*. It is surprising that Rawsthorne, ever conscious of the
shadow over Eden, should not have set more Hardy, and the contrast between
the Vaughan Williams setting, amiable and consolatory, and the Rawsthorne,
wintry and bleak, is considerable. This little miniature is a perfect vignette, its
overlapping melismas and words conveying a chamber-music richness of
texture with the utmost economy, signifying again that Rawsthorne has a
special place in the English choral repertoire which we ignore to our own loss.
His last choral work, *The God in the Cave*, was more ambitious. It is a setting
for mixed chorus and orchestra of a text by his old friend Randall Swingler,
and was commissioned by Edinburgh University Madrigal Society, who gave
the first performance in 1967, shortly before the poet's death. The poems had
been written twenty years earlier, after a visit to the Lascaux caves in France,
and deals with primitive caveman and the psychological urge to create cave-
art, as a metaphor for the relationship between man and nature.

This 'speliological cantata', as Rawsthorne described it,[8] divides into three
movements. The orchestral introduction to 'Incantation' recurs briefly at the
end of the third movement, 'Landscape', to close the work with a reminder
of the womb-cave from which man emerges. 'Incantation' describes the mys-
teries of the cave and the beast depicted on its walls, and the powers of creation and destruction inherent in the beast. The central movement, 'The

---

[8] Handwritten note to Alan Frank (undated).

Cave-Artist's Prayer', is a more violent baritone solo declaiming the poem's opening line: 'Keep me mine enemy before mine eyes | That I may know my fear!' The tone is vehement and turbulent, with just two quieter, muttering sections. 'Landscape' suggests initially a peaceful scene of rivers and hills, but the contemplation of man's destiny and his power to alter the face of nature leads to a crackling climax before the brief epilogue. There is much in common with *A Canticle of Man*, and even with *Carmen vitale*, in some of the concerns expressed in this work—the relationship of man with nature, the potential for destruction, the possibility of peace. There are some splendid moments: the orchestral opening, with its atmosphere of mystery and of man stirring in the womb-cave, the magnificent (and well-sustained) power of the music for the beast's appearance in whatever form it may take, the ineffably lovely landscape, and the majestic final affirmation of man's power. Harmonically and melodically the work is very consistent, the aggregated chord comprising two three-note cells (for instance, G-A-C plus E♭-F♯-G♯, as at the beginning) being the vital ingredient providing the essential unity, and there is some effective use of wordless chorus. But it does not add up to quite the moving experience one might anticipate. There is a sense of coming to rest on an open fifth every so often not as a focus but because the music has lost direction and needs to regroup. It is also quite difficult. For a piece written for amateur forces (with which Rawsthorne was never fully at ease), some of its instrumental melismata are rather tricky, and intonation for the strings must be a problem in places. It falls between two stools, that of the expression of a powerful vision expressed at a level demanding the highest professional expertise in performance, and that of music written for good amateurs, where the vision needs to be contained in a more direct expression. One senses that Rawsthorne, for whom this was obviously an important work (he was most anxious it should be performed at the Proms, though that never happened), was constrained by the imposed limitations and unable to give his instinct free rein.

Of much higher quality are many of the instrumental works from this period, with the *Elegiac Rhapsody* for strings among the finest. It is headed 'In Memoriam Louis MacNeice', and its first performance was by the Hirsch String Orchestra in January 1964. This tribute to an old friend and colleague brings out the best in Rawsthorne's formal mastery and detailed integrity of material. It is also notably resourceful in its handling of the string orchestra, with some brief but telling use of solo instruments, much divisi writing, and contrasts of register (used with immense skill as a colour and not merely as part of the development of the material) to create a score that is 'orchestrated' quite superbly. The music alternates slow and quick tempos, the former being dominated by two cells present in the opening bar, one rising, the other falling (Ex. 8.7(*a*)). The gradual spread of instruments creates a silvery web of sound, the music descending to a low B (the basic tonality) only in the fourteenth bar. The harmonies built up during this opening section clearly give rise to a more chordal theme in the fifth section (Ex. 8.7(*c*)), and there is throughout the piece careful, highly organized use of small cells to provide melodic lines or the basic components of the harmony. Another important figure, a falling fifth and semitone, is heard at the start of the first quick section, Allegro strepitoso; this is played forte in a double-dotted rhythm (Ex. 8.7(*b*)), the jagged outlines of the theme and the inner parts conveying the anguish that gave rise to the work's composition. The rhythmic device itself is later picked up and developed both with its associated melodic-harmonic cell and with other ideas. But for all the technical skill of the work's construction, two other features stand out as particularly noteworthy. One is the extraordinary number of imaginative textural ideas—a shivering octave minor second (C–B) near the start, savagely repeated chords, overlapping five-note chromatic groups (for all the world like the later Penderecki or Lutosławski in their sliding mode), very short but evocative use of trills or tremolandos, high keening phrases on cello or viola, overlapping canonic treatment of wandering phrases to create a tapestry

Ex. 8.7. *Elegiac Rhapsody*: (*a*) bars 1–8; (*b*) from letter C; (*c*) from letter L; (*d*) last 5 bars

(*a*)

against which other developments can take place, and innumerable other devices. It would be foolish to deny the passing influence of Bartók or Vaughan Williams here and there, but there is never any doubt that this is Rawsthorne himself, speaking with heartfelt intensity. The piece is a virtuoso demonstration, almost a thesaurus, of string orchestral writing at its most brilliant; clearly, to pay tribute to MacNeice, only the best would do. The other outstanding feature is the depth of feeling expressed in the *Rhapsody*. This is not in any way a self-indulgent lament, but a sad, noble testament, an expression of personal loss made more universal by the clarity of the vision. The B major final cadence, typically delayed until the last note, transcends mere subjective sorrow (Ex. 8.7(*d*)).

A number of chamber and instrumental works dating from this period are also of high quality, though they perhaps do not have quite the same emotional intensity as the *Elegiac Rhapsody*. The Third String Quartet (actually, of course, his fifth) was the result of an enterprise by Harlow New Town, which engaged the Alberni String Quartet as quartet-in-residence, before such positions became fashionable, and commissioned a number of outstanding quartets for it. Rawsthorne's Third was first performed in July 1965. More even than his Second Quartet, this is concentrated music of great density, without the relative relaxation afforded the listener by the Second Quartet's intermezzo-like third movement. Divided into two halves, separated only by a pause and themselves subdivided into sections, it is an extremely concise exploration, in the space of about seventeen minutes, of material stated in the Allegro deciso with which it starts; this leads after a few bars into the flowing 6/8 Allegretto that forms the first main section (Ex. 8.8(*a*)). Even in this short extract, the immediate development of the opening theme can be seen in the first violin (Allegretto, third bar) and then the second, while the Allegretto's opening bars create new material out of a three-note figure which, from the Second Violin Concerto, has been used with increasing ubiquity to create both melodies and harmonies (here on the viola, it starts D-C-A and then proceeds through various transpositions and inversions). The Allegretto's apparently free-flowing, rhapsodic style is actually a thorough examination of this material, and when the Allegro deciso returns to provide the second main section, opening with a greatly extended development of the first few bars, it soon reveals how the material pervades every new twist and turn of the music, including a vehement secondary theme on the cello. The second subject's series of chords (Ex. 8.8(*b*)) combines the two cells from the beginning of the work, the top line relating to the first phrase and the chords being built out of aggregations of notes derived from the three-note Allegretto phrase (the first chord, for instance, combines A–G–E with C♯–G♯, omitting for the moment the B or A♯ which would complete the lower three-note group). It is worth noting that there is an unusually complete recapitulation, bringing this movement closer than almost any other in his output to classical sonata form: both main subjects receive full repetition, albeit altered and further developed as is Rawsthorne's wont. But significantly enough, this departure from his structural norm is explained by a remark in a manuscript programme note: 'I myself feel that the composition of the form of a piece of music is as much a creative act as the invention of the material; the two things clearly go hand in hand.'

Ex. 8.8. Third String Quartet: (*a*) bars 1–11; (*b*) from letter H

Chopin, Brahms, and Schönberg would wholeheartedly have agreed with this precept.

The second half of the work is marked 'Andante (Alla Ciacona)', but in contrast to the chaconnes in the First Piano Concerto and *Carmen vitale*, no rigorous tonal plan is built into the subject: Rawsthorne is content to let it rotate around the same series of notes for most of the movement, allowing the expressive counterpoint (much of it based on the cell at the start of the quartet) to build up the tension. It is the inner intensity that breaks the formal bounds of the chaconne, leading to two powerfully rhetorical climaxes and a diminuendo. The opening (Ex. 8.9(*a*)) is a fascinating introduction in which a highly schematic harmony is built upwards while the phrases of the chaconne theme are anticipated by pizzicato fragments. These are then put together as a single, seven-bar theme to provide the ground bass for the chaconne, into which the music flows seamlessly (unwary listeners will find themselves in the midst of the chaconne before they know it). This introduction returns briefly to provide a moment of stillness before the Molto vivace finale breaks in, quietly at the start, with a 6/8 tarantella. There is nothing lightweight about this finale, however. From the start, it is made clear that there is going to be much interplay between the instruments, and while the main theme is based on the opening of the Allegretto, the opening Allegro deciso material gradually comes to play an increasingly important part. Rawsthorne's delight in rhythmic crosscurrents is given full rein (Ex. 8.9(*b*)), and eventually a powerful climax is reached at which the Allegro deciso theme wrests control from the Allegretto material, culminating in Beethovenian octaves (Ex. 8.9(*c*)). The path to the end of the quartet is strewn with references either direct (with appropriate changes of tempo) or indirect (by almost hidden quotation embedded in the

Ex. 8.9. Third String Quartet: (*a*) from letter P; (*b*) from 5th bar of letter BB; (*c*) from 3rd bar of letter EE

(*a*)

(b)

(c)

texture) to earlier parts of the work: the aggregated chord at the start of the chaconne, for instance, figuration or chords from different sections, and the superimposition of 6/8 and 2/4 versions of the opening argument, heard here as two dialogues (viola and cello versus two violins). The final cadence makes it clear that F sharp is the ultimate destination for a work that began, unequivocally, on a unison C (immediately contradicted by C♯-F♯, of course, thus concisely providing the ground-plan of the quartet in a nutshell). Even the final descending scale on first violin, leading down to the F♯, is anticipated in the fourth and fifth bars of the quartet (second violin), with the strong suggestion of whole-tone leanings. The quartet is a splendid, vital piece of chamber music, with real quartet writing throughout, and though it never tries to be ingratiating, there is such resourcefulness in the deployment of the material, such joy in writing a concise but highly developed work, that the music fizzes with life.

Five days before the première of the Third String Quartet, *Tankas of the Four Seasons* received its first performance at the Cheltenham Festival. Written to a commission from the Macnaghten Concerts, and dedicated to Anne Macnaghten, this is a remarkably different piece, so different, indeed, that it belongs stylistically among the almost austere, sparsely written last works rather than to a period when Rawsthorne's invention was still burgeoning. A setting for tenor, with ensemble of oboe, clarinet, bassoon, violin, and cello, of poems translated by J. L. Gili from the anarchist Catalan poet Carles Riba (an old friend of Rawsthorne's), it is a short (eight-minute), continuous piece. The poems are linked by instrumental interludes, but the effect is of a single movement, with ebbing and flowing intensity of counterpoint but little change of mood throughout. The tanka was a Japanese verse-form, similar to the haiku but with two extra lines, and Rawsthorne made no attempt whatever to give a Japanese or Catalan flavour to the music. His intention, he wrote, was 'to integrate the voice part with the instruments so as to produce a texture which can follow the images and moods of the poems, rather than to adopt a declamatory style'—an intention fully carried out.[9] The poems, delicate, elliptical disquisitions on love, death, and nature, maintain an almost abstract poise, which is matched by Rawsthorne's music. The tenor part is more instrumental both in outline and timbre than conventionally vocal, though when a particularly expressive melisma occurs it has a correspondingly greater effect.

The material of the work is economical in the extreme, and is stated in the oboe shortly after the start in a rising and falling phrase matching the work's overall rise and fall of intensity. The austerity arises from the uncompromising nature of the intervals. At the start, over an E harmonic on the cello, the clarinet hovers between E♭, D♭, and C, and this intervallic narrowness is the music's strongest characteristic, with the occasional angular leaps being mostly inversions of the closest intervals (sevenths and ninths becoming seconds, for instance). Once again, the influence of serial thinking can be felt on the ideas and their development, the tenor having, for the most part, the same material as the instruments. Unusually for this period, there is little hint of more diatonic implications: the influence of plainchant or diatonic harmony is almost completely avoided. There is much contrapuntal activity in the instruments, within which texture the voice part acts as a linking thread, but it is the terseness of material which dominates. *Tankas* is both fragile, in its instrumental delicacy and response to the words, and steely, in the close integrity of its thematic working, and is a unique addition to the genre of chamber music with

---

[9] Composer's programme note.

voice. Perhaps it lacks the ingredients for popular success, but its exceptional consistency of language and subtle expressive nuances make it a worthy programme companion of works like Stravinsky's *Three Japanese Lyrics*, with whose precision of thought and refusal to compromise it has much in common. Elizabeth Webster expressed a high opinion of it:

music of imagery and evocation, quietly and gently sketched in . . . an atmosphere as shadowy and gossamer-fine as a Japanese print . . . the last long, slow notes of the tenor on the words 'the boats are now returning, their sails colourless' against a quiet, held note on the clarinet and a few, faint pizzicato string notes like drops of falling water are masterly.[10]

Rawsthorne's approach to Schönberg and serial technique was balanced, unlike that of many of his contemporaries, who either embraced them unthinkingly or denied them utterly. In his interview with Malcolm Rayment, he said:

Music composed with twelve notes related only to one another has done away, to me, with the serious and wonderful idea that all these notes, or some of them, are related to another note which isn't there. That seems to me one of the most beautiful things about music, about melody—and also harmonically speaking of course. . . . the tonal centres as they change themselves become related again to one another and consequently again related to yet another that isn't there, if you see what I mean . . . I find the manipulation of small melodic units or cells an interesting and sympathetic method of setting about the business, but I certainly do not find that the adoption of this technique as a permanent and unique method of writing leads anywhere particularly . . . I think that teachings and certain practices of Schönberg have frequently been misunderstood. It is well to mould the teachings of Schönberg to suit yourself but I think it should always be understood that the results are yours and not Schönberg's . . . One [effect of serial technique] is this: it causes the present day composer, if he is at all sensitive to the methods of Schönberg, to examine his material very carefully and meticulously to see that it is doing the job which is it supposed to do. Schönberg, we know, was very insistent on getting the right sort of series or row from the start to see that it was going to be workable.[11]

In a letter to the present writer, then studying in Germany (5 April 1965), he summed it up thus: 'The Germans, at least, are still deep in their grand Romantic Tradition, don't you think?—and invented the 12-note system to make it nice and tidy. I often feel that Henze could break into the Ride of the Valkyries without much difficulty.' Perhaps, at heart, his 'dislike of orthodoxies' would have prevented him ever going along wholeheartedly with serialism, but in the Third Symphony he approached it more nearly than in any other major work.

---

[10] Cheltenham Festival review, *Musical Opinion*, 88 (Sept. 1965), 727.
[11] BBC radio interview for a series 'The Composer Speaks', recorded 24 May 1962.

The Third Symphony was commissioned by the Cheltenham Festival, and given there on 8 July 1964 by the then BBC Northern Orchestra conducted by George Hurst; it is dedicated to Isabel. Those of us enjoying a late lunch in the Town Hall bar after the festival midday recital were mildly astonished to hear occasional volcanic orchestral eruptions taking place in the rehearsal for the evening's symphony concert. 'What's the old boy up to?' we muttered. What Rawsthorne was up to was a symphony encompassing a spiritual journey from inner turbulence, flaring up into explosions of passion, to final peace and fulfilment. The Arcadia of the *Pastoral Symphony* is regained at the close, but only after a titanic struggle. There are moments when the outbursts of raw emotional intensity bring Rawsthorne nearer than in any other composition to the art of Francis Bacon.

The symphony follows an apparently conventional four-movement plan, with the Scherzo placed third and every appearance of sonata form for the opening Allegro and rondo form for the finale. However, thanks to the exceptionally complex and closely worked handling of the basic material, the formal divisions are by no means obvious. The basis of the work is a twelve-note row, which clearly contains within it several devices of vital importance: the main tonalities of the work are E (with a Neapolitan second, or Phrygian F, to inflect the first three notes), E flat (see notes 4–7), and C (in which, if one includes both major and minor, the first six notes also fit). In addition, notes 2–4 provide the kind of three-note harmonic and melodic cell now so familiar as one of Rawsthorne's newer resources, as do notes 5–7, thus implying the bitonality that underpins many of the chord structures. Notes 9–12 (sometimes omitting note 11) feature a cell that will achieve great prominence as the work progresses. The opening bars clearly illustrate the way Rawsthorne approaches the use of this row (Ex. 8.10(*a*)), with the woodwind solos gradually introducing it in fragments, an E on timpani and double basses constantly underlining the home key. In the sixth and seventh bars, clarinet and then flute indicate the melodic properties of notes 9–12 of the row, in different transpositions. Ian White's detailed analysis examines the treatment of the row throughout the work, more thoroughly than is possible here.[12] The second theme, stated on the horns (Ex. 8.10(*b*)), clearly derives from the row, harmonically from the three-note cell and melodically from the leap of a sixth (notes 10 and 12 in the original row), but it introduces one new element (in its third bar), a three-note cell G-F-G-E♭ which is not present in the series (there is no sequence of two whole tones in it) but which is characteristic of

12 'Rawsthorne's Orchestral Sound', *The Creel*, 3/2 (spring 1995), 7–18.

the plainchant from *Carmen vitale* and other similar phrases in Rawsthorne's recent work. Even more significant is the way it is not actually *heard* as a clearly differentiated second subject. Instead, thanks to the almost perpetual motion of semiquavers through this whole section of the movement, it simply seems part of the music's ongoing narrative, though clearly an important part. The

Ex. 8.10. Third Symphony, first movement: (*a*) bars 1–7; (*b*) horn theme, from fig. 3; (*c*) from fig. 9

(*a*)

(*b*)

Ex. 8.10. *Continued*

(*c*)

phrase marked *x* in (Ex. 8.10(*b*)) assumes an important unifying element throughout the work (cf. Ex. 8.14, from the finale).

This utterly seamless flow of invention turns on its head the traditional concept of sonata form, with easily identifiable themes and sections. Here, not only do the themes run into each other, but so do the sections. Only the transition (including a codetta), following the extensively developed first section, adjusts the motion of the music and slows it down to half-bar beats and occasional changes of harmony, with slow-moving melodic lines above (still, of course, derived from the row). The development starts almost immediately, returning to the fragmentary nature of the beginning but leading to a development of the second theme in quietly intense counterpoint for viola and cello (Ex. 8.10(*c*)). This development section contains an episode of lighter, almost waltz-like, character (anticipating the scherzo) but the turbulence of the earlier music revives, building to dramatic, dissonant brass chords (Ex. 8.11), a vehement explosion once again derived straight from the row and already anticipated during the course of the Allegro; this is the most sustained outburst of anger. A simple, quite spare transition leads to the recapitulation, which is again a natural part of the flow and not clearly marked out as a signpost on the journey. It is also characteristically brief, referring to the main themes before the short coda, in which lyrical beauty is disrupted very quietly by one more return of the opening texture and a trill between two luminous polytonal chords based on the three-note cell. The bottom note (in the cellos) is G♯, and it is, in effect, a first-inversion E major chord at heart, inflected by an E flat

Ex. 8.11. Third Symphony, first movement, from 5th bar of fig. 14

grouping at the top. It should be added, however, that the tonality of A, the subdominant of E, is also an important feature of the work, standing at either side of the development section of this movement as a significant marker.

A point ignored in some performances has been the marking 'attacca' at the end of each of the first three movements. It is clearly intended to reinforce the sense of absolute continuity throughout the work, which has been so superbly manifested in the seamless progress of the first movement, where even changes of motion have been a natural part of the music's ebb and flow. To make a conventional hiatus at this point is particularly disruptive, since the dark, obsessive second movement *must* follow the first's coda without a break. Marked

'Alla Sarabanda—Andantino', it is ostensibly in ternary form, the return of the first section being typically brief and telescoped. However, the central part of the movement consists of a threefold build-up of waves of intensity, bursting out into dissonant brass chords and anguished violin phrases and extending the tension by means of an important fortissimo passage of brass and violin counterpoint above a repeated fall of F-E in the tuba and double basses, a reminder in the bass of the Neapolitan relationship in the symphony's first bar (Ex. 8.12(c)). It is entirely characteristic of the wealth of detail embedded within the music that in Ex. 8.12(b), the violin's descending phrases (filling in a phrase occurring as early as the Theme and Variation for two violins; cf. Ex. 3.3) also *rise*: the first notes on successive beats are F♯, G, G♯, and then A. The opening of the sarabande emphasizes the pull between E and E flat, the flute's lonely meditation reminding one of the Allegro's second subject (Ex. 8.12(a)). Serial elements are present in this movement throughout, though the emphasis is different. The ending is memorably mysterious and bleak, the celesta's only appearance in the whole work (a mere five bars)

Ex. 8.12. Third Symphony, second movement: (a) bars 1–9; (b) strings from 3rd bar of fig. 29; (c) from 3rd bar of fig. 31

(a)

serving to reinforce the pull down from F to E. It is impossible verbally to express the brooding power of this wonderful movement, but to mention that the note E is embedded in the texture almost throughout does at least give some indication of its obsessional character. It is the darkest of all Rawsthorne's sarabandes.

The E at its close is far from conclusive. It is therefore necessary again to go straight into the Scherzo without a pause, especially since the opening (Ex. 8.13(a)) is so hesitant and indeterminate. The rocking thirds, the harmony based on the three-note cell, and a melodic oboe phrase all clearly relate to the original row, and there are brief passages where the working-out is if anything more purely serial than in the first movement. However, it is the extraordinary world of what the composer described as 'hints rather than state-ments'[13] that demands the attention; with strings muted throughout, and brass frequently muffled, this is a world of half-lights, of flickering shadows, at times remarkably like the atmosphere of the Cortège from Busoni's *Two Studies for 'Doktor Faust'*. There is only one brief outburst, restrained by the mutes, but

Ex. 8.13. Third Symphony: (*a*) third movement, bars 1–10; (*b*) fourth movement, bars 1–8; (*c*) fourth movement, main theme from 5th bar of fig. 56 (chords omitted)

---

[13] Composer's programme note.

(c)

otherwise this is all quiet, scurrying, whispering, indicative of 'life below the surface', in Rawsthorne's words. The opening material forms a kind of ritornello, whose reappearances are interspersed with episodes, including a ghostly waltz and a trio tune employing a marked dotted rhythm and moving down, tonally, from F through E to E flat (all three of which are sustained simultaneously). Rawsthorne brings back a brief reference to this trio before the final, equally brief reference to the ritornello, somewhat in the manner of the Scherzo in Beethoven's Seventh Symphony. The movement fades with the rocking minor third, to the accompaniment of an eerie E♭ rattling on the xylophone.

The finale, Rawsthorne's longest symphonic movement, bursts in suddenly (Ex. 8.13(b)): three dramatic chords and a diminuendo on E (timpani and cellos) are followed by a slow section which resumes the melodic serial style of the first movement. Just as in the first movement, where he played around with sonata form, extending transitional and codetta sections, so here Rawsthorne plays tricks with rondo form: the chords act as a ritornello phrase, recurring after this brief Andante and then again at the start of a kind of developmental recapitulation of the main material. In addition, he encapsulates the shape of the movement by quickly introducing the Andante material, which will form the essential basis of the episodes as the rondo unfolds. The episodes themselves become longer as it proceeds. A further refinement is that the main tune, which he described as 'obstreperous, emphatic and a little vulgar' (Ex. 8.13(c)), is not heard until the movement has already been under way for some time, developing its material as it goes and preparing the way for a firmer, more decisive tune such as this to take control. It is marked by wide leaps and the occasional dispersal of its line between different instruments which, combined with octave displacements, brings it as near as he ever came to the style of the post-Schönberg school. Interestingly, he reverts, for its final appearance, to deconstruction as a means of dissipating its energy and leaving the way clear for a powerful chordal climax culminating in a (decorated) E major, the lengthy coda emerging out of the collapse of the symphony's aggression. The serial components are clear from the start of the finale: the top three notes of the opening chords are notes 3–2–1 of the original row, while the Andante starts (on clarinet) with the same notes in their prime order (1–2–3). This principle is maintained throughout the movement, especially in the contrapuntal workings of the episodes. For instance, the first three notes of the main theme itself are 1–2–3 of the row, transposed to start on C instead of F, and the harmonies through the movement once again exploit the three-note cell, with the first movement's second theme also playing its part. This last is of particular significance when there is a move towards the resolution to which the symphony is progressing. There is a hint of relaxation during the first episode (Più tranquillo), which occurs after the main theme has been announced and extensively developed. Another turbulent and aggressive development of the ritornello material is succeeded by a second lyrical episode, and here, in a golden glow of E flat major/minor horns and strings (Ex. 8.14), a most moving sense of valediction is introduced briefly and extended, in a passage of Busonian restraint and inner majesty coming to a kind of false ending on C sharp major, until the opening chords burst in to thrust the music forward again.

The valediction has merely been postponed, not banished, however, and in the work's coda (revised and extended after the première) Rawsthorne ties together all the main strands: the note row, the three-note cell, the whole tones of the first movement's second subject, and above all the tonal scheme. The coda moves towards the final E major through a variety of keys which push each other aside in a logical progress towards the central key, recalling motifs heard earlier in tranquil remembrance and closing with quiet reminders first of E flat and then C to leave E major untroubled. It is a deeply moving conclusion. Furthermore, it brings to a satisfactory resolution the conflict which his First Symphony had begun but failed to resolve, the conflict of symphonic argument. In itself, this Third Symphony is a magnificent achievement, seemingly conceived in a single instant of white-hot inspiration. Taken as the culmination of Rawsthorne's symphonic career, it is even more remarkable. The

Ex. 8.14. Third Symphony, fourth movement, from fig. 68

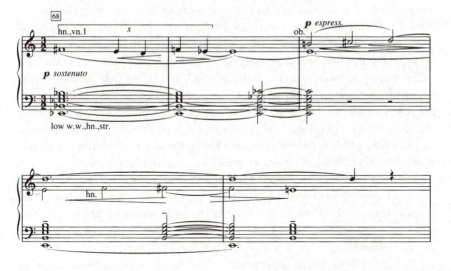

journey from the beginning of the Symphonic Studies, through the three symphonies, to this conclusion is a genuine spiritual odyssey. Peter Evans hints at the formal aspects of this in his article in *The New Grove*: 'Rawsthorne's recourse to pitch serialism is simply one aspect of a developmental process that is ubiquitous. Though first and last movements are sectional structures in matters of tempo, both are sustained by concentrated musical thinking: comparison with the Symphonic Studies shows how far Rawsthorne had escaped from neat structural frames.' The orchestration of the Third Symphony should also be given special praise: it ranges from massive tuttis of exceptional power to a great deal of delicate chamber-music writing, especially for woodwinds, and the use of string harmonics is inspired. There are times when separate blocks of sound are placed against each other, and other times when the counterpoint has unusual intensity and full-bodied sound. Above all, the percussion are used with exquisite precision. The ghostly tappings of side-drum and xylophone in the Scherzo, the celesta at the close of the sarabande, the perfectly placed cymbal clashes, some delicate touches of triangle (a most difficult instrument to use with subtlety)—these all show a composer in complete imaginative command of the medium. The vivid array of orchestral colourings, while always arising out of the content and the expressive needs of the music, is staggering in its variety; moreover, it is all beautifully balanced so that, no matter how complex the texture, everything can be heard clearly.

The symphony received much praise after its first performance, though with reservations. One cannot help feeling that some of the critics were listening to it as if it were by the Rawsthorne of 1951, rather than trying to understand how he had changed. Donald Mitchell described it with some sympathy as 'a tense, nervous, often brooding piece—subdued and quiet for much of the time and yet every so often erupting into violence', and stated that Rawsthorne 'at moments of climax certainly does not shrink from extremes of dissonance', but he refers to a 'gap between the big emotional gestures and the generally reticent character of most of the invention'.[14] Surely that is part of the purpose of the work, which is to build up intensity by the obsessive working with material (for which 'reticent' seems an inadequate description) through occasional massive outbursts? He goes on: 'All those running semiquavers . . . do they work up enough tension to warrant the impassioned climaxes?' It is a fair question, but only if one is listening in the expectation of hearing another version of the Second Piano Concerto, in which case the puzzlement would be understandable. This is a different animal, and must be appreciated as such. Lennox Berkeley, in a memorial tribute in *The Listener*, made clear his admiration for it. Describing the sarabande as 'one of the most beautiful and haunting pieces Rawsthorne ever wrote', he wrote of the conclusion: 'thus the note around which much turmoil has raged finds at last its fulfilment and resting-place'.[15]

It is no surprise that Alan Frank made such sterling efforts, extending beyond Rawsthorne's lifetime, to gain a live London performance for the work: he believed it to be one of the composer's finest works. Yet it never happened, which is remarkable in view of some of the conductors, orchestras, and entrepreneurs who showed genuine interest. Glock, who remained a loyal supporter to Rawsthorne even while he was casting so many non-modernist composers to outer darkness, tried to get it included in the BBC Symphony Orchestra's American tour in 1965, and Colin Davis, then in charge of the orchestra, was said to be keen to perform it. Among others were Lord Harewood (Philharmonia Orchestra), Charles Groves, one of Rawsthorne's most devoted interpreters (Royal Philharmonic Orchestra), and Harold Lawrence, General Manager of the London Symphony Orchestra. Groves did, indeed, put the work in the Royal Liverpool Philharmonic Orchestra's concert celebrating their society's 125th anniversary (1965), though such a difficult work was a controversial choice for a celebratory occasion, despite a magnificent performance. Rawsthorne wrote about it to Frank (15 March 1965): 'The Liverpool

----

[14] *Musical Times*, 105 (Sept. 1964).
[15] (30 Dec. 1971).

concert went well, I think. The hall was packed, but mostly with Mayors, all rattling their chains and applauding in the wrong places.'

Glock provisionally promised to perform the Third Symphony at the Proms, according to a letter from Alan Frank, but never succeeded. However, he did place the Cello Concerto, following its first performance in 1966 at a concert of the Royal Philharmonic Society (whose second Rawsthorne commission this was) in the Royal Festival Hall. The première was not a success, partly because Sir Malcolm Sargent, who conducted, was clearly out of sympathy with the work; Walton's First Symphony, of which he gave a brilliant performance after the interval, was much more his kind of music. As a result, the memorable quality of much of the thematic invention did not come across clearly (the orchestral playing needing more careful balancing and more precise playing), a point seized upon by critics, who, as usual in such cases, blamed the composer. Not everyone was unsympathetic, however. David Cairns, in his *Financial Times* review, described the opening of the first movement as 'pure enchantment—an exquisite cool pattern of interlacing woodwind phrases subtly preparing for the soloist's entry with the gently sinuous main theme whose characteristic rise and fall runs clearly through the entire work' (Ex. 8.15(*a*)). The most notable features of the theme are its wavering between notes, the outline of a scale which it presents (G-F-E in the woodwind, D-C-B in the cello solo), and the fourths which are introduced almost immediately to decorate it, but which become with thirds a vital interval in the development of the work. Alun Hoddinott noted an important chord in bar 15, describing it as 'the first inversion of a minor seventh (with a major third) coloured with bitonal additions that either sharpen the dissonance or make for an opaque sound . . . almost the entire middle section of the [slow] movement derives from the proliferations and exploring of the possibilities inherent in the chord.'[16] On its initial appearance in bar 15 it can also be described as a combination of two transpositions of the three-note cell (minor third plus tone— here, C♯-B-G♯ superimposed on F-E♭-C). Both views are valid, since both kinds of usage are made of the chord as the work progresses.

The first movement is subtitled 'Quasi Variazioni' and presents another subtle version of variation technique, so effortless in its flow that it sounds more like an exceptionally well-integrated sonata form; indeed, Rawsthorne in his programme note warns us that 'it should be heard as a continuous piece rather than as a set of variations in the formal sense'. He also points out that the last of the seven sections 'is in the nature of a recapitulation'. The key-

16 *Tempo*, 77 (summer 1966), 18–19.

centre of the work is C, but it would be difficult to sense this clearly from the first section. It is not until the beginning of the third section that this tonality is affirmed, and not until the last, after a brief cadenza, that it is really established firmly by the cello's accompanying figure, revealing that it was really C even from the very start. With hindsight, one realizes that the first note of the concerto, G, is the dominant, and repeated hearings bring a new sense of adventuring from the start of the work. The style is a curious mixture of the openly diatonic (somewhat akin to the *Pastoral Symphony*) and the extremes of dissonance stated so boldly in the Third Symphony and with almost equal

Ex. 8.15. Cello Concerto: (*a*) first movement, opening; (*b*) first movement, from fig. 20; (*c*) second movement, bars 1–2

(*a*)

(b)

(c)

ferocity in two substantial orchestral sections here. One says 'curious' because the material, though characteristically cellular and integrated, is freer than that in the symphony: there is no obsession with particular elements, nor such a fierce concentration on the motivic and other development. It is more rhapsodic in style. This is true even when, as in Ex. 8.15(b), Rawsthorne telescopes the theme to provide an intensely contrapuntal orchestral variation. The climaxes, therefore, seem less an eruption of subterranean turbulence than a sudden outpouring by way of contrast; in short, they seem to arise less spontaneously from the material itself, more from the confrontation between soloist and orchestra and the need to provide variety in a movement of this length.

In the first movement, the ebb and flow of intensity, matching the kind of fluctuation one would expect from a sonata form, adds to the subtlety with which Rawsthorne handles the free variation form he is employing. The D (minor) slow movement, marked 'Mesto', is equally rhapsodic in feeling, but far more concentrated in thought. Whereas the introduction and main theme of the Allegro Lirico had a basic downward urge, here the music gropes uncertainly out of the darkness, and is forced upward by the piling-up of minor/major thirds (Ex. 18.15(*c*)). A little upward waltz-like phrase which is to play an important part later in the movement is intoned in the clarinets (end of bar 2, also using the thirds), culminating in a massive, tragic outburst and, later, a powerful inversion of this little phrase. The cello's entry is an impassioned descending phrase that sets the imploring tone of the soloist's relationship with the orchestra, and Rawsthorne intensifies the emotion by gradually increasing the number of notes per beat in the cello part, so that the growing elaboration of the writing helps to sustain the tightening of the emotional screw. David Cairns is eloquent on this slow movement:

Nothing is more moving in the work than the way the sustained melodic sweep of the movement's first half declines, after a sombre and genuinely grand climax, into a pathetic passage . . . in which the soloist stammers and stutters, as if struggling to break free into fresh flights of lyrical expansion, but can only repeat with quiet resignation the sighing figures of the work's main theme. The movement ends with a sense of intense solitariness, silence and sadness. It is the essence of Rawsthorne's deep, stoical melancholy.

It is a far cry from the black bitterness of the Second Violin Concerto's slow movement, but no less profound. The change from the first movement's variety of orchestral colourings to this darkening purple is remarkable, and there is little to lighten the darkness.

Difficulties arise when considering the finale, Allegro, which starts with a resounding fanfare-like version of the opening main theme, wrenching the tonality from D back to C in the space of three notes. The first subject proper, accompanied by an oom-pah polka bass, is an extraordinarily blatant assumption of cheerfulness, attractive enough in its own terms. Hoddinott was in no doubt about its appeal, commenting that it 'bowls along in Rawsthorne's most vital, genial, and invigorating manner. The buoyancy and good humour of the thematic ideas and developments allied with the compellingly propulsive rhythmic patterns and an uninhibited C major tonality make this finale the perfect foil for the more introspective mood of the previous two movements.'[17] The tonality has gradually been strengthened throughout the work, so that its openness in the finale seems natural, and there is much splendid invention through what sounds like a rondo. It looks like one too, but it also contains strong signs of being another kind of variation movement, more elusively

[17] 'Rawsthorne's Concertos', in 'BBC Music Review', *Listener* (31 Mar. 1966).

derived from the work's main theme. There is even, hidden away in one of the episodes (or variations) a discreet fugal section on the brass (but quietly, almost self-effacingly, if one can imagine a self-effacing brass fugue). The real problem is the first subject itself: its bare effrontery is an almost brutal contrast to the Mesto's sombre mood. However, it is less uncomfortable when it reappears, and though this is an extensive movement, with much decorative solo writing, it shows great imagination, especially in a section near the start which is pure chamber music, involving the solo cello in duets with clarinet, bassoon, and oboe. The cello entry itself is splendidly alert and businesslike, too. Rawsthorne wisely cut a substantial section (no less than eighty-three bars) after the first performance, thereby excising some unnecessary repetition and note-spinning, reserving a new triplet style for the final Vivace 3/8 section. This emerges brightly to sweep the concerto to an imposing conclusion. One of the work's most distinctive features is the range of cello writing it employs. Though Rawsthorne is exceptionally well suited to the more melancholy, yearning tones at the instrument's command, he is able also to write admirably apt scherzando passages, light and airy in character, and there is much crisp, urgent solo writing as well. The finale's cadenza is a beautifully managed bit of sleight of hand; it is quite short and rhapsodic, but serves not only to accomplish the usual purpose of such things but also to bring the tonality back to C and, in addition, to prepare the way for a change to triplet rhythms for the final section; Rawsthorne never indulged in virtuosity for its own sake, but was always concerned to make it serve a useful musical purpose as well as that of mere display.

9

THE LAST YEARS (1967–71)

RAWSTHORNE's last work in concerto form, the Concerto for Two Pianos, was much terser in expression than the Cello Concerto. It was commissioned by the BBC for the 1968 Proms, where it was given its première by John Ogdon and Brenda Lucas. It was subsequently revised, as usual with his major works, the finale's introduction being omitted (even before the first performance) and the ending extended. Rawsthorne wrote that a difficulty lay 'in the appalling number of notes one has to contend with. Such is the range of the keyboard and the agility with which it can be manipulated that two grand pianofortes plus a symphony orchestra present an array of resources which can at times become bewildering.'[1] His response, however, is typically resourceful, and in many passages he responded to the challenge with vitality and imagination. If the work is, ultimately, less than completely satisfactory, this must lie in the gradual diminution in his energies. It is a tribute to his strength of purpose that, despite all his problems, he had maintained such creative vigour until the mid-1960s, but there is no doubt that even he could no longer fully withstand the ravages of ill health and alcohol. The conclusion of this work, another example of his offhand use of contrary-motion chromatic scales, reveals the crucial loss of energy.

The economy of the concerto is shown by the duration, eighteen minutes (fifteen minutes shorter than the Cello Concerto). Such terseness is emphasized by the essentially sectional nature of the work, which, unlike the Third Symphony, with its strong sense of forward momentum through all four movements, or the Cello Concerto, with its concern to achieve continuity of thought, falls into a series of vignettes. This is particularly true of the finale, another theme and variations. The closest unity is shown by the opening Allegro di bravura. Here, the ABCBA form which has become one of his solutions to the task of developing sonata form has a brilliant, showy opening and final section, with a 6/8 Allegro providing the most extended and developmental part of the whole work. The central section is a declamatory 3/4, full

---

[1] Composer's programme note.

of romantic fire and passion but giving way first to some deliciously decorative writing and then to almost static reflection before the 6/8 creeps back in to build the movement to its thunderous return of the opening material. The movement is rounded off with a simple and most beautiful slow coda, preparing the way for the second movement (Adagio ma non troppo). This is a straightforward ternary form, in which sombre, almost fragmentary themes with accompanying harmonies of quiet dissonance frame a dramatic, almost rhapsodic central section.

In the Theme and Variations, an amiable 6/8 theme somewhat reminiscent of the Allegro tune from the first movement (though marked 'Allegretto con moto', and thus steadier in pace) receives immediate decoration from the pianos (variation 1) and then a variety of treatments in clearly differentiated sections. The second variation, at the same basic pace, is in 3/4, with some delightful piano arabesques and a more intensely dissonant, but always quiet, orchestral variation of the tune. Variation 3 is an Allegro energico, exploiting the percussive sound of the piano in excitingly dissonant chords (one senses Rawsthorne's pleasure in the unity between this kind of keyboard sound and this particular aspect of his harmonic style) but running out of steam before long. Each variation, indeed, descends to a quiet pause, suggesting either that a strong through-line was unimportant to Rawsthorne in this movement, or that he had himself lost the ability to sustain intellectual energy through a continuous piece of any size. The fourth variation, however, is a lovely expression of typical melancholy, with a brief passionate outburst in the middle (the process of the slow movement miniaturized, as it were, making the variation seem to be the repetition of an idea already explored), and the fifth is a fairly raucous 3/8 Allegro which several times seems to run out of vigour; the third time it gains a fine burst of excitement and leads to the concerto's virtuosic coda. This is extremely brief (too brief?), and not entirely convincing, though it is at least better than the original, which was even shorter and led to an extraordinarily banal final B flat major chord. Alan Frank was perturbed: 'Can I ask you a crude question? Do you really believe in that final chord? It baffles many of us.'[2] Rawsthorne's answer was to provide a slightly longer finish, but one that is not really much more satisfactory.

The tonal scheme of the work is odd: first movement on an ambiguous A, but immediately introducing a B flat major scale to indicate that this is really the tonal centre of the whole work, second movement ambiguously on G but never really establishing any basic key, and finale starting with a theme

---

[2] Letter to Rawsthorne, 16 Aug. 1968.

indicating B flat but immediately cancelling it. The ending, in both versions, is unambiguously in B flat major, however. What is of more interest is the use of a different series of twelve notes for each movement (rather than one series for the whole work, as in the Third Symphony). It emerges only in the first movement's 6/8; the opening is based more on clashes of bitonality and a main theme owing much to plainchant inspiration (Ex. 9.1(*a*)). In the slow movement, the opening section shows clearly how Rawsthorne uses a different series to provide the harmonies and melodic lines of the pianos' entry (Ex. 9.1(*b*)), while in the finale the series contains a group of whole tones linking it with the 'plainchant' tune in the first movement, but otherwise does not seem related to the material of the first two movements. Rawsthorne's handling of this serial element is freer and less rigorous than in the Third Symphony: he uses it merely to provide a reservoir of melodic material, so that he can provide the different themes in each movement with a unifying element. It becomes, in short, more of a serial gesture than an instinctive use of the method.

The most exciting features of the concerto are the sheer physical exhilaration of the more virtuosic sections, the unity of keyboard sound and harmonic content both in the louder sections (see Ex. 9.1(*c*) for an excerpt from the finale) and in the quieter ones (where the harmonies are similar but equally pianistic as soft, delicately coloured textures), and the genuine poetry to be felt in the slower reflective passages. There is, too, some marvellous exploitation of the ability of the two pianos to produce wonderfully fluid, fast-moving

Ex. 9.1. Concerto for Two Pianos: (*a*) first movement, from 5 before letter B; (*b*) second movement, opening; (*c*) third movement, from letter J

(*a*)

(b)

(c)

textures, full of colour and life; Rawsthorne did not normally overwork colouristic ideas, and this work provided him with the opportunity to create sounds he had never before been able to make. Overall, though, there are too many similarities between one passage and others in the same vein, both quick and slow: it suggests that the composer's store of ideas was running out. The work has much attractive music, and deserves revival, but is not the culminating contribution to the two-piano concerto repertoire for which, knowing Rawsthorne's wonderful solo piano concertos, one might have hoped.

Only three minor vocal pieces stem from this last period. Of these, 'Streets of Laredo', a setting of Louis MacNeice's surrealist poem for voices and guitar, was written for a recording of new ballads by various composers, and is an amusing but perhaps over-long exercise in writing a latter-day popular ballad of the kind that might have been heard (with equivalent topical or political content) a couple of centuries or so earlier. It is a bitter little piece with a deadly sting in the tail, using the guitar almost entirely chordally (there is only a tiny bit of counterpoint) and firmly centred in D major. The undated 'Two Fish', the manuscript of which was discovered after Rawsthorne's death, is a setting of a translation of a poem by the sixteenth-century writer Guillaume du Barthas contrasting two fish, 'Th'adult'rous Sargus' and 'the constant Catharus'. The piano part is massive (so heavy, indeed, that it has been suggested it was intended for orchestral treatment), the bitonal harmonies at the start being the basis for the invention. The vocal part is attractive, the two stanzas sufficiently contrasted (the second a gentler variation of the first), and the sounds pleasant enough, but this ironic little fable did not draw his most subtle response. The remaining vocal piece, 'Scena rustica' for soprano and harp, was commissioned in 1967 by the Summer Music Society of Dorset. It was written for Sheila Armstrong and Marisa Robles, but illness prevented the first performance taking place, and though the work was published and presumably has been performed somewhere, there seems to be no record of this. It is a setting of a characteristically forthright and ironic poem by John Skelton about rustic love, rather heavy-handed harmonically and texturally (there is much near-contrapuntal harp writing that gets in the way of the vocal line), with, as in 'Two Fish', an emphasis on bitonal harmony. There are touches of rustic jollity here and there, but the melodic line lacks a sense of either memorability or, more crucially, direction.

The Ballade for piano, Rawsthorne's last solo piano work, was commissioned by the Cardiff Festival of 20th-Century Music, an admirable initiative started by the then Professor of Music at University College, Cardiff, Alun Hoddinott, a long-standing admirer of Rawsthorne (he also commissioned the Piano

Quintet at the university), and John Ogdon, who later made a fine recording, gave the première in March 1967, taking it to the USA shortly afterwards. There were many links between the participants in this event. Both Rawsthorne and Ogdon studied at the RMCM, the latter for a time with Gordon Green, and Rawsthorne's love of Chopin, which Ogdon shared, was a vital ingredient in the composition. Indeed, it was originally intended to be a four-movement work, each movement taking its title from various Chopinesque genres (nocturne, polonaise, and so on). In the event, Rawsthorne chose to write a single movement in the form to which he was particularly close, the ballade, a choice which feels instinctively right for him. In his programme note he refers to the introductory section as being 'in the gently moving six-eight which Chopin has so irrevocably associated with a "narrative" style'. This introduction immediately sets out the main cells (Ex. 9.2(*a*)), a diatonic (C major) wavering over three notes and a phrase built out of fourths, establishing

Ex. 9.2. Ballade for piano: (*a*) bars 1–12; (*b*) p. 2, bars 1–5; (*c*) p. 2, Allegro furioso, bars 1–3; (*d*) from p. 15, bar 20

(*a*)

Ex. 9.2. *Continued*

(*b*)

(*c*)

Allegro furioso

(*d*)

bitonality as a strong element straight away. In the eighteenth bar, the music, having spread over the whole upper range of the keyboard, circles around to return magically and beautifully to middle C, the first note of the piece. (When asked why C was his favourite key, Rawsthorne replied that middle C was the easiest note on the piano to find after a few drinks!) The right-hand arabesque in bar 10 clearly derives from the fourths of bar 3, filling them in with an extra note to produce the by now ubiquitous three-note cell (starting G-F-D in this case). This is a vital component in the harmonies heard a few bars later (Ex. 9.2(*b*)), which fill in an inverted statement of the opening motif with silvery chords perfectly imagined for this register of the piano but also fulfilling the harmonic ideas already mooted, above a C pedal note.

The slow sections of the Ballade are marked by an acute sensitivity to pianistic colouring, more perhaps than any of his other solo works, with Debussy a strong influence, though the close integration of the sound with thematic material gives an added strength of purpose and sense of unity to what, in other hands, might simply be a pretty noise. Somewhat in the manner of Chopin's Second Ballade, the one of Chopin's four ballades that this work most closely resembles, a fast virtuoso section bursts in (Ex. 9.2(*c*)), the rising fourths in the bass being derived from the introduction but developing them into what seems like a new theme. The virtuosity demanded of the pianist is staggering: exploring an exciting variety of textures, it builds to a powerful passacaglia in which the composer clarifies the unity behind the various ideas of the first two sections. This Allegro furioso is a large-scale movement of almost symphonic power, so much so that it can make the rest of the Ballade seem almost anticlimactic unless the performer keeps something in reserve. A return of the opening, altered of course, leads to a sprightly section varying the sequential fourths of Ex. 9.2(*c*) with the aid of the three-note chords, to maintain the unity between the ideas, and after a brief reference back to the slower music, the final section commences with a polka-like variation of the Allegro furioso material, building in brilliance and intensity until it achieves perhaps the most awesomely virtuosic writing of Rawsthorne's career (Ex. 9.2(*d*)), in which the keyboard style of the Second Piano Concerto's finale (also fearfully difficult) is recalled. The ending revives the simplicity of the opening section, and after a brief Debussyan arpeggio, middle C once again quietly holds sway.

It is a considerable feat to revive in so authentically personal a manner the form and style of the Chopin ballade. Rawsthorne's contribution to this tradition is successful because he understood both Chopin and the piano itself so well. His skill at registering the sound is particularly acute: he allows chords to be close in the upper registers, where clarity is more easily obtained, spacing the notes more widely in the bass except where extra power is required, a technique Chopin also used. The relationship between the two, in terms of their often deceptively fast-moving harmonic motion, can be illustrated by referring to Chopin's Fourth Ballade, at the lead into the new theme in the centre of the piece; the movement of harmony and tonality here is eminently comparable to Rawsthorne's own manner (see Ex. 9.3). However, the form of the piece, even though it derives from a consideration of Chopin's ballades, is entirely Rawsthorne's own extension of the idea. James Gibb also sees the addition to Rawsthorne's keyboard style of 'a Lisztian *bravura* and a persistently inventive transformation of thematic material that suggests a further influence from the same source',[3] to which entirely convincing point one might add the shadow of Busoni, both in the virtuoso writing and in the harmonic otherworldness, derived from the vestiges of the whole-tone scale running through the music, often under the surface. There is also a poignant aspect to the Ballade: at one point or another, all of Rawsthorne's previous piano solo works are recalled, however momentarily. Perhaps, subconsciously, he was bidding farewell to his own instrument. Certainly, it conveys the impression of a revival of the intellectual and emotional energy which had already begun to dissipate in the works of the previous year (1966), and which he was never fully to recapture in succeeding works, fine though some of them are.

Ex. 9.3. Chopin, Ballade No. 4 in F minor, bars 80–6

[3] 'The Piano Music', Poulton iii. 63.

Among the orchestral works from this late period, two are for youth orchestras. The shorter one, *Overture for Farnham*, was commissioned for the 1967 Farnham Festival (which specialized, under the direction of Alan Fluck, in commissioning a large number of new works for local schools and amateurs), and as noted before, one detects a certain restriction on the composer's imagination when writing for young people. The style is entirely recognizable, but more diatonic than usual (as if he feared to write too chromatically), and the ending, the contrary-motion chromatic scales, is a bad sign, as is the reliance on a number of other devices, including canonic treatment of a broader secondary tune, familiar from *Street Corner* (but without its freshness). The introductory theme is a pompous, neo-Handelian flourish, developed quite extensively, and the main theme itself has a disarming nursery-like innocence. The attempt to combine these two towards the end is self-conscious, and scored with unusual clumsiness. It is not, in the last resort, a piece likely to win converts to Rawsthorne's cause, for all the incidental delights here and there. The Theme, Variations and Finale of 1967, written for the Essex County Youth Orchestra, who took it to Berlin after the first performance, is more successful, though one has some reservations; perhaps the larger canvas enabled him to relax somewhat. Of course, writing for a good youth orchestra is easier than composing for schools: one may reasonably have higher expectations of their expertise.

The Theme itself, announced gently after a brief slow introduction, is one of Rawsthorne's amiable compound-time tunes, 12/8 in this case, not especially memorable either as a tune or in orchestral texture, but with potential for variation. The most interesting feature orchestrally is some prominent but quiet tapping for side-drum (muffled) and tambourine, though this spotlighting of the percussion is not followed through in the rest of the work save for one brief and effective use of Chinese block. Otherwise, percussion is used fairly conventionally. The first and last (sixth) variations have strong rhetorical phrases, though their implications are developed with insufficient thoroughness. Instead, the first gradually dissipates the energy in some rather ordinary development, and the sixth opts merely for hints of a possible extra variation in a gently flowing 5/8 before, instead of following this up, plunging into the Finale. 'Plunging' is perhaps not the right word, since each variation peters out to a silence before the start of the next. The best of them is the fifth and penultimate one, a lively, sometimes raucous 3/4 at a speed bringing it close to the spirit of the Beethoven one-in-a-bar scherzo before it becomes apparent that it is really a somewhat crazy waltz, a highly entertaining one at that. There are few such movements in Rawsthorne's output, which is perhaps why it seems fresher than the previous sections. Freshness is a characteristic of the Finale, too, a rather hornpipey and very diatonic piece based on a theme of rising and falling fourths which has an engaging openness. Unfortunately, its effect is somewhat vitiated by the closing bars, which, once again, fall back on contrary-motion scales to bring the piece to a thoroughly manufactured conclusion.

Perhaps Rawsthorne's intellectual energy was finally vanishing. After a three-year period of abstinence, he had started drinking wine again in 1964, and was in any case extremely disappointed by the relatively poor reception accorded his Cello Concerto of 1965, as well as the infrequent broadcasts of his music. He must also have been aware that Alan Frank's determined efforts to achieve a London performance of the Third Symphony after its successful Cheltenham première in 1964 had so far been unsuccessful (at the time of writing, 1997, it still awaits a public London performance, which is a disgrace)—though the extent of Frank's efforts would probably not have been known to him. He must also have felt increasingly that, however much of an accommodation he had made in his own way with serial technique, received opinion had largely relegated him to a category of distinguished but unfashionable names. The new Establishment certainly showed no sign of any awareness of the numerous developments that had occurred in his style over the years, continuing to regard him as utterly set in his ways. Thus to deny the achievements of his later years, and to ignore the continuing development shown by the Third Symphony and Cello Concerto, was a blot on British critical writing and entrepreneurship that must have depressed him a good deal.

February 1969 saw the first performance of another BBC commission, Rawsthorne's last orchestral work *Triptych*, whose original title was 'Prelude, Fantasia, and Fugue', under which name Norman del Mar and the BBC Northern Symphony Orchestra gave the première at a BBC Music Weekend in Lancaster. The title was changed, with 'Postlude' replacing 'Fugue' before Rawsthorne arrived at the final title of the published work, suggesting that he was not completely sure of his aims in the writing of the work. This seems clear from the finale, in which the fugue is commenced but not developed in any meaningful way after an exploratory introduction; the final section is fragmentary and inscrutable, with vestiges of melodic ideas floating in and out above low, brooding chords. There is something poignant about the final cadence, onto a single pizzicato C (his favourite tonality), and a genuine air of finality about it, as if he knew it was his farewell to the orchestra, whose repertoire he had so marvellously enriched during his career. But this work is not worthy of that inheritance. The ideas are patchy, and while Rawsthorne was incapable of writing a work without giving us some beguiling orchestral colours, including a prominent reminiscence of the atmosphere of the *Medieval Diptych* near the start, the vigour of the central Allegro is fitful. Since so much depends on the success of this, the most substantial part of the work, its failure to maintain a line or develop material convincingly is most disappointing. How sad that both Rawsthorne and his friend Walton should each, in his last orchestral work, no longer have the energy to pursue the ideas that were still there to be expressed. Walton's *Prologo e Fantasia* shows more promise than *Triptych*, but falls tragically short of its potential, and so does this work. Fortunately, Rawsthorne during the period of the Concerto for Two Pianos and the *Triptych* wrote other, more modest works which represent him if not at the peak of his powers, then at least still able to command both intellectual force and emotional fire.

The 1968 Piano Quintet, commissioned by University College, Cardiff, is almost first-class—almost, because at the end, the repeat of a 'brash' (Rawsthorne's word) tune heard earlier in the work seems a touch automatic. It succeeds in being engaging, however, and most of the quintet is a good deal more than that. There is poetry in the quieter music, depth in the slow movements, and much inventive writing in the quicker sections. The ground-plan is relatively simple: after an introduction setting forth the main themes (Ex. 9.4(*a*)), there are four sections, an amiable, translucent Allegretto, a purposeful Allegro (including the 'brash' theme already mentioned), an unusually spacious Lento non troppo ranging from reflective gloom to fiery passion, and a final reworking of two ideas from the Allegro, possibly too brief to make a completely satisfactory peroration. One's sense of anticlimax, however, must be put in context. This is a composer who positively disliked exact repetition, and who regarded straightforward complete recapitulation as unnecessary restatement of something that had already been fully stated. Viewing him in that light, one can understand and perhaps appreciate the brevity of Rawsthorne's repetition of these ideas in this last section; nevertheless, it is unlike him to repeat bits of them so exactly. When his imagination was working at full power, he would have subtly varied the material, as well as allowing himself a little more time to give such reworking its proper effect. To this criticism must be added the comment that occasionally some of the cadences are a little half-hearted.

But this is to be perhaps too severely critical of a work that is, in proportions and scope, relatively modest, at only just over a quarter of an hour. The quintet is continuous. Though Rawsthorne himself described the division into four main sections, that does not convey the richness of structural imagination displayed in, especially, the Allegretto. This opens with a characteristically amiable tune (Ex. 9.4(*b*)) of a kind usually heard in 6/8; here, it is in 9/8, and its shape and rhythmic contour bring it unusually close to Bartók's Sixth Quartet. But after developing this idea, which is clearly related to the initial eleven-note row, and the secondary opening theme, with much variety, he allows the music to expand its essentially narrative style, undergoing numer-

Ex. 9.4. Piano Quintet: (*a*) bars 1–8; (*b*) Allegretto, bars 1–3; (*c*) Lento non troppo, from fig. 24

(*a*)

(*b*)

(c)

ous changes of tempo (including a powerful restatement of the opening cells) with the aid of accelerandos, before the easygoing Allegretto motion is resumed, this time with delightful piano decoration. The quintet deploys all the variety of harmonic structures that Rawsthorne had acquired in his vocabulary over the years, from complex multitonal chords through usage of the familiar three-note cell to simple fifths or major thirds, and in the Poco lento that closes this first movement, he thins the texture out to a minimum. It is curious that this Poco lento, ostensibly a coda to the first 'movement', is sufficiently extended to have the feeling of being a brief, semi-fledged slow movement in its own right, even to its peaceful C major conclusion: in that sense, it anticipates the real slow movement perhaps too strongly, robbing it of some of its meaning before it has really started.

The Allegro which follows is extensive and develops the material with great ingenuity and charm, the shift of mood from the extrovert vulgarity of the 'brash' tune to something more powerfully intense being managed with great skill, though instead of recapitulating its opening idea, with its contrapuntal vigour, it merely thins out at the end once more to a sparse cello line. The Lento non troppo follows as an exploration of some of the implications of these thinner, slower ideas, including the heart of the work, a beautiful evocation of immense space (Ex. 9.4(c)) and a subsequent outburst of rhetoric. The final Allegro brings the work into something resembling an eccentric sonata form. Thus, the first 'subject' could be said to be the Allegretto, and its restatement, after the increase in tempo has run its course, the recapitulation thereof; the Allegro acts as a kind of second subject group, whose recapitulation forms the last section of the work. In replacing single themes by whole sections, which almost justify the description 'movement', Rawsthorne is once again playing Haydnesque games with form, and it very nearly comes off with brilliant success.

There are otherwise few innovations in the quintet: most of the thematic and harmonic ideas have been heard before. But they remain for the most part fresh and engaging, and Rawsthorne is particularly successful at balancing the string group with the piano, normally regarded as one of the most difficult problems in writing for this medium. Malcolm Boyd was more convinced of the structural integrity of the work, which he summarized as 'in a single movement, bringing together elements of the traditional four-movement pattern and at the same time achieving a convincing unity by constant back-reference to two contrasted and, as it happens, 12-note themes heard at the opening of the work'.[4] Rawsthorne changed the metronome marks, as he often did, after performance, but stated in a letter prior to the première, 'please don't take them too literally', an indication of his general approach to such things.[5]

There were a few more chamber works to come. From the same year, 1968, there is a charming, surprisingly light and airy Suite for flute, viola, and harp, written for the Robles Trio. Though containing a serial element (a twelve-note series emerges gradually as one of the principal thematic and harmonic ideas), it also has some diatonic themes and chords. The last of the three movements begins with a vigorous idea, almost a pounding rustic dance in C major accompanied by brisk thirteenth chords on the harp which have been anticipated in the opening Allegro moderato (preceded, as usual, by a slow introduction setting forth the note row, in exploratory fashion). The central movement is an expressive Intermezzo, marked 'Andantino', with delicate hints of both siciliano and waltz, though a more romantic interlude on harp looks for all the world like Rawsthorne's familiar style of piano writing. The harp part is effective, recalling at times the sound-world of the superior *Lament for a Sparrow*, and Rawsthorne resists the temptation to indulge in glissando washes of sound: the only glissando, at the end of the first movement, is part of a single, marvellously imagined texture. This is hardly an important work, and the melodic material is in itself not particularly memorable, but as a divertissement it is sweet and charming, with a vernal freshness reflecting Rawsthorne's pastoral side. Doubtless this derives partly from the medium itself, but his ideas are perfectly suited to it.

After the lesser quality of the works from 1968–9, and the disappointment of *Triptych*, 1970 saw at least a partial return to form with an Oboe Quartet

---

[4] First performance review, *Musical Times*, 109 (May 1968), 456.
[5] Letter to the author, 25 Feb. 1968.

(actually, of course, his second, though the early one from 1935 remains unpublished). The first performance, in May 1970, was given by the London Oboe Quartet, whose oboist, Janet Craxton, had long been an admirer of Rawsthorne's music; this quartet was commissioned by the City Music Society. It marks a further exploration of serial technique, more thoroughgoing than in the Concerto for Two Pianos, for the same set informs all three movements, though he takes care to depart from it to allow his lyrical impulses full freedom when necessary. He is as always careful, of course, to select a note row that will give him the kind of phraseology and harmonic content with which he is in sympathy. The row is stated contrapuntally between oboe and violin in the slow introduction; the 6/8 Allegretto which forms the body of the first movement uses it freely but with variety within an extremely terse utterance. There is not an ounce of unwanted fat on the music, but it develops a fine romantic intensity, and the ebb and flow of feeling is beautifully managed. The essence of the work is the oboe's plaint above the workings of the string trio, whether as contrapuntal accompaniment or as a primary source of interest to which the oboe adds a commentary. Rawsthorne's own personal musical fingerprint, the four-note tag (for instance, A♯-B-C♯-D), figures more prominently in this work than in almost any since the 1950s, suggesting a nostalgic glance backwards. This feeling of nostalgia, of a reflective survey of elements from the past, is heightened by the slow movement, which begins (as did the second movement of his 1935 Oboe Quartet) with oboe recitative passages and gives a particularly lamenting flavour to the oboe part. The finale, which begins with a contrapuntal gesture reminiscent of the opening of the Third Quartet, is a rondo in feeling, if not precisely in form, ending with a flourish.

Commentators are divided about the stature of this work. Sebastian Forbes is critical particularly of the last movement, finding the energy 'sometimes shortlived and contrived',[6] but it seems to the present writer more satisfying. The anonymous annotator for the Redcliffe Ensemble's compact disc recording describes it as a 'vintage' work:

It displays the typical Rawsthorne lyricism, which by now is refined. The fire is still there, but it is kept under control . . . here there is also to be found a personal, sombre quality. The counterpoint is clean and classical, while the individual harmonic progressions give the music a forward impulse and a power which is denied to music based on static harmonies.[7]

The use of a single set throughout the work, though not as rigorous as in the Third Symphony, gives it quiet strength through unity. The deliberate use of

---

[6] 'The Chamber Music', Poulton iii. 38.   [7] Redcliffe Recordings RR 006 (London, 1991).

familiar ideas in a context of unusual, often elliptical spareness and the combination of lyrical plaintiveness with contrapuntal development (see Ex. 9.5,
from the finale) all seem attractive and moving, and if the vigour of the ending
may seem a touch contrived, it does not detract from a work of considerable
quiet authority. It makes, incidentally, a perfect programme companion for the
Mozart Oboe Quartet, to the marvellous classical lyricism and subtlety of
which the economy and concentration of this late Rawsthorne work is an excellent foil.

The lyricism of the 1970 Oboe Quartet is, however, not anodyne.
Rawsthorne, though he might sometimes have fallen into traps of self-repeti-
tion of his own making, was never one to take the easy way out as far as the
listener was concerned, save in a few lesser works which are unlikely to have
lasting value. Unfortunately, one of these is his last completed work, the
Quintet for clarinet, horn, violin, cello, and piano, commissioned by the Music
Group of London and written in 1970, with the first performance early the
following year; this was almost certainly the last première he attended. It is
sparse in the extreme, and has been praised by some critics for its exceptional
economy of means. In the course of less than ten minutes, it explores, through
three slow sections interspersed with two Allegros, material similar to that of

Ex. 9.5. Oboe Quartet (1970), finale, from fig. 26

the Oboe Quartet, with a similar inclination for the melodic lines to investigate a freely chromatic line of distinctly serial bent. The writing is extremely austere: there are only ten bars in the entire piece in which all five instruments play simultaneously (and the piano is restricted to left hand in one of those), while the strings have very few passages of double-stopping. Instead, the instruments are confined to linear writing, sometimes vigorously contrapuntal in implication (though this is not carried through), sometimes with overlapping melodic lines, while the piano, often playing in octaves (especially in the Allegros), also provides the harmonic colouring as well as the occasional percussive edge; the reminder, in the Allegros, of the scherzo from his much finer Quintet for piano and wind, brings with it an unfortunate comparison with that more dynamic piece. There is nothing wrong with austerity, provided it results in a particular kind of lyricism (as the Oboe Quartet does, for instance), but here there is only a wandering kind of line which seems not to have a distinct aim in view. The two Allegros are based on the same material, but the second contains some attempts at cheerfulness which are, frankly, embarrassingly unfounded in the material from which they suddenly spring so intrusively. There are moments of lyrical beauty, or even a strange kind of remote warmth, but as a whole this is the poorest of Rawsthorne's three quintets, and one of his least interesting chamber works. The final cadence, into A major, is a weak resolution, typical of the work's lack of conviction.

Rawsthorne had always been a painstaking composer, but his health was sadly deteriorating. In February 1971 Alan Frank wrote to Hoddinott, who had asked for a string trio from Rawsthorne, that he had started but 'works very, very slowly these days'. Fortunately, he left one more work, though it was unfinished, and it proved to be one of his most moving, the Elegy for guitar. It was being written for Julian Bream, with whom Rawsthorne collaborated from the start, and when the composer died, the opening slow section and what was to be the central quick one were complete, up to bar 131, with a few sketches to show how he intended to continue. Bream was convinced that the work could be completed; he was also anxious that Isabel 'should receive the commission money in full, as her financial position at that time was pretty precarious'.[8] Both Bream and Gerard Schurmann, who was also consulted by Alan Frank, produced completed versions, Bream's published edition varying in some details from Schurmann's (it is slightly shorter). They both pursue a similar basic course, however, and should not be regarded as alternatives. It would certainly have been entirely characteristic for Rawsthorne

---

[8] Julian Bream, letter to the author, 4 Oct. 1997.

to have repeated the opening section, varying and abbreviating it as he did so, a precedent followed with great care in both completions (Bream comments that 'it took me two agonized days to sort out the last bar!'). In the form in which it has reached us, it is a noble lament, 'of a melancholy, haunting beauty', as Walton affectionately described it.[9] The Elegy is based on another series of notes which has clear serial implications (Ex. 9.6(a)), which are for the most part followed through freely rather than strictly. The C minor/major ambiguity in bar 5 and the side-slip down from C to B in bar 6 are also characteristic, and occur as a ritornello in the first section; Bream chose not to recapitulate it in his closing section. The theme is also notable for the fourths in bars 2–3. The fourth had been a favourite interval for many years, but lately had been less noticeably part of Rawsthorne's intervallic armoury—its reappearance as a prominent feature in this work is a mark, surely, of his practical mind at work, since the guitar tuning is dominated by fourths, and the piece would thus be idiomatic for the instrument. The fourths are particularly useful in the excitable central Allegro di bravura e rubato, where they provide a virtuosic inner decoration of the main theme (Ex. 9.6(b)). The return of the opening Andante brings back the grave, sombre tone of the first section, a feeling hardly to be encountered anywhere in Rawsthorne's output prior to this work; there are dark, melancholy, tragic movements in numerous works, with different degrees or kinds of anguish, but this is more removed from the passionate intensity of his earlier music. At the last, Rawsthorne reached back over the centuries to the contemplative world of the pavans of William Byrd. The Elegy is a fit companion piece to the many other fine works inspired by Julian Bream's playing, such as those by Walton, Tippett, Richard Rodney Bennett, Henze, and, of course, Britten's masterly *Nocturnal*. The final cadence may be Bream's invention, but it is entirely of a piece with the rest of the Elegy, and fits perfectly into its noble lament (Ex. 9.6(c)).

In 1971, Rawsthorne braved some exceptionally hot weather to attend the ceremony for the award to him of a Doctorate of Letters at Essex University, one of the numerous honorary awards he received during his last decade, including also doctorates from the universities of Belfast and Liverpool and an honorary Fellowship of Downing College, Cambridge, as well as the CBE in 1961. His fragile health had left him unable to withstand the effects of the heat, and after contracting pneumonia he died on 24 July. Among letters received by Isabel after Alan's death, Basil Wright's paid tribute to his genius and economy of means as a composer for films. John Ogdon's letter included

---

[9] 'Preface', Poulton iii. 1–2.

Ex. 9.6. Elegy for guitar: (*a*) bars 1–6; (*b*) bars 90–4; (*c*) bar 160 to end

(*a*)

Andante molto serioso

(*b*)

(Allegro di bravura e rubato)

(*c*)

a delightful, revealing vignette: 'I always remember 'phoning Alan and asking "Is that Alan Rawsthorne speaking?" His reply, "Well, yes, I think so", seemed very typical of him.'[10] Possibly the most touching came from Elisabeth Lutyens: 'I think when a dear friend dies one is more conscious of *waste* than anything and—in their name—one re-news one's vow not to waste time but, as all such vows, it is too soon forgotten. I plant rosemary, for remembrance, in my back garden and salute the gods.'[11] In his memorial poem, Roy Fuller summed Rawsthorne's work up thus:

> ANGST through an upper lip
> Stiff with Lancashire phlegm.[12]

[10] Letter to Isabel Rawsthorne 2 Aug. 1971.
[11] Letter to Isabel Rawsthorne, dated 'Sunday'.
[12] *Listener* (26 Aug. 1971).

In the programme book for the Memorial Concert at the Wigmore Hall in November 1971, Gordon Green wrote:

In his last years, less committed politically, he achieved, despite the hazards of health, something near serenity. Significantly, the last expression of musical faith I heard from him was one of awe and reverence for the late Beethoven quartets. In those last years the conversation, though now, perhaps, somewhat slower, was still witty, wise and often sparkling, but the underlying character was profoundly and imaginatively discerning—imaginative, because while many of us can sympathize with the neglected and deprived, he could also pity the debased; and this, surely, is the ultimate in human understanding.

For many children, one of the great joys of life is to create within a small patch of ground (it might be a small area of unregarded and apparently insignificant waste-ground) an entirely personal world, peopled with characters and events of the child's own making; as children, Alan and Barbara Rawsthorne had 'a small spinney which became [in our imaginations] a dense forest' full of adventures, in the garden at Sykeside House.[13] Such make-believe is an important element of a creative artist's quest to find some private ground and turn it into a coherent, fully realized personal world, whether on the grand scale of a Bach or a Bruckner, or on the smaller, more enclosed scale of a Ravel or a Delius. This is precisely what Alan Rawsthorne did: his music reflects a vision of a world that is uniquely his own, which no other composer could have created. In the process of doing this, he produced through his career a body of works which, however variable at times in inspiration, contributed something of special value. He gave expression, as many great English artists have done, to a passionate romanticism which is paradoxically expressed through a filter of emotional reticence, wit, and honour. The passion may break through to the surface (Third Symphony, *Carmen vitale*) or it may be contained within self-imposed confines (Second String Quartet), where, though its presence is quite apparent, one has to work harder to penetrate to its heart. When it is lacking, perhaps because a commission became a burdensome task, the art will nearly always be barren of any significance. When the passion is diminished by exhaustion, as in some of Rawsthorne's last works or one or two in the mid-1950s, then again the music will be less convincing. But these failings are remarkably rare. Rawsthorne's world was much wider than he has been credited with: he gave expression to his concerns with generosity of spirit and a willingness to take risks in broadening and deepening his style, an achievement that is of the highest order.

[13] Barbara Rawsthorne, 'For his Friends—from his Sister Barbara' (undated MS memoir).

A benchmark of a composer's stature is the number of compositions of the highest quality that can stand alongside the works of the most celebrated composers, and it might be worth closing by listing my own personal choice of those works of his that, whether large or small, stand in my mind as masterpieces by any standard. This is a highly personal list, and does not include pieces (like the First Violin Concerto, the Cello Concerto, or *Practical Cats*) which might well be chosen by other commentators: Symphonic Studies, Second Symphony (*Pastoral*), Third Symphony, First and Second Piano Concertos, Second Violin Concerto, *Street Corner*, *Cortèges*, *Elegiac Rhapsody*, Concerto for String Orchestra, *Concertante pastorale*, Concerto for Ten Instruments, Quintet for piano and wind, Clarinet Quartet, Second and Third String Quartets, Violin Sonata, Cello Sonata, Viola Sonata, Theme and Variations for two violins, Piano Sonatina, Ballade for piano, Elegy for guitar, *Lament for a Sparrow*, *A Rose for Lidice*, and *Carmen vitale*. Consideration of this list, bearing in mind the omission of a number of fine works which might have been included, brings one to the conclusion that Rawsthorne's contribution to the music of the twentieth century was not merely distinguished but more important than is currently realized: justice will only be done when the range and quality of his output is properly recognized. His was a voice unlike any other, speaking not at the top of his voice but quietly, persuasively, with intensity—a precious musical resource which we must not ignore.

Alan's funeral was on a balmy midsummer day at Thaxted Parish Church. When it came Isabel's turn to lay a flower on the grave, she threw it with all her power—raging against the dying of the light, perhaps. Their devotion to each other was well known, and undoubtedly gave him the strength to persevere and enlarge his musical vision during their years together. The music played at the service was the slow movement of his Piano Sonatina, on the organ (which it hardly suited). One could not suppress the thought (and cannot still) that perhaps the most ideal choice would have been the last movement of his *Pastoral Symphony*, with its haunted Arcadian beauty (Compact Disc, track 14). That song, almost more than any other piece, was perhaps the purest expression of the most personal of all his musical visions, the awareness of time future (autumn) contained within time present (spring).

Ex. 9.7. Symphony No. 2 (*Pastoral*), conclusion

A CHRONOLOGY OF ALAN RAWSTHORNE

Compiled by Geoffrey Thomason

Performance dates are for known first performances; an asterisk preceding details of a work or event indicates that it is attributed approximately to the year indicated.

1905 AR born 2 May, Haslingden, Lancs., second child of Hubert and Janet Rawsthorne

1911 AR shows early interest in wanting to compose

1914 AR becomes a pupil at Winterclyne School, Southport, Lancs.

1918 AR leaves Winterclyne School and enters Sandringham School, Southport. Plays the cello in Southport Orchestral Society

1919 *AR makes his first appearance as a solo pianist in Southport

Works: *Passepied and *Sylvan Sketch* for piano (lost). Performed Southport, *c*.1919: AR

1920 Works: *Three songs to texts by Blake and de la Mare for voice and piano (Blake setting lost; others unpub.)

1922 AR enters Liverpool University to read dentistry

1923 AR abandons dentistry to read architecture

1924 AR leaves Liverpool University

1925 AR enters the Royal Manchester College of Music. Studies cello with Carl Fuchs, piano with Frank Merrick, and composition with Thomas Keighley

1927 Death of AR's mother Janet, aged 49. Jessie Hinchliffe enters the Royal Manchester College of Music

Works: Valse for piano in C minor (unpub.). Performed in a BBC radio broadcast, January 1928: Gordon Green

Violin Sonata (lost). One movement performed Manchester, July 1927: Maurice Ward, AR

*Three Songs to texts by de la Mare, Shakespeare, and Villon (lost). Performed Manchester, March 1927: Marjorie Lyon, AR

1929 AR graduates from the Royal Manchester College of Music with the teacher's and performer's diplomas. Approaches Arnold Bax for lessons but is unsuccessful. The Rawsthorne family move to Fallowfield, Manchester

Works: Ballade for piano in G sharp minor (unpub.). Performed Liverpool, autumn 1930: Gordon Green

Tzu-Yeh Songs for voice and piano (Waley, from the Chinese: unpub.). Performed Manchester, March 1929: Margaret Collier, AR

1930   AR goes to Zakopane, Poland, June–September to study with pianist Egon Petri. Moves to London on his return to England

1931   AR continues his studies with Petri in Berlin

Works: *Four Poems of Richard Church* for voice and piano (unpub.)

*'Fain would I change that note' for voice and piano (anon.; unpub.)

*'Le Moulin' for voice and piano (Verhaeren; unpub.)

1932   AR returns to England. At Bax's suggestion studies composition with Adam Carse. Takes up post of pianist and composer at the School of Dance-Mime, Dartington Hall, Devon. Hubert Rawsthorne moves to Colwyn Bay

Works: String Quartet (unpub.). Performed Dartington, June 1933: Griller Quartet

* *Esquisses* for voice and chamber orchestra (Waley, from the Chinese; unpub.)

*'Come unto these yellow sands' for voice and orchestra (Shakespeare; unpub.)

1933   Works: Six Songs to texts by Herrick, Hardy, and Shakespeare for voice and piano (lost, except for a setting of Herrick's 'To Daffodils' (unpub.)). Performed Dartington, June 1933: Norman Stone, AR

Incidental music to *The Women from the Voe* (Bottomley; lost). Performed Dartington, June 1933

*Violin Sonata, A major (unpub., incomplete)

1934   AR involved in a road accident. Leaves Dartington and returns to London. Marries Jessie Hinchliffe, July. Comes to the notice of London audiences after the 1932 Quartet is performed at the Macnaghten–Lemare concerts by the Macnaghten Quartet

Works: Concertante for violin and piano (version 1 as Concertante No. 2; slightly revised, 1935). Performed London, November 1934: Jessie Hinchliffe, AR

Incidental music to *The Women of Ghent* (Ling; lost). Performed Dartington, March 1934

Incidental music to *Alice in Wonderland* (Caroll; lost). Performed Dartington, June 1934

Incidental music to *Subject to Alteration* (Goffin; lost). Performed Dartington, summer 1934: Trude Rittmann, Edmund Rubbra, Walter Kinsman

Fra Lippo Lippi for tenor and chamber orchestra (Browning; lost). Projected performance London, February 1935: Steuart Wilson, Lemare Orchestra, cond. Iris Lemare

*Violin Sonata, A minor (unpub.)

1935   AR freelances as a copyist and arranger for the BBC. Political sympathies bring him into contact with like-minded others, notably the poet Randall Swingler. Jessie is a violinist in the BBC Symphony Orchestra

Works: Overture for Chamber Orchestra (lost). Performed London, February 1936: Iris Lemare Orchestra, cond. Iris Lemare

String Quartet (unpub.). Recording released, 1997: Flesch Quartet (ASV CDDA592)

Oboe Quartet (No. 1; unpub.). Performed London, October 1935: Helen Gaskell, Jean Pouget, William Primrose, Bernard Richards

1936   Works: Clarinet Concerto. Performed London, February 1937: Frederick Thurston, Lemare Chamber Orchestra, cond. Iris Lemare

Sonatina for flute, oboe, and piano. Performed London, 1936: Sylvan Trio

Studies on a Theme of Bach for string trio (unpub.)

The Enemy Speaks for tenor and orchestra (C. Day Lewis; unpub.)

* *Weep you no more* for chorus (anon; unpub.)

1937   Concertante for violin and piano appears in print as AR's first published work (as Concertante No. 2). The Theme and Variations for two violins becomes his first recorded work after its success at the ISCM Festival in London

Works: Theme and Variations for two violins. Performed London, January 1938: Jessie Hinchliffe and Kathleen Washbourne

Viola Sonata (revised 1954). Performed London, 1938: Frederick Riddle, Adolph Hallis[1]

---

[1] Dating from the printed score (OUP, 1955). Poulton gives a composition date of 1935 and refers to a BBC broadcast of March 1937.

Music for the Shell Film Unit documentary *Power Unit* (lost)

*Chamber Cantata on medieval texts for voice, string quartet, and harpsichord (lost). Performed London, February 1937: Betty Bannerman, Shadwick String Quartet, Alice Ehlers

*'Pierette' for violin and piano (unpub.)

*'Lullaby' arr. for solo voice, women's chorus and orchestra (trad.; unpub.)

*'Infant Joy' for voice and piano (Blake; unpub.)

1938   Constant Lambert publishes the first printed discussion of AR's music in the *Monthly Musical Record*, September

Works: Symphonic Studies for orchestra. Performed Warsaw, April 1939: Polish Radio Symphony Orchestra, cond. Stanley Chapple

Four Bagatelles for piano. Performed in a Radio Oslo broadcast, Oslo, August 1938: Gordon Green

Three French Nursery Songs for voice and piano or orchestra (trans. Cohen). Piano version performed London, February 1938: Sophie Wyss, Adolph Hallis. Orchestral version performed London, January 1939: Sophie Wyss, BBC Symphony Orchestra, cond. Clarence Raybould

Three Catalan Tunes for string orchestra. Published in 1958 as *Light Music*. (?) Performed London, c.1938: Workers' Music Association Orchestra, (?) cond. David Ellenberg

1939   AR collaborates with Alan Bush on the song cycle *Prison Cycle* and with Bush and others on the left-wing 'Pageant for the People'. Produces several arrangements for Bush's London String Orchestra. Symphonic Studies premièred at the Warsaw Festival of the ISCM. The Venice Festival commissions a string quartet, the MS of which is lost after the cancellation of the festival owing to the outbreak of war. AR reconstructs the finale as the 'Theme and Variations'. Moves to Bristol following the outbreak of war to be close to the BBC Symphony Orchestra, which also moves there

Works: Concerto for piano, strings, and percussion (Concerto No. 1; version 1). Performed London, March 1939: Adolph Hallis, London Symphony Orchestra, cond. Iris Lemare

First String Quartet ('Theme and Variations'). Performed London, September 1940: Blech Quartet

Two Songs to texts by Ernst Toller for voice and piano, for *Prison Cycle* (unpub.). Performed London, December 1939: Anne Wood, Alan Bush

'Homeland Mine' and Finale for chorus, wind orchestra and percussion, for 'Pageant for the People' (Swingler; lost). Performed
London, April 1939

100 Years of the Viennese Waltz for string orchestra (lost). Performed
London, January 1930: London String Orchestra, cond. Alan
Bush

Music for the GPO documentary *The City* (lost)

Music for the documentary *Cargo for Ardrossan*: released *c.*July
1939 (lost)

1940   Adrian Boult conducts the London Symphony Orchestra in the
British première of the Symphonic Studies. In Bristol AR
lectures at the university and teaches English to foreign students.
Several MSS are lost when the Rawsthornes' flat is destroyed in
an air raid, including the first version of the First Violin Concerto.
As a result they stay with Julian Herbage in Chew Magna,
Somerset

Works: *The Creel* for piano duet. Performed *c.*1940: Helen Pike,
Paul Hamburger

'We Three Merry Maidens' for voice and piano (Calvocoressi, from
the French). Performed Sophie Wyss (no further details)

Two songs to texts by Fletcher for voice and piano

First Violin Concerto (version 1, possibly sketches only; lost)

Kubla Khan for solos, chorus, and orchestra (Coleridge; MS lost:
vocal score survives). Performed in a BBC broadcast, June 1940,
cond. Reginald Redman

Incidental music to *The Happy Hypocrite* (Beerbohm; version 1 lost,
version 2 unpub.). Version 1 performed in a BBC radio broadcast, January 1940: BBC Revue Orchestra, cond. Hyam Greenbaum. Version 2 performed in a BBC radio broadcast, November
1944: cond. AR

* Theme and Four Studies for piano. Performed London, October
1971: John Ogdon

*Suite for recorder and piano (unpub). Performed Cheltenham,
1992: John Turner, Peter Lawson

*'Left, Left': socialist songs arr. for two pianos (lost; recording sur-
vives). Performed *c.*1940–2: Geraldine and Mary Peppin

1941   AR called up for active service and enters the Royal Artillery but is
moved to the Education Corps. Tries to form a military band and
symphony orchestra

Incidental music to *The Golden Cockerel* (Pushkin, trans. Dillon; unpub.). Performed in a BBC radio broadcast, December 1941: BBC Northern Orchestra, cond. AR

*'All through the Night' (Welsh trad.) arr. for tenor solo, men's chorus, harp, and string orchestra or quartet (unpub.)

1942   The BBC Symphony Orchestra moves its wartime HQ to Bedford. AR commissioned to provide music for *Radio Newsreel*. Rescores the Concerto for piano, strings, and percussion for full orchestra, in which version it is given at the Henry Wood Promenade Concerts. Oxford University Press, which has published several earlier pieces, becomes AR's sole publisher, 17 June

Works: First Piano Concerto (revised from Concerto for piano, strings, and percussion, 1939). Performed London, July 1942: Louis Kentner, London Philharmonic Orchestra, cond. AR

Music for the Army Film Unit films *Street Fighting*, released *c*. December 1942, and *Tank Tactics* (lost)

Music for *Radio Newsreel* (unpub.). First broadcast July 1942

*Suite for viola d'amore and piano (unpub.), arr. from the Suite for recorder and piano

1943   Death of Hubert Rawsthorne. AR awarded a Fellowship of the Royal Manchester College of Music

Works: *Ode* for soprano and baritone solos, chorus, and orchestra, from *Salute to the Red Army* (MacNeice; lost). Performed London, February 1943: Joan Hammond, Dennis Noble, Royal Choral Society, London Philharmonic Orchestra, members of the BBC Symphony Orchestra, cond. Malcolm Sargent

Incidental music to *The Story of my Death* (MacNeice; unpub.). Performed in a BBC radio broadcast, October 1943: London Symphony Orchestra, cond. AR

1944   ENSA commissions the Overture *Street Corner*.

Works: Overture *Street Corner*. Performed Leamington Spa, September 1945: New London Orchestra, cond. Constant Lambert

Incidental music to *Sitting on the Fence* (Gubbins: unpub.). Performed in a BBC radio broadcast, June 1944: BBC Revue Orchestra, cond. Charles Groves

Incidental music to *He had a Date* (MacNeice: unpub.). Performed in a BBC radio broadcast, June 1944

1945   The Rawsthornes' London flat is damaged by a German doodle-bug. AR is demobbed from the army. His relationship with Jessie begins to decline. *Cortèges* premièred at the Henry Wood Promenade concerts

Works: Fantasy Overture *Cortèges*. Performed London, July 1945: London Symphony Orchestra, cond. Basil Cameron

Music for the Ministry of War documentaries *USA: The Land and the People* (lost) and *Burma Victory*: released November 1945

Music for the Ministry of Information film *Broken Dykes*: released August 1945

*'Precursors' for voice and piano (MacNeice; unpub.)

1946   The British Council sponsors a recording of the Symphonic Studies with Constant Lambert conducting the Philharmonia Orchestra. *Cortèges* played at the London Festival of the ISCM. First String Quartet played at the Cheltenham Festival

Works: Film scores for *School for Secrets*, released April 1946, and *The Captive Heart*, released December 1946

'Jennie's Bawbee' arr. for orchestra (unpub.). Performed in a BBC radio broadcast, April 1946: London Radio Orchestra, cond. AR

'Prisoners' March' from music to *The Captive Heart* for orchestra. (?) Performed London, December 1946: London Symphony Orchestra, cond. Muir Mathieson

Orchestration of the overture to Purcell's *Ode for St Cecilia's Day* for modern orchestra (unpub.). Performed London, November 1946: London Philharmonic Orchestra, London Symphony Orchestra, trumpeters from the Royal Military School of Music, cond. Adrian Boult

Incidental music to *The Insect Play* (Capek; unpub.). Performed in a BBC radio broadcast, February 1946: BBC Symphony Orchestra, cond. AR

Incidental music to *King Lear* (Shakespeare; unpub.). Performed London, September 1946: Old Vic Theatre Company Orchestra, cond. Herbert Menges

Incidental music to *Circle on Circle* (Rodgers; unpub.). Performed in a BBC radio broadcast, December 1946: cond. AR

1947   AR and Jessie separate but remain on amicable terms

Works: Oboe Concerto. Performed Cheltenham, July 1947: Evelyn Rothwell, Hallé Orchestra, cond. John Barbirolli

First Violin Concerto (version 2, reconstructed from sketches after the loss of version 1 in 1940). Performed Cheltenham, July 1948: Theo Olof, Hallé Orchestra, cond. John Barbirolli

Film score for *Uncle Silas*: released November 1947

'Carol' for voice and small orchestra or piano (Rodgers)

Incidental music (with Gerard Shurmann) to *The Pied Piper of Hamelin* (Browning; lost). Performed Amsterdam, late 1947: cond. Gerard Schurmann

*'Alla marcia' for orchestra (unpub., incomplete)

*Incidental music to *The Stone in the Midst* (Dickinson; lost, recording survives). Performed in a BBC radio broadcast February 1948: Ronald Smith

1948   Works: Clarinet Quartet. Performed London, November 1948: Frederick Thurston, Harry Blech, Keith Cummings, Douglas Cameron

Cello Sonata. Performed London, January 1949: Anthony Pini, Wilfrid Parry

Film score for *Saraband for Dead Lovers*: released September 1948

Music for the Shell Mex documentary *X-100* (lost)

Incidental music to *No Other Road* (MacNeice; unpub.). Performed in a BBC radio broadcast, September 1948: London Symphony Orchestra, cond. AR

Incidental music to *Trimalchio's feast* (MacNeice; lost, recording survives). Performed in a BBC radio broadcast, December 1948: cond. AR

1949   Basil Cameron conducts the British première of the Concerto for String Orchestra at the Henry Wood Promenade Concerts

Works: Concerto for String Orchestra. Performed in a Radio Hilversum broadcast, Netherlands, June 1949: Dutch String Orchestra, Gerard Schurmann

Piano Sonatina. Performed London, April 1949: James Gibb

Cadenza for Mozart's Concerto for two pianos and orchestra K. 365 (unpub.)

1950   AR's reputation broadens after the success of Symphony No. 1 leads to numerous performances abroad

Works: First Symphony. Performed London, November 1950: Royal Philharmonic Orchestra, cond. Adrian Boult

Music for the Crown Film Unit documentary *The Dancing Fleece*: released *c*.July 1951 (lost: unpub. short score survives as *Wool Ballet*)

Film score for *Pandora and the Flying Dutchman*: released March 1951

1951   The Arts Council commissions a new piano concerto for the Festival of Britain, which proves to be an instant success with the public and receives many performances over the next few years. The film *Where No Vultures Fly*, with music by AR, is chosen for the Royal Film Performance. Death of Constant Lambert

Works: Second Piano Concerto. Performed London, June 1951: Clifford Curzon, London Symphony Orchestra, cond. Malcolm Sargent

Concertante pastorale for flute, horn, and string orchestra. Performed Hampton Court, August 1951: Gareth Morris, Dennis Brain, New London Orchestra, cond. Alec Shermann

Film scores for *Waters of Time*, released spring 1951, and *Where No Vultures Fly*, released January 1952

1952   Growing relationship with Lambert's widow Isabel

Works: *A Canticle of Man* for baritone solo, chorus, flute, and string orchestra (Swingler). Performed Bryanston, August 1952: members of the Bryanston Summer School, cond. Norman del Mar

Film score for *The Cruel Sea*: released April 1953

1953   AR and Isabel Lambert move to Sudbury Cottage, Little Sampford, near Thaxted, Essex. He suffers a severe haemorrhage in December and is hospitalized

Works: Four Romantic Pieces for piano. Performed London, March 1953: Frank Merrick

'Canzonet', for 'A Garland for the Queen', for soprano solo and chorus (MacNeice). Performed London, June 1953: Cambridge University Madrigal Society, cond. Boris Ord

Film scores for *The Drawings of Leonardo da Vinci*, released September 1953, and *West of Zanzibar*, released April 1954

Coronation Overture for orchestra (unpub.). Performed London, April 1953: National Youth Orchestra, Walter Susskind

1954   AR and Jessie divorce. AR visits Canada to lecture at the Toronto Conservatory Summer School

Works: Second String Quartet. Performed Cheltenham, July 1954: Griller Quartet

Practical Cats for speaker and orchestra (Eliot). Performed Edinburgh, August 1954: Alvar Liddell, BBC Scottish Orchestra, cond. Ian Whyte

Film score for *Lease of Life*: released November 1954

1955   AR marries Isabel Lambert. She collaborates as designer for the
        Sadler's Wells commission *Madame Chrysanthème*
        Works: *Madame Chrysanthème*: ballet (Ashton, after Loti). Per-
        formed London, April 1955: Orchestra of the Royal Opera
        House, Covent Garden, cond. Robert Irving
        Film score for *The Man who Never Was*: released March 1956
        Variation from the joint composition (with other British composers)
        Diabelleries for orchestra (unpub.). Performed London, May 1955:
        Macnaghten New Music Group Ensemble, cond. Iris Lemare
1956   Disappointing première of the Second Violin Concerto
        Works: *A Rose for Lidice* for soprano solo and chorus (Swingler).
        Performed Thaxted, 1956: Purcell Singers, cond. Imogen Holst.
        Simultaneous première in Lidice rose-garden Czechoslovakia.
        Four Seasonal Songs for chorus (anon., Davies, Sylvester, Fletcher).
        Performed in a BBC broadcast, December 1956: Purcell Singers,
        cond. Imogen Holst
        Second Violin Concerto. Performed London, October 1956: Endre
        Wolf, BBC Symphony Orchestra, cond. Pedro de Freitas Branco
        Film score for *The Legend of the Good Beasts*: released summer 1956
1957   Works: Suite from *Madame Chrysanthème* for orchestra. Performed
        London, August 1957: BBC Symphony Orchestra, cond. AR
1958   Works: Violin Sonata. Performed London, May 1959: Manoug
        Parikian and Lamar Crowson
        Overture *Hallé*. Performed Manchester, February 1958: Hallé
        Orchestra, cond. John Barbirolli
        Film score for *Floods of Fear*: released December 1958
        Incidental music to *Noah* (Obey, trans. Wilmurt; unpub.).
        Performed Saffron Walden, May 1958: Norman Knight (flute)
        Macnaghten String Quartet
1959   Works: Second Symphony (*Pastoral*). Performed Birmingham,
        September 1959: April Cantelo (soprano), City of Birmingham
        Symphony Orchestra, cond. Meredith Davies
        Music for the documentary *The Port of London*: released *c.* Septem-
        ber 1959
1960   Works: *Improvisations on a theme by Constant Lambert* for orches-
        tra. Performed Newcastle, January 1961, Northern Sinfonia,
        cond. Michael Hall
        Music for the Kuwait Oil company documentary *Sweat without
        Tears*: released August 1960

1961   AR made a CBE. Suffers another haemorrhage and is made to give
        up alcohol for three years
        Works: Concerto for Ten Instruments. Performed Cheltenham, July
            1961: Prometheus Ensemble
        Incidental music to *Hamlet* (Shakespeare: unpub.). Performed
            Stratford-upon-Avon, April 1961: Royal Shakespeare Theatre
            Wind Band, cond. Brian Priestman
1962   Revisions to the Second Violin Concerto
        Works: Divertimento for chamber orchestra. Performed Cambridge,
            April 1962: London Mozart Players, Harry Blech
        Piano Trio. Performed London, July 1962: Louis Kentner, Yehudi
            Menuhin, Gaspar Cassadó
        Lament for a Sparrow for chorus and harp (Catullus). Performed
            London, June 1962: Elizabethan Singers, cond. Louis Halsey
        Medieval Diptych for baritone and orchestra (anon.). Performed
            London, August 1962: Peter Glossop, BBC Symphony
            Orchestra, cond. Norman del Mar
1963   Revised version of the Second Violin Concerto premièred in Chester
        by Manoug Parikian with the BBC Northern Orchestra under
        George Hurst, January. AR visits the Soviet Union with Alan
        Bush as a representative of the Composers' Guild, September.
        Conducts there the Second Symphony and Concerto for String
        Orchestra
        Works: Quintet for piano and wind instruments. Performed in a
            BBC broadcast, April 1963: Wilfrid Parry, Roger Bennet, Jack
            Brymer, Gwydion Brook, Alan Civil
        Carmen vitale for soprano solo, chorus, and orchestra (medieval
            English anon.). Performed London, October 1963: Heather
            Harper, BBC Symphony Orchestra and Chorus, cond. Norman
            del Mar
1964   The first performance of the Third Symphony at the Cheltenham
        Festival is greeted with critical acclaim
        Works: *Elegiac Rhapsody* for string orchestra. Performed London,
            January 1964: Hirsch String Orchestra, cond. Leonard Hirsch
        Third Symphony. Performed Cheltenham, July 1964: BBC
            Northern Orchestra, cond. George Hurst
        Third String Quartet. Performed Harlow New Town, July 1965:
            Alberni String Quartet
        Film score for *Messenger of the Mountains*: released *c.* January 1964

Suite for brass band (unpub.). Performed Edinburgh, July 1964: National Youth Brass Band of Scotland, cond. Bryden Thomson

'He does not die' for chorus and two pianos (Belloc; unpub.). Performed Edinburgh, December 1964: choir of George Watson's College, Edinburgh

1965   Works: Cello Concerto. Performed London, April 1966: Christopher Bunting, New Philharmonia Orchestra, cond. Malcolm Sargent

'The Oxen' for chorus, for the OUP anthology *Carols of Today* (Hardy). Performed London, December 1965: Elizabethan Singers, cond. Louis Halsey

Tankas of the Four Seasons for tenor, oboe, clarinet, bassoon, violin, and cello (Riba, trans. Gili). Performed Cheltenham, July 1965: Wilfred Brown, Peter Graeme, Gervase de Peyer, William Waterhouse, Emanuel Hurwitz, Terence Weil

Music for the BBC dramatization of *A Tale of Two Cities* (Dickens; unpub.). Broadcast April–June 1965: cond. AR

'Streets of Laredo' for two voices and guitar (MacNeice; unpub.)

1966   Works: *The God in the Cave* for chorus and orchestra (Swingler). Performed Edinburgh, 1967: Edinburgh University Madrigal Society, cond. Edward Harper

1967   Works: Theme, Variations and Finale for orchestra. Performed Chelmsford, September 1967: Essex County Youth Orchestra, cond. Graham Treacher

Overture for Farnham for orchestra. Performed Farnham, May 1967: orchestras of Farnham Grammar School and Tiffin School, Kingston on Thames, cond. Alan Fluck

Ballade for piano. Performed Cardiff, March 1967: John Ogdon

'Scena rustica' for soprano and harp (Skelton)

1968   Works: Concerto for Two Pianos. Performed London, 1968: John Ogdon, Brenda Lucas, London Philharmonic Orchestra, John Pritchard

Piano Quintet. Performed Cardiff, March 1968: John McCabe, Cardiff University Quartet

Suite for flute, viola, and harp. Performed London, November 1968: Robles Trio

Concertante for violin and piano (version 2)

1969   AR awarded an honorary D.Mus. by Liverpool University and Queen's University, Belfast

Works: *Triptych* for orchestra. Performed Lancaster, February 1969: BBC Northern Symphony Orchestra, cond. Norman del Mar

1970 Works: Oboe Quartet (No. 2). Performed London, May 1970: London Oboe Quartet

Quintet for clarinet, horn, violin, cello, and piano. Performed London, February 1971: Music Group of London

*'Two Fish' for voice and piano (Barthas, trans. Sylvester). Performed Cookham, May 1973: Helen Salva, Keith Bosley

1971 AR awarded an honorary D.Litt. by Essex University and made a Fellow of Downing College, Cambridge. Contracts pneumonia and dies at Addenbrookes Hospital, Cambridge, 24 July. Memorial concert held in the Wigmore Hall in November

Works: Elegy for guitar (unfinished; completions by Julian Bream and Gerard Schurmann). Performed London, February 1972: Julian Bream

INDEX

302 INDEX

Brahms, Johannes (*cont.*):
WORKS:
Horn trio 10
Piano concerto no. 2 10, 138–9
String quartet, op. 51 no. 1 158
Symphony no. 3 132
Variations on theme of Handel 10
Violin sonata, op. 100 160
Brain, Dennis 151, 295
Brass, Denis 103
Bream, Julian 281, 282, 299
Bridge, Elizabeth 4, 13, 14
British Broadcasting Corporation, *see* BBC
British Council 65, 293
Britten, Benjamin 17, 28, 84, 103, 112, 131, 199, 222, 234, 282
WORKS:
A boy was born 17
Nocturnal 282
Quartetto serioso 17
Sinfonietta 17
String quartet no. 2 131
The turn of the screw 222, 234
Violin concerto 112
Brodsky, Adolph 12
Brooke, Gwydion 297
Brott, Boris 199
Brown, Wilfred 298
Browning, Robert 289
Bruckner, Anton 284
Brymer, Jack 297
Bunting, Christopher 298
Bush, Alan 14, 60–2, 235, 290, 291, 297
WORKS:
Dialectic 62
Busoni, Ferruccio 13–14, 23, 49, 60, 89, 93, 231, 254
WORKS:
Doktor Faust 231
Rondo arlecchinesco 93
Two studies for 'Doktor Faust' 49–50, 254
Violin concerto 49
Butt, Clara 8
Byrd, William 148, 282

Cairns, David 259, 262
Calvocoressi, Michel 291
Cambridge Evening News 157
Cambridge University 282, 299

Cambridge University Madrigal Society 295
Cameron, Basil 98, 131, 293, 294
Cameron, Douglas 294
Campbell, Roy 104
Cantelo, April 192, 296
Capek, Karel 293
Cardiff Festival of 20th-century music 268
Cardiff University Quartet 298
Carnegie Hall 104
Carroll, Lewis 289
Carse, Adam 12, 288
Casella, Alfredo 17
Cassadó, Gaspar 205, 297
Catullus 208, 297
Cecilian Press 23, 26, 27
Celibidache, Sergiu 144
Chaplin, Charlie 77
Chapple, Stanley 64, 290
Cheltenham Festival 76, 111, 112, 158, 202, 246, 248, 274, 291, 293, 295, 297, 298
Chisholm, Eric 26, 27, 54, 59, 62
Chopin, Frédéric 10, 11, 86, 97, 106, 113–15, 153, 243, 269, 271–2
WORKS:
Ballades 113–14, 271
Fantasy in F minor 113
Church, Richard 15, 16
Churchill, Winston 28
City of Birmingham Symphony Orchestra 192, 296
City of London Festival 205
City Music Society 279
Civil, Alan 297
Clark, Edward 105
Clementi, Muzio 17, 27
Coleridge, Samuel Taylor 76, 79, 291
Collier, Margaret 288
Cologne Ballet 205
Composers' Guild 105, 235, 297
Concertgebouw Orchestra 112
Cooke, Arnold 62
Corelli, Arcangelo 107
Couperin, François 27, 96
WORKS:
Passacaille in B minor 96
Coward, Noel 28–9
WORKS:
Cavalcade 28